Domestic Violence in the Anglophone Caribbean

Ann Marie Bissessar · Camille Huggins
Editors

Domestic Violence in the Anglophone Caribbean

Consequences and Practices

palgrave
macmillan

Editors
Ann Marie Bissessar
Faculty of Social Sciences
University of the West Indies
St Augustine, Trinidad and Tobago

Camille Huggins
Department of Behavioural Sciences
University of the West Indies
St Augustine, Trinidad and Tobago

ISBN 978-3-030-88475-8 ISBN 978-3-030-88476-5 (eBook)
https://doi.org/10.1007/978-3-030-88476-5

This Palgrave Macmillan imprint is published by the registered company Springer Nature Switzerland AG
The registered company address is: Gewerbestrasse 11, 6330 Cham, Switzerland

This Book is dedicated to all our sisters who have been victims of Domestic Violence/Intimate Partner Violence

Prologue

Domestic violence continues to be a social problem that is rarely understood or discussed in many parts of the world. The same holds true in the Anglophone Caribbean. The Caribbean context is unique as it was birthed out of colonization, which was violent and brutal for those who were forced to migrate from another country as enslaved labor, as well as for those who were conquered out of their lands. Most Caribbean islands' societies were created and developed by slaves, colonizers and indentured servants. This history has left an indelible scar on all involved, which is exemplified by the antagonistic way people interact, whether it is between races, ethnicities, religions or gender. Traditionally, domestic relationships and causal factors for domestic violence have been investigated from a myriad of perspectives including the ethnic lineage of the participants. However, in the Caribbean due to its historic origins, domestic violence should also be examined through the lens of its colonial past. This Book examines the consequences of allowing domestic violence to perpetuate in the region. It then looks at some of the practices used to provide support and find justice for victims and perpetrators in a Caribbean cultural context.

Locally, intermittently, on each island there are newspaper headlines of women killed due to a domestic dispute. It may leave a small island in shock and dismay, but there are many victims who suffer without such a drastic outcome. But what of their consequences for enduring violence in their domestic settings. From a societal perspective, if domestic violence is left unchallenged and not properly managed it will continue to perpetuate violence in society. This book examines the impact of laws instituted to protect perpetrators and leave victims shuddering for cover. It investigates the consequences of such laws and their cumulative impact on vulnerable populations such as children. This book also delves into the consequences of domestic violence on women's physical and mental health; on older adults; on children who are the offspring of these relationships and its perpetrators. The second part of this proposed book explores approaches utilized in the Caribbean to deal with the aftermath of domestic violence. It investigates practices currently utilized such as, domestic violence shelters and community approaches used to help women who want to keep their families intact.

The first section of this book contains four chapters in which authors examined the impact of Domestic Violence or Intimate Partner Violence on Children, on women's health, on older adults and the financial hardships experienced. Section Two focussed some of the prescriptions that have been introduced to minimize this kind of violence.

Chapter 1, *The Impact of Domestic Violence on Children in the Caribbean* by authors Akeem Modeste-James and Camille Huggins, argued that little is known about the impact of domestic violence and its adverse effects on children in the Caribbean region. They noted that despite ongoing efforts by social workers to address the issue of domestic violence it continues to plague every segment of the population. They contended that while significant emphasis has been placed on the victims and perpetrators of domestic violence, statistics have failed to recognize the children who are exposed to these toxic environments. In their chapter they reviewed the contextual background of the Caribbean, children growing up in bacchanal and confusion, the effects of domestic violence on children, the changing relationships and finally children's resilience against domestic violence and the adult survivor.

In Chapter 2 by Randy Seepersad, Linda Mohammed and Michele Thomas, the emphasis was on the impact on women's health. In their piece entitled *Intimate Partner Violence and Its Impact on Women's Health: The Moderating Role of Family Support and Educational Attainment* they commenced by suggesting that violence against women has reached epidemic proportions making women the primary victims of intimate partner violence (IPV). The authors contended that while IPV had many negative impacts on victims it was one of the major contributors to women's poor health. Their chapter examined the nature and extent of IPV in Trinidad and Tobago and assessed the impact of IPV on women's health. In their chapter they employed two primary data sources. These were: (1) official crime data from the Trinidad and Tobago Police Service and (2) survey data from the Inter-American Development Bank (IDB) 2018 Survey of Women's Health in Trinidad and Tobago. Multiple regression analysis was the primary means of assessing the relationship between IPV and women's health. The study provided information on how various dimensions of IPV affect health outcomes and it was hoped that this analysis would assist in determining which dimensions of IPV are critical in developing interventions where health outcomes are concerned.

In Chapter 3 by Akeem Modeste-James entitled *Older Adults and Intimate Partner Violence in Trinidad & Tobago: A View from Health Professionals*, the focus was on the experiences of intimate partner violence (IPV) for older adults. The author suggested that the experiences of older adults have been absent from many IPV studies as most of the focus has been placed on the needs of younger women. As a result, it was noted that little was known about the experiences of older adults in abusive relationships and the effectiveness of the healthcare professionals to respond to it. The author, contended, however, that healthcare professionals are on the front line and are in a unique position to identify, assess and intervene for older adults who are experiencing some forms of violence. This chapter utilized a narrative method, to interview healthcare professionals on their perspective of IPV and its impact on older adults.

Chapter 4 entitled *Financial Hardships of Domestic Violence Survivors in the Caribbean* by authors Camille Huggins and Vidya Mungal-Bissessar examined the financial hardships faced by domestic violence survivors in the small island state of Trinidad and Tobago. They utilized the theoretical framework post-colonial feminist theory which focussed on the textures of everyday life to understand race, gender and sexuality. Their chapter is a case study of a female named Rose and her lived experience of domestic violence during her marriage. It examined her understanding of what domestic violence meant within her cultural context of the Caribbean. The findings by the authors indicated Rose's understanding of domestic violence did not include financial abuse and furthermore that her cultural understanding of her gender role identity made her susceptible and vulnerable to incidents of domestic violence.

Section Two of the Book, the prescriptions or remedies to combat Domestic Violence commenced with a Chapter (5) by Ann Marie

Bissessar entitled *The Challenges in Enforcing Domestic Violence Prescriptions in the Case of Trinidad and Tobago*. The author noted that during the period 2007–2013, there were 11,520 reported cases of domestic violence in Trinidad and Tobago, a small twin-island republic comprising a total of 1.3 million persons. Approximately 300 women were killed in what officials termed 'domestic violence disputes' during the period 2005–2015 and according to all reports, these statistics have been increasing. This chapter examined some of the measures and prescriptions that have been introduced in this twin-island republic to minimize incidents of domestic violence and some of the challenges experienced in implementing these measures.

In Chapter 6, The Legislators themselves, namely Charmaine Pemberton and Avason Quinlan-Williams, two presiding judges in Trinidad and Tobago, in their Chapter entitled *A Prospective Legal Framework for Equitable Treatment of Domestic Violence Victims and Perpetrators in a Caribbean Context* engages the reader in some of the practicalities of introducing or reforming laws. Factors such as public pressure, economic issues or political decisions, they advised all impact. However, they acknowledged that change is a constant feature when looking at Caribbean history and society. They advised that modern legislation focussed on what constituted abusive behaviour and the effect on relationships and how those relationships were affected adversely by that behaviour.

In Chapter 7, *A Sociological Perspective of Men's Underreporting of Domestic Violence and a Lack of Appropriate Interventions in the Caribbean* by Camille Tamara Cummings, the author argued that historically, domestic violence programmes were born from the women's liberation movement of the 1970s and 1980s to address the needs of female survivors. She contended that the violence against women and domestic violence movements have operated on a gender binary with men as perpetrators and women as victims. However, this has created a female-centred approach to advocacy which only addresses the needs of one group of survivors and largely fails to acknowledge and address the other group of survivors which are male. She advised, therefore, that addressing this stigmatized topic in an open and supportive way is a mandatory prerequisite to identifying male victims of domestic violence in any practice. She suggested, as well, that more training measures for service providers as well as law enforcement should be made available in order to raise awareness of the issues facing male victims.

Cheryl Ann Sarita Boodram in Chapter 8 entitled The *Use of the Social-Ecological Model of Intervention for Addressing Domestic Violence in Trinidad and Tobago* emphasized that traditional models of domestic violence intervention have focussed on empowering victims with knowledge and skills to cope with violence. However, she noted that literature has documented the role that community and family beliefs play in both exacerbating as well as mitigating violence against women. Her argument is that efforts targeting only the victim do not address the broader context of women's lives and that the context called for an all-of-society approach to domestic violence prevention, aimed at breaking the social, cultural and historical systems that support violence against women within communities. This chapter focussed on the value of the social-ecological model in addressing violence against women in Trinidad and Tobago and provided a discussion for implementing such action. The chapter argued that a social-ecological approach has the potential for disrupting traditions of abuse at the individual, family, community and societal levels.

Chapter 9, in perhaps what may be a first in the area, explored Domestic Abuse in the Seventh Day Adventist Church. Edward Clarke in his chapter entitled *Exploring Domestic Abuse in the Seventh Adventist Church* commenced with the view that violence against women is not a novice phenomenon and rather it is a feature of various societies all around the world. He advised that a report from the United Nations contended that globally, one in three women will suffer abuse in their lifetime. In European Union countries it was estimated that one in three women (approximately 32%) have experienced psychologically abusive behaviour on the part of an intimate partner, either their current partner or a previous partner, making this form of abuse the most common type. Additionally, one in 20 women (approximately 5%) has been raped since the age of 15, either by a partner or by someone else. (Restored 2016). He suggested that these global statistics present a chilling story about what happens to women mainly in their homes. He questioned, whether domestic abuse could be occurring within the confines of the churches as well. He concluded that while it was challenging to believe that domestic abuse can occur in church, the citadel of love, grace and spiritual upliftment, domestic abuse has in reality entered the sanctuary, and women in congregations suffer silently while the rest of the parishioners celebrate God's goodness.

In their Chapter (Chapter 10) entitled *Escape to Safety: Seeking Shelter from Domestic Violence the Case of Madinah House (1999–2019)* by Amina

Ibrahim-Ali and Nura Amina Ali the case of a shelter by the name of Madinah House is presented. The authors noted that *Madinah House*, a temporary shelter, was founded in 1999 in Trinidad to respond to the needs of battered women and their children who, having escaped their abuse, were forced to deal with practical issues such as housing and safety. In 2019, after having housed more than 1,200 clients and their children, the shelter was closed due to insufficient funding to manage its daily expenses and to complete outstanding repair work on its building. This chapter provided information on the day-to-day operations of *Madinah House*, and, in so doing, contributed to an under-researched area related to gender-based violence in the Caribbean, i.e. safe houses. The two authors, former board members, followed a narrative approach in examining individual client files, journals and letters and conducting interviews with former shelter managers. Findings documented the 20-year contribution of *Madinah House* and deepened the understanding of the circumstances of battered women, and the key interventions which afford them support.

The final Chapter (Chapter 11) by Jewel Amoah, in her chapter entitled the *Shifting from Domestic Violence to Transformative Gender Justice: A Template for Public Accountability and Inclusion* explores the evolution of domestic violence in Trinidad and Tobago and highlights the international human rights obligations of the State to address same. She observes that while the State has fulfilled some of its obligations regarding the legislative establishment of fair and effective legal procedures to address domestic violence, she argues that full compliance must include the adoption of international best practices for a gendered human rights approach that eliminates gender stereotypes that promote notions of inferiority and superiority.

Contents

Notes on Contributors

Nura Amina Ali (L.L.B., L.E.C) was admitted to practice as an Attorney-at-Law in the Courts of Trinidad and Tobago in November 2015. She also holds an ADR Mediation Training Certificate covering both negotiation and mediation training skills. From 2016 Ali worked as a Legal Associate at the Children's Authority of Trinidad and Tobago. During this time, she assisted in the implementation and maintenance of the case management and administration systems required to support the effective conduct of court matters and secure the welfare of 'at risk' and abused children. Until 2018, she also provided legal advice, guidance and representation on matters relating to children in need of care and protection, family services matters, adoption matters and foster care matters. In 2019 Ali completed a Writing for Children course at the Toronto Public Library. She is currently an Overseas Member of the Law Association of Trinidad and Tobago.

Jewel Amoah is a Canadian-Trinidadian human rights lawyer, activist and academic. She is committed to research, advocacy and activism to inspire and produce systemic change, enhance access to justice and the full enjoyment of rights. She joined the Faculty of Law at UWI St. Augustine and is currently on a leave of absence and serves as the Human Rights and Equity Advisor for the Halton District School Board and also serves as a part-time Commissioner with the Ontario Human Rights Commission.

Jewel has more than 20 years' experience in human rights advocacy in Canada and throughout West and Southern Africa. She has facilitated organizational change in various public sector environments by raising awareness of harassment, discrimination, human rights and workplace equity. Dr. Amoah is a member of the Law Society of Ontario, the University Rights Advocacy Program at UWI (U-RAP) and the Canadian Association of Black Lawyers. Dr. Amoah's research interests include intersectionality, Critical Race Theory, Feminist Legal Theory, legal pluralism, public international law and international human rights law. She is a graduate of McMaster University, the University of Ottawa and the University of Cape Town.

Ann Marie Bissessar is a full-tenured Professor with the Department of Political Science, Faculty of Social Sciences, The University of the West Indies, St Augustine, Trinidad and Tobago. She was awarded the 2019 prestigious Vice Chancellor's Award for research and university service. She served as a Dean of the Faculty of Social Sciences (2015–2019) and the Head of the Department of Behavioural Science (2010–2013). She served as a Member of the Integrity Commission of Trinidad and Tobago (2010–2013). She is the author/co-editor of approximately 26 books and of over 100 articles/chapters/entries.

Dr. Cheryl-Ann Sarita Boodram is a Social Work educator and scholar who is passionate about community-engaged teaching that promotes the co-production of learning with students, teachers and communities. Her research interests are unified by a focus on collective trauma in the Caribbean as it relates to issues such as the forced displacement of persons or those considered 'out of place', all forms of violence and experiences of disasters. Her professional experiences include working with families, vulnerable youth, forced migrants and communities that have experienced loss following natural disasters. Dr. Boodram currently serves as Lecturer/Practicum Co-ordinator at UWI, St. Augustine. Her teaching portfolio at the undergraduate and graduate levels includes courses such as International Social Work and Research Design and Methodologies for Social Work. She also coordinates the undergraduate and postgraduate field instruction components of the social work programme. Dr. Boodram has published in the areas of migration, disaster resilience and work/life balance. She is keen on working in communities to widen the use of participatory action methods and to harness these methods to transform and humanize research and stimulate action.

Dr. Edward Clarke was educated in England, works in Trinidad and currently resides in South Africa. He is the founding and current Dean of the School of Social Science, Professor of Social Psychology, at the University of the Southern Caribbean. He is qualified in the areas of Counselling, Sociology, Psychology, International Relations and Business Management. He was educated at the Universities of London, Surrey and Oxford Brooks in England.

He has lived and worked in many Southern African countries, including, Lesotho, (where he was a senior lecturer in Sociology at the University of Roma, Lesotho), Swaziland, Namibia, Botswana, Zimbabwe, Angola etc.

In addition, his African experience included being a part-time research consultant for WHO, UNICEF, UNFPA and USAID. He has been a senior executive and entrepreneur in the cosmetics and oil industry in South Africa; Marketing Director of Renaissance Petroleum, MD of Amka Products and owner of The Ultimate Hair System. He is very committed to the academic development of the University of the Southern Caribbean and enjoys being active in the church. He has undertaken significant research in the area of Gender Studies, Childhood Sexual Abuse and Negligence, Suicide Ideation, Homosexuality, Absent Fathers and Present Fathers, Mental Ill Health and Stigma and Prostate Cancer. He has co-authored, a chapter, 'Dying Too Young in the Caribbean: In Legacy of the Crossing', edited by Thomas A. LaVeist.

Dr. Clarke is a founder member and co-facilitator of Leading from Above the Line (LFATL) Leadership programme, from its inception. He credits the LFATL as the catalysis for his current specialization and expertise in the area of Emotional Intelligence.

Camille Tamara Cummings is a Ph.D. Candidate at the University of the West Indies, St. Augustine, who recently passed her oral defence. Her work focusses on emotions, sex and physical abuse in the context of partner conflict. Ms. Cummings has a B.Sc. in Sociology with a minor in Social Policy and a M.Sc. in Sociology with a specific focus on sociology of health. Her Master's thesis focussed on health care and domestic violence against women. She is multilingual and is interested in conducting social research among diverse populations. Her research interests include partner conflict, healthcare response to domestic violence, male domestic violence victimization, migration in the context of domestic violence and human trafficking.

Dr. Camille Huggins was born and spent most of her life in New York City in the United States. She moved to Trinidad, West Indies, in 2013 and became a lecturer at the University of the West Indies at St. Augustine with the Faculty of Social Science since 2015. During her tenure at UWI, she was appointed Deputy Dean of Planning and Programs for the Faculty of Social Sciences from the academic year 2018 to 2019. She secured two monetary grants from Quinnipiac University and the International Association of Schools of Social Work to establish various initiatives. Her research interest is older adults, grief, loss and trauma. She currently has co-authored one book and two book chapters and eight peer-reviewed articles.

Prior to her academic career, Dr. Huggins obtained a Ph.D. in social work from New York University; a Master's degree in Social Work from Columbia University and a Bachelors' degree in Sociology from the State University of New York at Buffalo. She worked as a crisis intervention social worker for eight years and nine years as a social work director in long-term care facilities.

Amina Ibrahim-Ali (Ph.D. Linguistics) served as coordinator, assistant lecturer and instructor of English as a Second Language (ESL) at the Department of Liberal Arts and the Centre for Language Learning (CLL), University of the West Indies (UWI), St. Augustine Campus from August 2003 to August 2020. During this time, she was actively involved at the practical level in the Diploma in Teaching English to Speakers of Other Languages (TESOL). In 2012 she was instrumental in establishing the International English Language Testing Systems (IELTS) test centre at the CLL and served as the administrator of this test until 2019. Ibrahim-Ali has written children's books, newspaper articles for a general readership and is a co-author of two academic book chapters. She currently teaches in the Academic Literacies Programme at the Department of Modern Languages and Linguistics (DMLL) at UWI St. Augustine.

Akeem Modeste-James is from the Twin Island Republic of Trinidad and Tobago in the Caribbean. He earned his Bachelor's and Master's degrees in Social Work from the University of the West Indies. Since graduating he was appointed as an adjunct faculty in Social Work at the University of the West Indies Open Campus. Akeem also worked as an outpatient psychiatric social worker at the community health centres focussing on the treatment of trauma and anxiety disorders. He is currently pursuing his

Ph.D. in Social Work at the Graduate School of Social Work, University of Denver. His research interest includes disparities in mental health care for young adults, marginalized populations and homelessness.

Dr. Linda Mohammed is the Programme Leader and Assistant Professor at the Institute of Criminology and Public Safety (ICPS) at the University of Trinidad and Tobago. She has authored and co-authored several peer-reviewed articles and has presented at academic conferences nationally and internationally. Her research interests include policing and police psychology, job stress, job satisfaction, gender-based violence and job burnout. Dr. Mohammed was the recent recipient of a Canada/CARICOM Faculty Leadership Scholarship tenable at Ontario Tech University, Canada. She currently serves on the Boards of Undergraduate Studies, Postgraduate Studies and Ethics at the University of Trinidad and Tobago. She is also a Co-Director of the Newsletter, 'Keeping it Real', which focusses on crime in Trinidad and Tobago.

Vidya Mungal-Bissessar is the former Deputy Mayor of the city of San Fernando and was a member of the City Council for six years. Mrs. Mungal-Bissessar is a prominent south business woman for the past 30 years as a Director and Chief Financial Officer of SNS Hardware Supplies Ltd., All Granite and Stone Works Ltd. and Twin Island Products Ltd. which are companies in the hardware, stone and construction industries, respectively. Mrs. Mungal-Bissessar is a former Trinidad and Tobago liaison of the Naparima Alumni Association of Canada and lifetime member, as well as a former public relations officer for the Stri Sevak Sabha one of Trinidad's oldest Hindu women's organizations. She is a member of the Trinidad and Tobago National Council against Alcoholism and other Addictions and was awarded the prestigious City of San Fernando Award in the fields of Business and Social Work in 2008.

She is a proud past student of Naparima Girls' High School and a Graduate of The University of the West Indies with a B.Sc. Sociology and a Master of Science Social Work with Distinction. Vidya is currently a M.Phil./Ph.D. student in Social Work. Mrs. Mungal-Bissessar was previously the Research and Teaching Assistant at the Social Work Unit of the Faculty of Social Sciences St. Augustine and currently a part-time lecturer of Social Development Policy.

Charmaine Pemberton received her education at Bishop Anstey High School; the University of the West Indies (LL.B. [Hons] 1991); The

Hugh Wooding Law School (L.E.C. 1993); The Institute of International Relations, St. Augustine (Dip. I.R. [Dist.] 1992) and the University of Nottingham (LL.M. 1993).

In 1983, she was admitted as a Solicitor to the Bar of Trinidad and Tobago where she served both in the public service and at the private Bar until 1999. She enjoyed a short stint as a sole practitioner until July 2000 when she joined the Eastern Caribbean Supreme Court as its first Master. In 2003, Justice Pemberton was elevated to Judgeship and served in St. Lucia and St. Kitts and Nevis, before becoming the first resident female Judge in Grenada, while serving in Dominica as well. In 2005, Justice Pemberton returned to her native Trinidad and Tobago to serve on the High Court Bench in the Civil Division. In 2016, she was welcomed to the Bench of the Court of Appeal of Trinidad and Tobago.

Justice Pemberton's passion is ADR and continuing legal education. She holds certification as a Mediator and Mediation Trainer in Trinidad and Tobago. She is a Trained Family Law and Divorce Mediator; a Judicial Settlement Officer in both Civil and Family Divisions and holds the designation FCIArb. She is a certified Judicial Trainer having received that designation from the University College, London, and is a Fellow of the Commonwealth Judicial Education Institute. As such, Justice Pemberton continues to train Judicial Officers, not only in her native Trinidad and Tobago but also in the Eastern Caribbean and Guyana. She continues her involvement in community affairs by authoring and presenting several papers and sharing her thoughts on diverse topics to a variety of audiences. Justice Pemberton was elevated to the Court of Appeal and sits mainly in the Civil Division. Justice of Appeal Pemberton is a member of many Judiciary Committees and is currently a Board Member of the JEITT and the JLSC.

Avason Quinlan-Williams presides in the Civil Division of the High Court of Trinidad and Tobago since 2017. Before that, Justice Quinlan-Williams presided as a Magistrate of Trinidad and Tobago for 17 years. She presided in every magisterial jurisdiction in Trinidad and Tobago. She is the holder of a Bachelor of Laws Degree (with Honours) from the University of the West Indies and a Legal Education Certificate from the Hugh Wooding Law School. She is also the holder of an Executive Masters of Business Administration Degree with Distinction from the Arthur lok Jack Graduate School of Business, University of the West Indies.

Justice Quinlan-Williams is a Board Member of the Judicial Education Institute of Trinidad and Tobago and has been involved in the planning and execution of the continuing education of Judicial Officers, stakeholders to the Administration of Justice and other associations and groups of persons. Justice Quinlan-Williams is also a Fellow of the Commonwealth Judicial Education Institute. Before joining the bench, Justice Quinlan-Williams worked as a Senior State Attorney, in the office of the Director of Public Prosecutions for seven years. During that period, she was involved in prosecutions of diverse cases at the Magistrates' Courts, the High Court and the Court of Appeal.

Justice Quinlan-Williams is a member of numerous associations including the Commonwealth Magistrates and Judges Association, the Caribbean Association of Judicial Officers, the International Association of Women Judges, the Caribbean Association of Women Judges, the Trinidad and Tobago Association of Women Judges and the Magistrates Association of Trinidad and Tobago.

Dr. Randy Seepersad is a Criminologist and Head of the Criminology Unit at the University of the West Indies, Trinidad and Tobago. Dr. Seepersad holds a Ph.D. from the University of Toronto and an M.Phil. degree from the University of Cambridge. Dr. Seepersad specializes in research methodology and statistics and has a research interest in economic deprivation and crime, intimate partner violence, gang violence, youth crime and justice and penology. Recent books which were published by Dr. Seepersad include *Gangs in the Caribbean* (2013), *Making Deterrence Work: Problems and Possibilities* (2014) and *Crime and Security in Trinidad and Tobago* (2016). Dr. Seepersad has also published in a number of peer-refereed journals including the *Journal of School Violence*, the *Journal of Gang Research* and the *International Journal of Law, Crime and Justice*.

Dr. Michelle Thomas is an Associate Lecturer at Beijing Concord College of Sino-Canada in Asia. She completed her Ph.D. at Nova Southeastern University, Florida, in Conflict Management and Resolution Studies, and her Master's and undergraduate studies at the University of the West Indies, St. Augustine, Trinidad. Dr. Thomas specializes in interpersonal conflict management and intimate partner violence. Her research interests lie in the areas of interpersonal conflict, IPV and male perpetration in the Caribbean. Dr. Thomas is a national scholar and qualitative research expert.

List of Figures

List of Tables

CHAPTER 1

The Impact of Domestic Violence on Children in the Caribbean

Akeem Modeste-James and Camille Huggins

Discussion

Since the outbreak of the Coronavirus Disease 2019 pandemic (COVID-19), measures were implemented to safeguard citizens. For many, their daily lives were altered as governments around the world implemented stay-at-home orders confining nonessential personnel at home. While the restrictions on movement curbed the spread of the virus, victims of domestic violence were essentially imprisoned with their abusers for extended times, which led to an increase in violence (Bradbury-Jones and Isham 2020). Domestic violence is a significant problem that remains a

A. Modeste-James
Graduate School of Social Work, University of Denver, Denver, CO, USA
e-mail: Akeem.Modeste-James@du.edu

C. Huggins (✉)
Department of Behavioural Sciences, University of the West Indies, St. Augustine, Trinidad and Tobago
e-mail: camille.huggins@sta.uwi.edu

A. M. Bissessar and C. Huggins (eds.), *Domestic Violence in the Anglophone Caribbean*,
https://doi.org/10.1007/978-3-030-88476-5_1

threat to the health, well-being, and quality of life for individuals of all ages, socio-economic backgrounds, race, and culture. Historically, women and children have been longstanding recipients of the most severe forms of violence around the world, including the Caribbean. Globally, on average one in three women worldwide have either experienced physical or sexual intimate partner violence or non-partner sexual violence (UN Women 2010; World Health Organization [WHO] 2016).

Domestic violence does not only impact the victim but also the children as well, as many violent men who abuse their wives also abuse their children. It is suggested that 275 million children across the world have witnessed domestic violence (The United Nations Children's Fund [UNICEF] 2006). The early exposure to this traumatic ordeal is particularly concerning for children in the Caribbean region. Children who are exposed to acts of violence directly or indirectly can face adverse effects on their health and well-being. It is important to note that children are considered the silent victims of domestic violence as their pain often goes unnoticed and their voices are not heard. Could you imagine witnessing two of the most important persons in your life physically hurting the other causing injuries and destroying property?

A turbulent home environment can make children anxious, fearful, and unhappy. As a result, this can prevent them from thriving in school and psychosocial functioning. The impact of witnessing domestic violence on children in the Caribbean region goes unrecognized as they suffer from a range of physical and psychological harm even though they are not physically abused themselves. This chapter provides an understanding of domestic violence and its impact on Caribbean children.

Background of the Caribbean

The Caribbean consists of 100s of tiny islands, but only 30 islands are inhabitable. These islands are spread across the Caribbean Sea located between the North and South Americas. While there are 43 million people living on these small islands, 5.3 million people live on ten English-speaking islands (World Populations Review 2019). A few of the islands are governed by larger more developed countries (e.g. United States Virgin Islands), while others are sovereign small developing nations such as Trinidad and Tobago and Barbados (World Populations Review 2019). The Caribbean is diverse with cultural and religious practices and ethnicities. The main ethnicities are groups of Indigenous peoples, Africans,

Indians, Europeans, Chinese and Portuguese. Some of these ethnicities were forced on those islands through colonization and enslavement.

Children Growing up in Bacchanal and Confusion

Historically, remnants of domestic violence are deeply rooted throughout all Caribbean countries as this can be traced to the pre-independence of Caribbean islands during plantation economies, enslavement, and indentureship (Thornton 2015). During slavery and indentureship, violence was perpetuated to ensure political, social, and cultural ordering, which gave rise to the justification of boundaries between those men who could exercise power and control on those who are likely to be victims (women and children). Today the Caribbean is a product of its past, where violence remains prevalent, and its cultural practices influence how decisions are made when it comes to violence within the household (Morgan and Youssef 2006).

In the Caribbean, domestic violence is often considered a family secret. Both men and women are perpetrators of violence although, women are at a higher risk for experiencing violence. Domestic violence does not occur in isolation but often co-exists with other family difficulties such as the abuser feeling like they are being provoked and they lose control, alcohol addiction and drug misuse, mental illness, learning disabilities, infidelity, unwillingness to perform sexual acts, and unsatisfactory household chores. Most of the times women suffer in silence and when they do disclose about the abuse in their life it is to a close family member or friend. Often times, most react to the news of domestic violence in a similar manner, offering little to no support and encouraging the victim to pray about it and leave it to God as he would make a way. Despite the knowledge of the abuse, there has been an overwhelming silence as our Caribbean culture perpetuates see, hear, and speak no evil. This means "I'm not getting involved in that".

Older adults would encourage younger women to stay in the abusive relationship "for the sake of the children" leaving them with no other alternatives. As a result most Caribbean women stay in this tumultuous relationship to provide a false sense of stability for their children. Moreover, some women may not make an official police report or seek medical attention as they are fearful of the repercussions that may follow. Others may fight back, risking their lives and their children's to escape the abusive relationship. Some women who escaped continued to be at risk, as they were subjected to harassment, stalking, and threats of being killed. While there are legal remedies available for women and children living in violence such as the Domestic Violence Act which offers a protection order to ensure the safety and protection of the applicant (United Nations Regional Centre for Peace Disarmament and Development in Latin America and the Caribbean 2020), many women are afraid of that option as they refer to the protection order as a "piece of paper" that can exacerbate their vulnerability to violence.

Over the last two decades there have been instances where domestic violence has become fatal. Within the region it is noted that domestic violence accounts for half of all cases of murdered women (Sewll et al. 2010). Moreover, estimates show varied rates of intimate partner homicide within the region for Suriname (4.3), Guyana (2.1), Dominican Republic (1.6), and Jamaica (0.1) per 10,000 female population (United Nations Office on Drugs and Crime [UNODC], Global study on homicide: Gendered-related killing of women and girls 2018). In the most recent case in Trinidad and Tobago, three children all under the age of seven witnessed their father brutally chopping their mother. The oldest ran to his neighbour screaming "*Aunty Toya! Aunty Toya! Come and help mommy. Daddy Killing mommy*" (Felmine 2021). Could you imagine what was going through that child's mind seeing that gruesome image? What we do know is that this traumatic event will cause psychological distress for those children who now have to live without parents.

Many children hear or see their parents, screaming in anger, crying in pain, or begging for their life before being murdered. However, most mothers think that their children may not be aware of the violence or the extent of it or even doubt to themselves that they are aware of anything. It is a taboo topic for Caribbean parents to discuss the occurrence of violence with children because it's a norm within the West Indian culture that children should be seen and not heard and should not get involved in big people's business. This perspective does not facilitate opportunities for open discussions which leads children to speculate.

The Effects of Domestic Violence on Children

The statistics about the number of Caribbean children affected by domestic violence are limited. In recent times, however, there has been a noted high occurrence of childhood exposure to domestic violence within the Caribbean. These traumatic events have affected children's physical, psychological, emotional, social, behavioural, developmental, and cognitive well-being and functioning (Carpenter and Stacks 2009). It is noteworthy to mention that children exposed to domestic violence are more vulnerable to behavioural problems (Renner and Boel-Studt 2013) than children who have not endured the same circumstances. Additionally, children's responses to living with domestic violence may vary according to age and stage of development. Some children do not show obvious signs of stress or have developed their own coping mechanism. To begin with, infants are enormously vulnerable to attachment issues as they are solely dependent on their primary caregiver who is usually the mother, for love, care, and support (Huth-Bocks et al. 2001). The toxic and stressful environment can trigger psychological and behavioural issues in these children. For example, they can exhibit excessive irritability, emotional distress, sleep disturbance, fear of being alone, mood swings, problems with toilet-training, language, immature behaviour, and in extreme cases they suffer from failure to thrive (Nguyen and Larsen 2012). Furthermore, in this type of household the infant has difficulties developing attachments with his/her mother as she may be depressed and overwhelmed because of the situation.

For preschoolers, they also depend on their parent's care, safety, and security needs. However, at this age children who are exposed to violence tends to show more behavioural and social disturbances. Due to the constant exposure to violence, children of this age have difficulties developing empathy as they have become desensitized to aggressive behaviours and accept the use of violence as a means of conflict resolution or love. They struggle with sleep disturbances, headaches, display poor verbal abilities, and show a lack of interest in exploring and playing freely and lack of motivation (Holt et al. 2008). Often time they may regress developmentally and display behaviours such as bed-wetting, thumb-sucking, increased crying, and whining. Furthermore, children of this age may assume that they are the cause of the problems within the home. Also, they may make suicidal statements about how the world would be better without them.

School-age children are usually advanced in their emotional awareness of themselves and their immediate environment. As a result, they are fully aware that violence is occurring in the home. Some children blame themselves for their victim's abuse. These inaccurate beliefs give rise to poor social skills, low self-concept, isolation or avoidance of peer relations, oppositional-defiant behaviour in the school setting, poor academic performance, lashing out at objects, and sadness and depression (Nguyen and Larsen 2012).

Adolescence is a critical age, as they are discovering themselves and building intimate relationships with peers. However, due to the violence witnessed, this age group has difficulties forming healthy intimate relationships with peers. They also tend to feel lonely and isolated, develop stress-related medical and mental health problems, and have difficulties in school (Nguyen and Larsen 2012). Additionally, these adolescents are more likely to show the effects of the disruption in their lives through underperformance and they engage in more self-destructive behaviours such as having unprotected sex, drugs, alcohol, aggressive, and antisocial behaviour (Nguyen and Larsen 2012).

These adverse effects will continue to impact these children into their adult lives, resulting in negative health and behaviour outcomes (Baker 2013).

The Changing Relationships

Domestic violence is conceived as a private family matter. As a result, a culture of silence is perpetuated around it making individuals refuse to talk about the abuse. To protect their children from the trauma of violence, mothers often would try to deny or minimize the severity of the abuse, as many assume that the children are too young to understand what is happening. However, without creating an outlet for discussion about the incident(s), the children may misinterpret what happened or why it happened. Consequently, they may engage in self-blame behaviours since they often believe that they are responsible for the disputes occurring between their parents.

Witnessing acts of violence can disrupt a child's normal relationship with his/her parents. Some children may feel frustrated and confused by the abuser's behaviour, while some may try to protect the abused parent (mother) by refusing to leave their presence or inserting themselves in abusive altercations. The constant exposure to domestic violence, relationships, and bonds with parent(s) are disrupted and damaged (Howell et al. 2016). Damaged bonds usually result in a lack of social competence, which prohibits developing and maintaining healthy relationships with others (Hungerford et al. 2012). For example, some children as they grow older will avoid abusive relationships, while others may repeat the cycle of abuse. Moreover, some children take sides with the abusive adult and become disrespectful or aggressive to their non-violent parent since they believe they provoked it and, in some cases, prefer to live with their abusive parent instead (Groves et al. 2007; Radford and Hester 2006).

Children's Resilience Against Domestic Violence

Despite the multitude of negative consequences associated with children being exposed to domestic violence, while some children can maintain successful psychosocial functioning. These children are labelled as resilient. Resilience has been defined as:

> *the capacity of people to effectively cope with, adjust, or recover from stress or adversity. Resilience reflects the ability to confront and handle stressful life events, ongoing adversities and difficulties, and traumatic experiences. Resilience also reflects the ability to maintain a stable equilibrium and relatively stable healthy level of psychological and physical functioning, even in the face of highly disruptive stressful and traumatic events.* (Meichenbaum 2013, p. 10)

Resilience is an important factor to increase the likelihood that children will resist or recover from the negative effects they have experience because of witnessing or being abused. Children living in a household plagued with violence, quickly learn that to survive this type of environment, they must learn ways to minimize the trauma by developing unique ways to cope. At a first glance, children may display behaviours that may be deemed as odd or inappropriate, however, that is their way of surviving captivity. Researchers have identified several protective factors that can protect children from difficult experiences. Protective factors can be defined as "qualities of a person or context that predict better outcomes, particularly in situations of high risk" (Howell, Resilience and psychopathology in children exposed to family violence 2011). Moreover, these protective factors can be broken-down into two categories; (i) personal characteristics and (ii) family factors.

The first is the personal characteristics, which are inherent traits used to buffer children from their toxic environment. These protective factors include high self-esteem and internal sense of worth, strong determination to be different from abusive parents, positive emotionality, intelligence, an easy-going disposition, good problem-solving skills, internal locus of control, and strong connections with siblings and peers (Alvord and Grados 2005; Child Welfare Information Gateway 2009; Edleson 2004; Howell 2011; Howell and Graham-Bermann 2011; Meichenbaum 2013; Osofsky 1999).

The second is family protective factors; these increase a child's sense of security despite the trauma faced. These factors are parental social competence, having a parent, usually the mother who models resilience despite the abuse, and having positive support systems including other family members that bring stability to the child's high level of stress (Howell 2011; Mullender et al. 2002; Rossman et al. 2000; Hughes et al. 2001).

Both personal and family protective factors contribute to the child's ability to cope and mitigate the trauma of those unsavoury events creating an opportunity for them to thrive despite adversity.

The Adult Survivor

Surprisingly, there has been little to no research done examining the long-term effects of domestic violence on adult survivors. Witnessing and experiencing violence in childhood may lead to violence and instability in later years. While all children are not the same, not all who experience child maltreatment shows symptoms. Therefore, it is important to note that some children find functional coping behaviours during childhood such as seeking assistance from support adults and do not become symptomatic as adults. Sometimes these coping behaviours may be deemed dysfunctional, but it still serves an important function in the child's survival with ongoing abuse. The effects of witnessing domestic violence can continue well into adulthood resulting in poor health outcomes both physically and psychological. The most common adverse long-term effects adult survivors face are major depressive disorder, low self-esteem, and trauma-related symptoms (Levendosky et al. 2013). Additionally, some mothers may experience difficulties in parenting their own children as this may bring back flooding memories of the experiences they endured.

When most adult survivors think of health challenges because of domestic violence they envision a few bruises or broken bones from intervening between their parents or resulting from the physical abuse. While this may be true, it is only part of the story. Felitti et al. (1998) posit those adult survivors may suffer from a host of long-term health problems such as heart disease, cancer, chronic lung disease, liver disease, obesity, suicide attempts, and depressive disorders.

Many mothers who have challenges in leaving the abusive relationship are concerned with intergenerational violence in their children's own lives. Intergeneration violence is a consequence many adult survivors face. Coming from a household of abuse does not necessarily mean that one will become abusive, however, for those parents who abused their children they themselves were twice likely to have been abused as a child themselves. Therefore, being exposed you are at a higher risk of transmitting abuse. From a social learning perspective children learn what they see and display aggressive behaviours or alternatively accept aggression as a normative behaviour within the household by observing those behaviours from their parents (Bandura 1973, 1977). Specifically, female survivors who grew up in a household of violence are more likely to become victims and to a lesser extent question violence by men. Furthermore, these female survivors were found to have experienced higher psychological distress and limited social support (Henning et al. 1997), while male survivors who witnessed their fathers or other males perpetrating violence against their mothers have a risk of becoming a perpetrator. Additionally, these male survivors tend to commit the most frequent acts of violence and engage in abusive behaviours towards the next generation (Pears and Capaldi 2001; Murrell et al. 2007).

Conclusion

Violence against women and children continues to be an epidemic in Caribbean countries and around the world (UNODC Report and World Bank 2007). This is cause for concern because this impacts children across all developmental stages, who are exposed to violence within the home. Unfortunately, children witnessing or experiencing domestic violence can suffer from adverse effects such as poor socialization skills, educational functioning, and the continuation of the cycle of violence if it is not treated early. Additionally, these children also develop maladaptive behaviours such as violent outbursts or self-harm by cutting. To cope with the traumatic occurrence children develop their own coping strategies. Providing intervention for children can help to break the cycle of violence and prevent children from being exposed to this epidemic.

References

Alvord, M.K., and J.J. Grados. 2005. Enhancing Resilience in Children: A Proactive Approach. *Professional Psychology, Research and Practice* 36: 238–245.

Baker, Jeffrey R. 2013. The Failure and Promise of Common Law Equity in Domestic Abuse Cases. https://law.loyno.edu/sites/law.loyno.edu/files/Baker-FINAL.pdf. Accessed 2021.

Bandura, A. 1973. *Aggression: A Social Learning Approach*. Englewood Cliffs, NJ: Prentice-hall.

Bandura, A. 1977. *Social Learning Theory*. Englewood Cliffs, NJ: Prentice-Hall.

Bradbury-Jones, C., and L. Isham. 2020. The Pandemic Paradox: The Consequences of COVID-19 on Domestic Violence. *Journal of Clinical Nursing* 29 (13–14): 2047–2049.

Carpenter, G.L., and A.M. Stacks. 2009. Developmental Effects of Exposure to Intimate Partner Violence in Early Childhood: A Review of the Literature. *Children and Youth Services Review* 31: 831–839.

Child Welfare Information Gateway. 2009. Domestic Violence and the Child Welfare System. https://www.childwelfare.gov/pubs/factsheets/domestic_violence/domesticviolence.pdf. Accessed 2021.

Edleson, J. L. 2004. Should Childhood Exposure to Adult Domestic Violence be Defined as Child Maltreatment. In *Protecting Children from Domestic Violence: Strategies for Community Intervention*, ed. R.G. Jaffe, L.L. Baker, and A.J. Cunningham, 8–29. New York, NY: Guilford Press.

Felitti, V.J., R.F. Anda, D. Nordenberg, D.F. Williamson, A.M. Spitz, V. Edwards, and J.S. Marks. 1998. Relationship of Childhood Abuse and Household Dysfunction to Many of the Leading Causes of Death in Adults: The Adverse Childhood Experiences (ACE) Study. *American Journal of Preventive Medicine* 14 (4): 245–258.

Felmine, Kevon. 2021. Children Witness Mom's Brutal Murder, March 10. https://www.cnc3.co.tt/children-witness-moms-brutal-murder/. Accessed June 2021.

Groves, B.A., P.V. Horn, and A.F. Lieberman. 2007. Deciding on Fathers' Involvement in Their Children's Treatment After Domestic Violence. In *Parenting by Men Who Batter*, ed. J.L. Edleson and O.J. Williams, 65–84. New York: Oxford University Press.

Henning, K., H. Leitenberg, P. Coffey, T. Bennett, and M.K. Jankowski. 1997. Long-term Psychological Adjustment to Witnessing Interparental Physical Conflict During Childhood. *Child Abuse & Neglect* 21: 501–515.

Holt, S., H. Buckley, and S. Whelan. 2008. The Impact of Exposure to Domestic Violence on Children and Young People: A Review of the Literature. *Child Abuse & Neglect* 32 (8): 797–810.

Howell, K.H., and S.A. Graham-Bermann. 2011. The Multiple Impacts of Intimate Partner Violence on Preschool Children. In *How Intimate Partner*

Violence Affects Children: Developmental Research, Case Studies, and Evidence-based Intervention, ed. S.A. Graham-Bermann and A.A. Levendosky, 87–107. Washington, DC: American Psychological Association.

Howell, K.H. 2011. Resilience and Psychopathology in Children Exposed to Family Violence. *Aggression & Violent Behavior* 16: 562–569.

Howell, K.H., S.E. Barnes, L.E. Miller, and S.A. Grahman-Bermann. 2016. Developmental Variations in the Impact of Intimate Partner Violence Exposure During Childhood. *Journal of Injury & Violence Research* 8 (1): 43–57.

Hughes, H.M., S.A. Graham-Bermann, and G. Gruber. 2001. Resilience in Children Exposed to Domestic Violence. In *Domestic Violence in the Lives of Children: The Future of Research, Intervention, and Social Policy*, ed. S.A. Graham-Bermann, and J.L. Edleson. Washington, DC: American Psychological Associates.

Hungerford, A., S.K. Wait, A.M. Fritz, and C. Clements. 2012. Exposure to Intimate Partner Violence and Children's Psychological Adjustment, Cognitive Functioning, and Social Competence: A Review. *Aggression and Violence Behavior* 17 (4): 373–382.

Huth-Bocks, A.C., A.A. Levendosky, and M.A. Semel. 2001. The Direct and Indirect Effects of Domestic Violence on Young Children's Intellectual Functioning. *Journal of Family Violence* 16 (3): 269–290.

Levendosky, A.A., G. Anne Bogat, and C. Martinez-Torteya. 2013. PTSD Symptoms in Young Children Exposed to Intimate Partner Violence. *Violence Against Women* 19: 187.

Meichenbaum, Donald. 2013. Donald Meichenbaum's Handout for 2013. The Evolution of Psychotherapy Conference. Anaheim. 13.

Meltzer, H., L. Doos, P. Vostanis, T. Ford, and R. Goodman. 2009. The Mental Health of Children Who Witness Domestic Violence. *Child & Family Social Work* 14 (4): 491–501.

Morgan, P., and V. Youssef. 2006. *Writing Rage: Unmasking Violence through Caribbean Discourse*. University of the West Indies Press.

Mullender, A., G. Hague, U. Imam, L. Kelly, E. Malos, and L. Regan. 2002. *Children's Perspectives on Domestic Violence*. London: Sage.

Murrell, A.R., K.A. Christoff, and K.R. Henning. 2007. Characteristics of Domestic Violence Offenders: Associations with Childhood Exposure to Violence. *Journal of Family Violence* 22 (7): 523–532.

Nguyen, T.D., and S. Larsen. 2012. Prevalence of Children Witnessing Parental Violence. *Review of European Studies* 4 (1): 148–154.

Osofsky, Joy. 1999. The Impact of Violence on Children. *The Future of Children* 9 (3): 33–49.

Pears, K.C., and D.M. Capaldi. 2001. Intergenerational Transmission of Abuse: A Two-generational Prospective Study of an at Risk Sample. *Child Abuse & Neglect* 25 (11): 1439–1461.

Radford, L., and M. Hester. 2006. *Mothering Through Domestic Violence*. London: Jessica Kingsley Publishers.

Renner, L.M., and Shamra Boel-Studt. 2013. The Relation between Intimate Partner Violence, Parenting Stress, and Child Behavior Problems. *Journal of Family Violence* 28: 201–212.

Rossman, B.B.R., H.M. Hughes, and M.S. Rosenberg. 2000. *Children and Interparental Violence: The Impact of Exposure*. Philadelphia, PA: Taylor & Francis.

Sewll, C., J.S. Martin, and W.D. Abel. 2010. Domestic Violence: Its Prevalence and Profile. *West Indian Medical Journal* 59 (1): 1.

The United Nations Children's Fund (UNICEF). 2006. Behind Closed Doors: The Impact of Domestic Violence on Children. http://www.unicef.org.nz/advocacy/publications/UNICEF_Body_Shop_Behind_Closed_Doors.pdf. Accessed 2021.

Thornton, K.M. 2015. Power, Privilege and Patriarchy. Doctoral dissertation.

United Nations Office on Drugs and Crime (UNODC), and World Bank. 2007. Crime, Violence, and Development: Trends, Costs and Policy Options in the Caribbean. Report No. 37820, Vienna, Washington: UNODC AND World Bank.

United Nations Office on Drugs and Crime (UNODC). 2018. *Global Study on Homicide: Gendered-related Killing of Women and Girls*. Vienna: Austria.

United Nations Regional Centre for Peace, Disarmament and Development in Latin America and the Caribbean. 2020. Normative Study: Making the Link between Norms on Violence against Women and Small Arms Control and Regulation Norms: Analysis of CARICOM States. http://unlirec.screativa.com/wp-content/uploads/2018/05/Caribbean-Legal-Study-on-Gender-SALW-Sept.-2020.pdf. Accessed June 2021.

UNWomen. 2010. UNWomen Annual Report 2010–2011. United Nations Entity for Gender Equality and the Empowerment of Women, New York, NY.

World Health Organization. 2016. Violence against Women: Intimate Partner and Sexual Violence against Women [Fact Sheet]. http://www.who.int/mediacentre/factsheets/fs239/en/. Accessed 2021.

World Population Review. 2019. https://worldpopulationreview.com/countries/trinidad-and-tobago-population/. Accessed April 2020.

CHAPTER 2

Intimate Partner Violence and Its Impact on Women's Health: The Moderating Role of Family Support and Educational Attainment

Randy Seepersad, Linda Mohammed, and Michelle Thomas

Introduction

Deemed a grave public health problem, intimate partner violence (IPV) not only adversely affects society economically and socially, but it also negatively impacts the physical and psychological health of victims,

R. Seepersad (✉)
The University of the West Indies, St. Augustine, Trinidad and Tobago
e-mail: randy.seepersad@sta.uwi.edu

L. Mohammed
University of Trinidad and Tobago, Arima, Trinidad and Tobago
e-mail: linda.mohammed@utt.edu.tt

M. Thomas
Concord College of Sino-Canada, Beijing, China

A. M. Bissessar and C. Huggins (eds.), *Domestic Violence in the Anglophone Caribbean*,
https://doi.org/10.1007/978-3-030-88476-5_2

thereby affecting their ability to lead happy and fruitful lives (Kilpatrick 2004). This deep-rooted problem is pervasive across the globe (Garcia-Moreno et al. 2006), with developing nations like Trinidad and Tobago not being spared. The World Health Organization defines IPV as "behaviours within an intimate relationship that cause physical, sexual or psychological harm, including acts of physical aggression, sexual coercion, psychological abuse and controlling behaviours" (WHO 2010, p. 11). These subtypes of IPV have been shown to have detrimental effects on victims' physical, psychological, and reproductive health.

A healthy society is often regarded as a productive society and while there are many facets of a healthy society, the health of its people, especially its women, is paramount. This understanding is reflected in the title of an article published in the Health Care Women International issue, entitled "*The Health of Women and Girls Determine the Health and Well-being of our Modern World*" (Davidson et al. 2011). Given the importance of women's health, this chapter aims to examine whether IPV has an impact on this outcome, and if so, whether women's level of education as well as the provision of family support can serve to mitigate that impact. Data from the Inter-American Development Bank's (IDB) 2018 National Women's Health Survey for Trinidad and Tobago will be used in this study. The IDB survey collected data from a random representative sample of 1079 women in Trinidad and Tobago.

An examination of national trends in IPV helps to put the issue of IPV and women's health in perspective. Figure 2.1 shows the number of IPV incidents which were reported to the police in Trinidad and Tobago from 2000 to 2020. During this time, there was an average of 1399 incidents reported per year. The data show that there was a decrease in the number of incidents of IPV from 2000 to 2003, and then a consistent increase until 2012 when the number of reported incidents peaked at 2301. The number of incidents reported then declined consistently to reach 1032 incidents in 2018. The number then increased slightly to 1078 incidents in 2019 and increased sharply to 2438 in 2020. In all likelihood, the sharp increase in 2020 may have been due to government-imposed stay-at-home restrictions as a result of the COVID-19 pandemic. A larger proportion of persons at home implies that potential victims and offenders would have been in close proximity for prolonged periods of time, increasing the risk of victimization.

Table 2.1 shows domestic violence offences which were reported to the police for the period from 2010 to 2020. During this period, a total

Fig. 2.1 Total number of domestic violence incidents in Trinidad and Tobago (2000–2020) (*Source* Trinidad and Tobago Police Service)

of 17,860 offences were reported. The most prevalent offence was assault by beating. This accounted for 49.5% of all offences which were reported. This was followed by threats, which accounted for 29.3%, breach of protection orders (8.7%), and verbal abuse (3.0%).

The data in Table 2.1 also show that 1.8% of all domestic violence offences which occurred from 2010 to 2020 resulted in the murder of the victim. From 2010 to 2020 a total of 4847 murders were committed in Trinidad and Tobago, of which 328 or 6.8% were as a result of domestic violence. An examination of long-term trends suggests that there was a decline in the proportion of murders that was due to domestic violence. From 1995 to 2000 a total of 640 murders were committed of which 137 or 21.4% were due to domestic violence. For each year after 2000, less than 11% of all murders were due to domestic violence. From 2001 to 2020 a total of 7860 murders were committed of which 539 or 6.9% were due to domestic violence. The decrease in the proportion of murders due to domestic violence was due in large measure to an increase in the overall number of murders rather than to a decrease in the number of murders due to domestic violence.

While the data from the Police Service provides an idea of the extent to which IPV affects persons in Trinidad and Tobago, other research has suggested that police statistics underestimate the prevalence of IPV. For example, data from the UNDP (2012) suggested that the actual rate of IPV in Trinidad and Tobago is 6.3 times higher than reported in police statistics (Seepersad and Williams 2016). The findings from an

Table 2.1 Reported domestic violence offences in Trinidad and Tobago (2010–2020)

Offences	*2010*	*2011*	*2012*	*2013*	*2014*	*2015*	*2016*	*2017*	*2018*	*2019*	*2020*	*Total*	*Percent*
Assault by beating	560	1140	1042	821	823	808	642	553	559	511	1380	**8839**	**49.5**
Threats	244	650	787	493	727	526	305	347	250	274	630	**5233**	**29.3**
Breach protection order	159	180	177	108	116	95	88	101	121	190	215	**1550**	**8.7**
Verbal abuse	97	34	81	44	59	62	38	25	29	19	44	**532**	**3.0**
Wounding	176	69	53	46	0	2	0	0	16	26	86	**474**	**2.7**
Psychological abuse	52	5	36	45	125	71	17	32	6	0	4	**393**	**2.2**
Murder	33	21	13	27	27	15	35	43	37	37	40	**328**	**1.8**
Sexual abuse	31	41	74	14	35	38	5	2	6	1	6	**253**	**1.4**
Malicious damage	18	29	33	22	13	15	8	14	5	9	27	**193**	**1.1**
Child abuse	10	4	5	12	6	0	3	5	3	11	6	**65**	**0.4**
Total	**1380**	**2173**	**2301**	**1632**	**1931**	**1632**	**1141**	**1122**	**1032**	**1078**	**2438**	**17,860**	**100.0**

Source Trinidad and Tobago Police Service

IDB (2018) study are even more troubling. The IDB survey showed that 30% of ever-partnered women experienced physical and/or sexual violence by an intimate partner in their lifetime, and 6% in the 12 months prior to data collection. The study also found that 7% of all respondents reported having been forced into sexual intercourse by a non-partner in their lifetime (1% in the last 12 months).

The high rate of IPV in Trinidad and Tobago is cause for concern, and suggests that a large number of persons may be suffering from the consequences of such abuse. It is therefore important to examine the consequences of IPV and to determine whether measures can be taken to mitigate the negative effects. The physical and mental health consequences of IPV have been examined by several researchers. In a systematic review of the literature on the physical and mental health impact of IPV, Dillon et al. (2013) found that IPV was associated with a variety of mental health consequences which include depression, anxiety, self-harm, and sleeping disorders. Other researchers have identified post-traumatic stress disorder (PTSD), substance abuse, low self-esteem, and clinical depression as consequences of IPV (Kilpatrick 2004; Afifi et al. 2009; Bonomi et al. 2009; Anderson and Saunders 2003; Arboleda-Florez and Wade 2001). Physical consequences of IPV may range from minor to life-threatening, and can include cuts, bruises, scratches, and burns, to broken bones and even death (Sheridan and Nash 2007). Chronic pain as well as gynecological and gastrointestinal problems are also common consequences of IPV (Campbell 2002). Problems related to cardiovascular and neurological discomfort in addition to rheumatoid pain were also found to be associated with IPV (Lown and Vega 2001; Wijma et al. 2003).

In addition to the impact of physical and psychological IPV on women's health, the literature also underscores the importance of numerous socio-demographic variables as predictors and/or moderators of health outcomes. These include age, educational attainment, drug and alcohol abuse, social support and socio-economic status. In relation to age, the literature suggests that unlike their younger counterparts, older victims of IPV are more likely to experience psychological outcomes such as depression (WHO 2020). The research has also shown that more educated persons are not only predisposed to better health outcomes when they are victimized, but they are also better at navigating the health care system and are more inclined to make better personal and lifestyle choices regarding their health when compared to their less-educated counterparts (Zimmerman and Woolf 2014). Low socio-economic status has been found to correlate strongly with higher rates of mortality and morbidity for victims of IPV (Politzer et al. 2019). Social support has been found to positively impact women's quality of life both directly and indirectly, through friend and family support (Ahmadi 2016). The research suggests that the provision of social support may serve to mitigate the negative outcomes of IPV (ibid.).

The present study attempts to bring together the two main areas of research which have been identified above. While researchers have attempted to look at the health consequences of IPV, or have looked at the impact of other variables on health outcomes, they have rarely attempted to bring both strands of research together. The first strand suggests that it is important to verify whether IPV has an impact on women's health. This has not been previously done with a sample from Trinidad and Tobago. Where IPV is found to negatively impact women's health, it is important to determine how the negative effects could be mitigated. This chapter proposes that the provision of family support may serve to mitigate the impact of IPV on health. This study also proposes that education may serve as a second mitigating factor. It is expected that women who are more educated may be able to reduce the negative impact of IPV on their health. In this study, IPV is treated as an independent variable, while health is treated as a dependent variable. Several dimensions of IPV (physical, psychological, and IPV during pregnancy) as well as several health outcomes (physical health, reproductive health, perceptions of physical health, psychological health, and suicide ideation) will be utilized. This study uses family support and educational attainment as moderator variables.

Literature Review

IPV and Health

Several researchers have investigated the impact of the various subtypes of IPV (physical, sexual, and psychological) on women's health. In terms of women's health, a range of health outcomes have also been investigated. These can be broadly classified into two main areas; physical and psychological health. Campbell (2002) found that compared to women who were not abused by their partners, those who were physically and sexually abused were likely to suffer up to 60% more physical illnesses. Ruiz-Pérez et al. (2007) investigated the association between physical, sexual, and psychological IPV on women's physical health in a sample of 1402 Spanish women aged 18–65 years who were at the time seeking medical care. The study's findings revealed that the lifetime prevalence of IPV among the sample studied was 32%, with women who experienced either psychological or both physical and psychological IPV being more likely to suffer a chronic disease than their non-abused counterparts. Further, it was reported that a combination of physical, sexual, and psychological abuse resulted in a greater impact on the physical health of the women studied.

In an earlier, study Straight and Harper (2003) investigated the impact of psychological IPV on the physical health status and health behaviours of college-aged women. The findings suggest that psychological abuse was positively correlated with illegal drug use, negative perceptions of health, and physical and role limitations. Overall, poorer health has been reported in women with histories of physical and sexual abuse. Not only are they likely to visit the doctor more frequently, but they are also more prone to be hospitalized than their non-abused counterparts (Kimerling and Calhoun 1994; Eby et al. 1995). Physically and sexually abused victims have also been found to have negative health-related thoughts, to be dissatisfied with their health and to have negative perceptions about their health (Koss et al. 1991). Analogous to sexual and physical abuse, adult female victims of psychological partner abuse, recent or current, also reported greater regularity of serious and chronic illnesses, which resulted in greater use of psychotropic drugs (Marshall 1996).

While the research cited above focused on physical health, other researchers have attempted to determine whether IPV has an impact on psychological health. In their examination of the impact of physical, sexual, and psychological IPV on women's mental health, Pico-Alfonso et al. (2006) reported that depression, suicidal thoughts, and PTSD were higher among physically and psychologically abused women, compared to their sexually abused counterparts. However, when compared to non-abused women, depression levels were higher among sexually abused women. Herbert et al. (1991) asserted that when compared to physical abuse, psychological abuse is either just as damaging or more detrimental to the individual. These researchers found that psychological abuse was able to predict PTSD among battered women even after controlling for physical abuse (Arias and Papé 1999).

IPV During Pregnancy and Health

A notable body of literature emphasizes the adverse implications of IPV during pregnancy, ranging from jeopardizing a woman's reproductive health to harming the health of the unborn child. Research suggests that between 3 and 9% of women experience abuse during pregnancy (Martin et al. 2001; Saltzman et al. 2003) with a higher prevalence of around 50% being reported among low-income, single women (Bailey and Byron 2007). Several studies have reported that women who are abused during pregnancy are not only at higher risk of smoking, as well as alcohol and substance abuse, but their sexual health is also at risk through sexual risk-taking, induced abortions, and unplanned pregnancies (Alhusen et al. 2015; Anderson et al. 2002; Caetano et al. 2005).

According to Berhane et al. (2019), low birth weight and preterm babies are common among women who experience IPV during pregnancy. Women who experience non-physical forms of IPV during pregnancy are three times more likely to experience low birth weight and preterm babies. In contrast, those subjected to physical IPV are five times more likely to experience the same outcomes. Incidents of abuse during pregnancy also adversely impact women's mental health both during pregnancy and in the post-partum phase (Kiely et al. 2013; Connelly et al. 2013). Compared to their non-abused counterparts, women who experience abuse during pregnancy are 2.5 times more likely to report depressive symptomatology (Dunn and Oths 2004).

According to the WHO (2011), the majority of studies that have examined IPV during pregnancy have restricted their research to physical IPV. Despite this, sexual and psychological IPV are also threats to the health of the woman and her unborn child. IPV during pregnancy has both fatal (homicides and suicides) and non-fatal outcomes (depression, physical impairment, miscarriage, alcohol, and substance abuse). Antenatal care provides a window of opportunity for identifying IPV during pregnancy and health care workers have a responsibility to sound the alarm once abuse is suspected.

Overall, the research findings suggest that there are long-term as well as short-term impacts of IPV on health, and that the impact applies to physical as well as mental health. The research findings also suggest that IPV has several negative outcomes regardless of whether or not it occurs during pregnancy. Given the findings in this area, it is expected that IPV will have a negative impact on health outcomes in Trinidad and Tobago.

Family Support as a Moderator of IPV and Health Consequences

While the research cited above has shown that IPV can have a negative impact on women's health, this chapter argues that the presence of social support from the family can serve to mitigate the negative impact of IPV and thus reduce the likelihood of negative health outcomes. The provision of support implies that assistance and guidance is available when it is required. Such support may include tangible support such as the provision of resources or assistance, or intangible support such as counselling and the provision of advice in times of need. Research is supportive of the beneficial role of social support. For example, Ross et al. (1990) found that social support directly impacts mental health, inclusive of depression, physical symptoms, and several causes of mortality. Seeman (1996) also found that friend and family support were correlated with lower heart and blood pressure rates, lower cholesterol, and higher immune functioning.

Research on families has also provided indirect evidence of the importance of social support. George (2016), for example, found that in families with close social relationships there is a decreased likelihood of chronic disease, disability, mental illness, and even death. The key factor which may be operative in such families is the provision of support. Families which share close social relationships have a higher likelihood of the provision of support to members. When such assistance is rendered, whether in times of need, or whether as a preventative mechanism, it serves to protect the well-being of the recipient, hence the beneficial outcomes which have been identified in research.

Despite the above, only a few studies have attempted to determine whether social support is important in the context of IPV. To examine whether support from family and friends could mitigate the impacts of IPV, Phuangkhem (2018) examined whether friend/family support moderated the association between IPV and the quality of life among 283 Thai women who were between 18 and 60 years of age. His findings suggest that both family and friend support moderated the relationship between IPV and the women's psychological health. This cushioning effect provided by family and friends was stronger for females than males. Moreover, psychological health was found to be poorer where victims of IPV received less friend and family support.

Educational Achievement as a Moderator of IPV and Health Consequences

In addition to family support, this chapter proposes that educational attainment may also serve to mitigate the negative effects of IPV. It is expected that a person's level of education can affect the coping mechanisms and strategies which they adopt if they experience IPV. Persons who are more educated may utilize more effective strategies such that they deal more effectively with health-related issues and other negative consequences of IPV.

While prior research has not examined the moderating role of education in the present context, the extant literature is suggestive that education can serve a moderating role. For example, a positive correlation has been found between education and several health outcomes, with more educated persons being more likely to seek diagnosis and follow up with treatment than their less-educated counterparts (Grossman 2000; Goldman and Lakdawalla 2001). Research has found that compared to persons with fewer years of education, persons who are more educated live longer and healthier lives (Zajakova and Lawrence 2018). Additionally, it has been found that better health is experienced by well-educated persons as indicated by higher levels of self-reported health and lower levels of morbidity, mortality, and disability (Raghupathi and Raghupathi 2020).

Research has also found that mental health is affected by educational attainment. For example, Chevalier and Feinstein (2006) found that the risk of poor mental health and depression is reduced by education, and suggest that investing in education has enduring benefits for mental health. The understanding here is that more educated persons may have more opportunities, greater control over their lives, and better security. These not only pave the way for less stress, but it also positively impacts the psychological health of those persons.

While research has consistently shown health disparities between more and less educated persons, researchers have not agreed on the precise mechanism through which education translates into better health (Kim and Durden 2007; Leopold 2016). The education–health relationship is a complex one due to the interplay of many factors such as sociodemographics, childhood health, resource accessibility, attitudes towards preventative care, and access to social networks (Feinstein et al. 2006; Raghupathi and Raghupathi 2020). Despite the fact that the processes which lead to better health for more educated persons are not fully understood, the findings from previous research suggest that persons who are more educated may make the types of decisions and may engage in the types of actions which lead to better health outcomes. It is, therefore, expected that where factors threaten their health (such as IPV) that more educated persons will engage in the types of actions which help to maintain their health status.

In investigating the impact of IPV on health, and the moderating role of family support and educational attainment, this study uses age, socio-economic status, and drug and alcohol use as control variables. Each of these variables will be examined next.

Age and Health

Research evidence suggests that there is an increase in chronic diseases as one ages, with a high degree of comorbidity between mental disorders and chronic illnesses (Keyes 2005). The literature on age and health points largely to a relationship between age and health-related behaviours such as screening (Siegrist 2005), rather than actual health status. Age is an important factor that is likely to influence health-related behaviours with older persons taking more precautionary measures than younger persons. The literature also suggests that more than 20% of adults aged 60 and older suffer from a mental or neurological disorder such as depression and dementia (WHO 2019). In fact, in 2016, in excess of 46 million adults in the United States were reported as having a mental disorder, of which 52% were women aged 18–49 years (Lin et al. 2020). Quite apart from the relationship between age and health-related behaviour as well as mental disorders, as persons get older they face an increasing array of health-related challenges. Physical strength and agility deteriorate while susceptibility to diseases and illnesses increase. Given the relationship between age and health, this variable was used as a control in the present study.

Socio-Economic Status and Health

A significant body of literature has found that the three primary dimensions of socio-economic status, education, occupation, and income, are key determinants of health (Adler and Newman 2002). According to Adler and Newman (2002), cardiovascular disease, low birth weight, diabetes, hypertension, arthritis, and cancer are all associated with socio-economic status. They further posit an association between lower socio-economic status and higher rates of mortality, with the strongest relationships occurring between the ages of 45 and 65 years. Overall, the research suggests that lower socio-economic status is likely to be associated with increases in morbidity and mortality. An unfortunate reality is that compared to their male counterparts, females have reduced access to socio-economic resources that may be used to support good health and well-being, a position shaped by cultural biases, discrimination, uneven labour divisions, and gender-based violence (Marmot et al. 2008). Given that socio-economic status is a predictor of health, and that females may be disproportionately affected by low socio-economic status, this variable is included as a control in the present study.

Drug and Alcohol Use and Health

Santelli et al. (2001) contend that among the negative psychological problems common in young women in the United States, alcohol and substance abuse is the most frequently reported. Several mental, physical, and social problems are associated with alcohol and substance abuse and include injuries, cancer, cardiovascular disease as well as psychiatric and neurological damage (ibid.). Substance abuse has also been reported to negatively affect women's sexual and reproductive health (Stidham Hall et al. 2013). More specifically, alcohol and substance abuse among women has been associated with non-use of contraceptives, an increased number of sexual partners, and an increase in sexually transmitted diseases (ibid.). Poor fertility outcomes have also been associated with alcohol and substance abuse, and range from unintended pregnancies to preterm birth and increased probability of maternal and infant mortality and morbidity (Reardon et al. 2004; Cornelius et al. 2002).

An unfortunate reality about substance use in women is that women who are victimized may turn to the use of alcohol and drugs as a coping mechanism (Cormier et al. 2004). According to Coker et al. (2002), such women are more likely to suffer from depression, suicidal ideation, lower self-esteem, and PTSD. While IPV may result in these outcomes, ironically, the use of alcohol and drugs can serve to further exacerbate such outcomes. Given that alcohol and drug use has been linked to poorer health outcomes, this variable is included as a control in the present study.

Methodology

The data used in this study derived from the IDB's (2018) National Women's Health Survey in Trinidad and Tobago. This was a cross-sectional survey which was designed to provide a diagnosis of IPV. The survey collected information on the prevalence, frequency, severity, associated factors, circumstances, and consequences of IPV as well as the reasons for and results of survivors seeking help. The IDB study aimed to assess the prevalence of IPV, to document the health consequences, to examine risk and protective factors, and to examine coping strategies of victims of IPV.

The target population was English-speaking females ages 15–64, residing in households in Trinidad and Tobago. These women represent approximately 35% of the total national population according to the 2011 Population and Housing Census. In Trinidad and Tobago, a national representative sample was selected using a three-stage design. In the first stage, 127 enumeration districts (EDs) were randomly selected.[1] Systematic sampling was then used to select 15 households per ED using a random start point and calculated selection interval. In the final stage of sampling, the Kish Selection Grid was used to select a single eligible respondent from each selected household. In total, 1515 households were selected from which 1079 females were successfully interviewed. The findings from the survey provided estimates with a 3% margin of error and 95% confidence interval. Ethical protocols were adapted from the guidelines developed by the WHO (2001) for conducting research on IPV against women while ethical approval for the study was provided by the University of the West Indies Research Ethics Board.

The sample ranged in age from 15 to 64 years of age, with a mean age of 40.8 years. The largest proportion were Evangelical (25.7%), Roman Catholic (18.5%), and Hindus (17.6%). Of the sample 43.4% were of African descent, 34.1% were East Indians, 15% were mixed,[2] and 7.5% were of other ethnicities. When educational attainment was considered the results show that 16% had up to primary school education, 51.4% had secondary school education, while 32.6% had university, vocational, or other types of education beyond secondary education. The results also show that 69% of the sample resided in rural areas while 31% resided in urban areas. Respondents were also asked to indicate their partnership status. Of the sample 5.6% never had a partner, 59% were married, 13.6%

had a partner but were not currently married and 21.8% previously had a partner but were not currently partnered.

Results

Regression models were used to examine the relationship between IPV and health. The variables which were used appear in Table 2.2. There were three measures of IPV; psychological, physical, and incidents which occurred during pregnancy. These were used as independent variables. Five aspects of health were used as dependent variables. These were physical health, reproductive health, perceptions of health (subjective health), psychological health, and suicidal ideation. Separate regression models were computed for each dependent variable (Table 2.3). Control variables included age, socio-economic status, and drug and alcohol usage. Family support and level of education were used as moderator variables. It was expected that while IPV would lead to poorer health outcomes, that persons who received higher levels of family support or persons who had higher levels of educational attainment would have fewer negative impacts upon their health. Moderation effects were tested through the use of interaction terms following the method developed by Aiken and West (1991).

Table 2.2 Variables

	Variable	*Mean*	*SD*	α
Control variables	Age	40.83	13.41	–
	Socio-Economic Status	4.46	1.64	0.664
	Drug and Alcohol Usage	4.09	1.41	0.280
Moderators	Education	12.05	3.27	–
	Family Support	1.11	0.31	–
Dependent variables	Health (subjective)	3.75	0.753	–
	Health (physical)	23.01	1.35	0.595
	Health (psychological)	3.43	3.71	0.871
	Health (suicidal ideation)	0.265	0.692	0.638
	Health (reproductive)	0.501	1.08	0.071
Independent variables	IPV (Psychological)	0.714	1.24	0.822
	IPV (Physical)	0.834	1.68	0.873
	IPV (During Pregnancy)	0.087	0.375	0.820

Table 2.3 Intimate partner violence as a predictor of health outcomes

	Health (physical)	*Health (reproductive)*	*Health (subjective)*	*Health (psychological)*	*Health (suicidal ideation)*
Age	***−0.159	**0.084	***−0.119	***0.154	***−0.167
Education	***0.147	−0.024	***0.130	***0.101	−0.013
Socio-Economic status	**0.092	0.056	0.051	0.035	−0.042
Family support	−0.152	0.055	***−0.129	***−0.199	***0.130
Drug and alcohol usage	0.024	***0.159	−0.005	*−0.058	**0.081
IPV psychological	***−0.131	−0.001	−0.038	***−0.139	0.040
IPV physical	0.077	*0.096	−0.010	−0.052	***0.161
IPV during pregnancy	*−0.094	0.022	*−0.075	***−0.136	0.064
IPV psychological * family support	**0.119	0.004	0.034	0.005	0.070
IPV psychological * education	−0.001	−0.044	−0.051	−0.002	0.026
IPV physical * family support	*−0.116	0.019	−0.014	−0.056	−0.049
IPV physical * education	−0.002	*0.087	0.023	−0.053	0.016
IPV pregnancy * family support	*−0.076	−0.049	0.037	0.046	−0.052
IPV pregnancy * education	0.022	−0.057	0.043	0.018	0.007
Adjusted R^2	0.177	0.056	0.080	0.186	0.126

$N = 1079$

The regression models which appear in Table 2.3 simultaneously test the impact of IPV on health, and the importance of family support and educational attainment as moderators of the relationship between IPV and health. Variance inflation factors were computed to assess whether multicollinearity existed. The results show that multicollinearity was not a problem in any of the regression models.

The results provide strong evidence that experiencing IPV has a negative impact on health. Experiencing higher levels of psychological abuse was related to poorer physical health ($\beta = -0.131, p < 0.001$) and poorer psychological health ($\beta = -0.139$, $p < 0.001$). Experiencing higher levels of physical abuse was related to poorer reproductive health ($\beta = 0.096$, $p < 0.05$) and higher suicidal ideation ($\beta = 0.161$, $p < 0.001$). Experiencing abuse during pregnancy was related to poorer physical health (−0.094, $p < 0.05$), poorer perceptions of health ($\beta = -0.075$, $p < 0.05$), and poorer psychological health ($\beta = -0.136$, $p < 0.001$). The results suggest that all three types of IPV which were considered have a negative impact on health, and the impact applies to a range of health-related outcomes.

Two moderators were included in the regression models. These were family support and educational attainment. The overall premise of the study was that experiencing IPV has a negative impact on health. As indicated previously, this was supported. The core idea behind the moderators was that they can serve to mitigate the negative effects of IPV. As such, it was expected that persons who experience IPV but who receive family support will experience fewer negative health effects. It was also expected that persons who experience IPV but who are more educated will experience fewer negative health effects.

Overall, while there was some evidence to support the moderating role of family support and educational attainment, the evidence was not compelling in that very few moderating effects were found across the range of dependent variables. The results showed that persons who experience IPV during pregnancy but who have family support have better physical health ($\beta = -0.076$, $p < 0.05$). In addition, persons who experience physical IPV but who receive family support also have better physical health ($\beta = -0.116$, $p < 0.05$). The results also showed that persons who experience physical IPV but who have higher levels of education have better reproductive health ($\beta = 0.087$, $p < 0.05$). This was net of the direct impact of education on reproductive health.

Contrary to expectations, however, it was found that persons who experienced physical IPV and who received family support had poorer physical health ($\beta = 0.119$, $p < 0.01$). In addition, no moderating effects were found when perceptions of health, psychological health, and suicidal ideation were used as dependent variables. The absence of moderating effects for three of the dependent variables coupled with only a few moderating effects when physical and reproductive health were used as dependent variables suggest that family support and educational attainment do not adequately mitigate the negative impact of IPV on health outcomes.

Several variables were included as controls in the regression models in Table 2.3. The majority of relationships were in the expected direction. The results show that an increase in age was related to poorer physical health ($\beta = -0.159$, $p < 0.001$), poorer reproductive health ($\beta = 0.084$, $p < 0.01$), poorer perceptions of health ($\beta = -0.119$, $p < 0.001$), better psychological health ($\beta = 0.154$, $p < 0.001$), and lower suicide ideation ($\beta = -0.167$, $p < 0.001$). Higher socio-economic status was related to better physical health ($\beta = 0.092$, $p < 0.01$) while higher levels of drug and alcohol usage was related to poorer reproductive health ($\beta = 0.159$, $p < 0.001$) poorer psychological health ($\beta = -0.058$, $p < 0.05$) and higher levels of suicidal ideation ($\beta = 0.081$, $p < 0.01$).

In keeping with the method developed by Aiken and West (1991), family support and educational attainment, while used as moderators, were also included as controls. The results show that higher levels of family support were related to improved perceptions of health ($\beta = -0.129$, $p < 0.001$), better psychological health ($\beta = -0.199$, $p < 0.001$), and lower levels of suicidal ideation ($\beta = 0.130$, $p < 0.001$). Higher levels of education were related to better physical health ($\beta = 0.147$, $p < 0.001$), better perceptions of health ($\beta = 0.130$, $p < 0.001$), and better psychological health ($\beta = 0.101$, $p < 0.001$).

Discussion

The current chapter examined the impact of various forms of IPV on women's health as well as the possible moderating role of family support and educational attainment in this relationship, using data from the Inter-American Development Bank's (IDB) 2018 National Women's Health Survey for Trinidad and Tobago. The results provide strong evidence that experiencing IPV has a negative impact on women's health. Experiencing higher levels of psychological abuse was related to poorer physical health and poorer psychological health while experiencing higher levels of physical abuse was related to poorer reproductive health and higher suicidal ideation. Experiencing abuse during pregnancy was related to poorer physical health, poorer perceptions of health, and poorer psychological health. The results suggest that all three types of IPV which were considered have a negative impact on women's health. Contrary to expectations, however, family support and educational attainment did not adequately serve to mitigate the negative effect of IPV on women's health.

The findings of this study in regard to the role of social support (in this case family support) as a possible moderator of the IPV–health relationship is inconsistent with previous research undertaken in western societies. The fact that the IPV–health relationship is not mitigated by social support in the Trinidad and Tobago context could be attributed to the changing family structure of Caribbean families, inclusive of Trinidad and Tobago. Historically, Caribbean families were primarily of the extended type, and having such large families meant that there were sufficient persons to provide the necessary social support to family members who needed it. Over the last few decades, however, the structure of Caribbean families has moved away from a primarily nuclear or extended type to that of single-parent households with mainly women taking on headship roles (St. Bernard 2003; Hill 2011). Ultimately this translates to less social support being available in the family due to the sheer reduction in the number of family members. Unfortunately, the IDB survey did not capture data on family structure to allow for an assessment of the prevalence of single-parent households among respondents.

Another possible explanation for the failure of social support to moderate the IPV–health relationship could be due to IPV still being very much an undisclosed crime in Trinidad and Tobago, with persons not wanting to reveal that they are victims, not even to family members. Many persons try to hide the fact that they are victims due to factors such as fear of the perpetrator and embarrassment, while others may be led to believe that they are responsible for their victimization and so remain quiet about it. Yet others fail to disclose their victimization to their families or the authorities, in the hope that the situation would change for the better and the abuse would cease. Culturally, in Trinidad and Tobago, it is not the norm for IPV victims to disclose their abuse and they therefore may choose to deal with the issue privately (Zellerer 2000). Non-disclosure implies non-receipt of family support.

In Trinidad and Tobago, it is the norm for persons outside of the abusive circle to not get involved since they think that it is inappropriate to intervene in others' personal matters (Lazarus-Black 2007). Further, given that IPV may be taking place within the victim's family, the victim may not see their current family environment as being able to provide any level of support. In fact, it is not uncommon in some societies for female IPV victims to not turn to their families for help as was evident in a study among Mexican female IPV victims, in which it was found that 40% turned to public authorities rather than their own families for help

(Frias and Agoff 2015). Additionally, 11% did not seek help in order to hide their abuse from family members (ibid.).

The reasons cited above suggest that social support may not be sought, or may not be sufficiently provided for victims of IPV in Trinidad and Tobago. This implies that the variance of the measure used in the present study may be too low to detect reliable moderation effects. This does not mean that family support does not, or cannot serve to mitigate the negative impact of IPV. Rather, it means that in samples with higher variance in this measure, it may well be possible to detect statistically reliable moderation effects.

Educational attainment was also not found to be a moderator of the IPV–health relationship. While the literature suggests that persons with higher levels of education are not only more likely to make better decisions regarding their health, and are also more likely to seek the required health care and so mitigate the negative impact of IPV on health, this was not found in this study. A possible explanation for this finding may relate to the variance in the education measure which was used, that is, if the majority of persons were either very educated or not educated, detecting statistically significant moderation effects would have become more difficult. The data from the IDB study, however, do not support this explanation.

Another possibility may relate to the quality of healthcare that is available in Trinidad and Tobago. The healthcare system has often been described as one which provides a poor standard of healthcare. If this is indeed so, even where more educated persons seek care, the quality of care which is received, may not be sufficient to have a meaningful impact on the negative health consequences of IPV.

Another possibility is that educational attainment may not be related to health-seeking behaviour when it is related to IPV. It may be the case that educational attainment is related to health-seeking behaviour for other types of health concerns (e.g. diabetes, heart issues, etc.) but where persons experience IPV, they may not seek medical care in an effort to conceal the fact that they were a victim of such violence. If more educated persons do not seek medical attention, then the negative impacts of such victimization upon their health will not be mitigated. It was noted earlier that the need to conceal IPV may also have affected the moderating role of family support. This suggests that a cultural shift may be necessary so that persons become more willing to report incidents of domestic violence when they occur.

The findings of this study provide strong evidence that IPV results in a wide range of negative health outcomes for victims. Health outcomes can be physical or psychological, and can occur regardless of the type of IPV that is experienced. Contrary to expectations, however, family support and educational attainment did not adequately mitigate the negative health effects of experiencing IPV. These findings suggest that it may be worthwhile for future research to examine additional potential moderators of the IPV–health relationship. These include other sources of social support (e.g. co-workers, friends, etc.), health-seeking behaviour, the quality of health care which is available, and other such factors.

The negative health outcomes of IPV persist long after the abuse has ended, making IPV an issue which requires urgent attention. Fortunately, within the last five years, Trinidad and Tobago has made several advances in addressing the IPV problem, ranging from the National Strategic Plan on Gender-Based and Sexual Violence in Trinidad and Tobago being laid before the Parliament in 2016, to the launch of the Gender-Based Violence Unit (GBVU) within the Trinidad and Tobago Police Service (TTPS) in 2020. While other initiatives also exist, more needs to be done at the level of health care institutions. For example, it is imperative that medical personnel be adequately trained to identify IPV victims at the screening level and that systems be put in place to offer assistance to victims. At a cultural level, more needs to be done to reduce the reluctance of persons to report and deal effectively with IPV and its consequences.

Notes

1. Trinidad is divided into fourteen (14) administrative areas or municipalities: two (2) cities, three (3) boroughs, and (9) regional corporations; Tobago is subdivided into seven (7) parishes. These municipalities are made up of Enumeration Districts (EDs). Each ED consists of about 150–200 households, on average.
2. This refers to persons who have one parent of African and one parent of East Indian descent.

References

Adler, N.E., and K. Newman. 2002. Socio-Economic Disparities in Health: Pathways and Policies Inequality in Education, Income, and Occupation Exacerbates the Gaps Between the Health 'Haves' and 'Have-Nots.' *Health Affairs* 21 (2): 60–76.

Afifi, T.O., H. Mc Millan, B.J. Cox, G.J. Asmundson, M.B. Stein, and J. Sween. 2009. Mental Health Correlates of Intimate Partner Violence in Marital Relationships in a Nationally Representative Sample of Males and Females. *Journal of Interpersonal Violence* 24 (8): 1398–1417.

Ahmadi, A. 2016. Social Support and Women's Health. *Women's Health Bulletin* 3 (1): 1–6.

Aiken, L.S., and S.G. West. 1991. *Multiple Regression: Testing and Interpreting Interactions*. Newbury Park, CA: Sage.

Alhusen, J.L., E. Ray, P. Sharpe, and L. Bullock. 2015. Intimate Partner Violence During Pregnancy: Maternal and Neonatal Outcomes. *Journal of Women's Health* 24 (1): 100–106.

Anderson, B.A., H.A. Marshak, and D.L. Hebbeler. 2002. Identify Intimate Partner Violence at Entry to Pre-Natal Care: Clustering Routine Clinical Information. *Journal of Midwifery Women's Health* 47: 353–359.

Anderson, D.K., and D.G. Saunders. 2003. Leaving an Abusive Partner: An Empirical Review of Predictors, the Process of Leaving and Psychological Well-Being. *Trauma, Violence and Abuse* 4: 163–191.

Arboleda-Florez, J., and T.J. Wade. 2001. Childhood and Adult Victimization as Risk Factors for Major Depression. *International Journal of Law and Psychiatry* 24: 357–370.

Arias, I., and K.T. Papé. 1999. Psychological Abuse, Implications for Adjustment and Commitment to Leave Violent Partners. *Violence and Victims* 8: 17–28.

Bailey, B.A., and A.R. Byron. 2007. Factors Predicting Birth Weight in a Low-Risk Sample: The Role of Modifiable Pregnancy Health Behaviours. *Maternal Child Health* 11 (2): 173–179.

Berhane, M., N. Workineh, T. Girma, R. Lim, K.J. Lee, C.D. Nguyen, E. Neal, and F.M. Russell. 2019. Prevalence of Low Birth Weight and Prematurity and Associated Factors in Neonates in Ethiopia: Results from a Hospital-Based Observational Study. *Ethiopian Journal of Health Sciences* 29 (6): 677–688.

Bonomi, A.E., M.L. Anderson, R.J. Reid, F.P. Rivara, D. Carrell, and R.S. Thompson. 2009. Medical and Psychosocial Diagnoses in Women with a History of Intimate Partner Violence. *Archives of Internal Medicine* 169 (18): 1692–1697.

Caetano, R., C. Mc Grath, S. Ramisetty-Mikler, and C.A. Field. 2005. Drinking, Alcohol Problems and the Five-Year Recurrence and Incidence of Male to Female and Female to Male Partner Violence. *Alcohol and Clinical Experience Resources* 29: 98–106.

Campbell, J.C. 2002. Health Consequences of Intimate Partner Violence. *The Lancet* 359 (9314): 1331–1336.

Chavalier, A., and L. Feinstein. 2006. The Causal Effect of Education on Mental Health. LSE Online. Available at http://cee.lse.ac.uk/ceedps/ceedps/ceedp7/pdf. Accessed 15 Mar 2021.

Coker, A.L., P.H. Smith, M.P. Thompson, R.E. Mckeon, L. Bethea, and K.E. Davis. 2002. Social Support Protects Against the Negative Effects of Partner Violence on Mental Health. *Journal of Women's Health and Gender-Based Medicine* 11 (5): 465–476.

Connelly, C.D., A.L. Hazen, M.J. Baker-Ericzén, J. Landsverk, and S.M. Horwitz. 2013. Is Screening for Depression in the Perinatal Period Enough? The Co-Occurrence of Depression, Substance Abuse, and Intimate Partner Violence in Culturally Diverse Pregnant Women. *Journal of Women's Health* 22 (10): 844–852.

Cormier, R.A., C.A. Dell, and N. Poole. 2004. Women and Substance Abuse Problems. *BMC Women's Health* 4 (1): S8.

Cornelius, M.D., N.L. Goldschmidt, and C.L. Day. 2002. Alcohol, Tobacco and Marijuana Use Among Pregnant Teenagers: 6 Year Follow Up of Offspring Growth Effects. *Neurotoxicology and Teratology* 24 (6): 703–710.

Davidson, P.M., S.J. Mc Grath, A.I. Meleis, et al. 2011. The Health of Women and Girls Determine the Health and Well-Being of Our Modern World: A White Paper from the International Council on Women's Health Issues. *Health Care Women International* 32 (10): 870–886.

Dillon, G., R. Hussain, D. Loxton, and S. Rahman. 2013. Mental and Physical Health and Intimate Partner Violence Against Women: A Review of the Literature. *International Journal of Family Medicine* 28 (6): 1–13.

Dunn, L.L., and K.S. Oths. 2004. Prenatal Predictors of Intimate Partner Abuse. *Journal of Obstetrics, Gynaecology and Neonatal Nursing* 33: 54–63.

Eby, K.K., J.C. Campbell, C.M. Sullivan, and W.S. Davidson. 1995. Health Effects of Experience of Sexual Violence for Women with Abusive Partners. *Health Care for Women's Health* 16 (6): 563–576.

Feinstein, L., R. Sabatés, T. Anderson, A. Sorhaindo, and C. Hammond. 2006. What Are the Effects of Education on Health? Presentation at the Social Outcome of Learning Project Symposium, OECD's Centre for Educational Research and Innovation (CERI), in Copenhagen, 23 and 24 March 2006.

Frias, S.M., and C. Agoff. 2015. Between Support Vulnerability: Examining Family Support Among Women Victims of Intimate Partner Violence in Mexico. *Journal of Family Violence* 30 (3): 277–291.

Garcia-Moreno, C., H. Jansen, M. Ellsberg, L. Heise, and C.H. Watts. 2006. Prevalence of Intimate Partner Violence: Findings from the WHO Multi-Country Study on Women's Health and Domestic Violence. *The Lancet* 368: 1260–1269.

George, L.K. 2016. The Health Promoting Effects of Social Bonds. Department of Sociology, Centre for the Study of Aging and Human Development. Duke University, Durham, NC.

Goldman, D.P., and D.N. Lakdawalla. 2001. Understanding Health Disparities Across Educational Groups. NBER, Working Paper #8328.

Grossman, M. 2000. The Human Capital Model. In *Handbook of Health Economics*, ed. A.J. Culyer and J.P. Newhouse, 347–408. Amsterdam: Elsevier Science.

Herbert, T.B., R.C. Silver, and J.H. Ellard. 1991. Coping with an Abusive Relationship: How and Why Do Women Stay? *Journal of Marriage and Family* 50: 311–325.

Hill, K. 2011. Too Many Single Parents. *Jamaica Gleaner*, April 10. http://jamaica-gleaner.com/gleaner/20110410/news5.html. Accessed 10 Mar 2021.

Inter-American Development Bank. 2018. *National Women's Health Survey in Trinidad and Tobago*. Washington, DC: Inter-American Development Bank.

Keyes, C. 2005. Chronic Physical Conditions and Aging: Is Mental Health a Potential Protective Factor? *Aging International* 30 (5): 88–104.

Kiely, M., M.G. Gantz, M.N. El-Khorazaty, and A.A. EL-Mohandes. 2013. Sequential Screening for Psychosocial and Behaviour Risk During Pregnancy in a Population of Urban African Americans. *British Journal of Obstetrics and Gynaecology* 120: 1395–1402.

Kilpatrick, D.G. 2004. What Is Violence Against Women? Defining and Measuring the Problem. *Journal of Interpersonal Violence* 19 (11): 1209–1234.

Kim, J., and E. Durden. 2007. Socio-Economic Status and Age Trajectories of Health. *Social Sciences and Medicine* 65 (12): 2489–2502.

Kimerling, R., and K.S. Calhoun. 1994. Somatic Symptoms, Social Support and Treatment Seeking Among Sexual Assault Victims. *Journal of Consulting and Clinical Psychology* 62 (2): 332–340.

Koss, M.P., P.G. Koss, and M.S. Woodruff. 1991. Deleterious Effects of Criminal Victimization on Women's Health and Medical Utilization. *Archives of Internal Medicine* 151: 342–347.

Lazarus-Black, M. 2007. *Everyday Harm: Domestic Violence, Court Rites and Cultures of Recognition*. University of Illinois Press.

Leopold, L. 2016. Education and Physical Health Trajectories Later in Life: A Comparative Study. *Demography* 55: 901–927.

Lin, S.C., N. Tyus, M. Maloney, B. Ohri, and A. Sripipatana. 2020. Mental Health Status of Women of Reproductive Age from Underserved Communities in the United States and the Association Between Depression and Mental Health: A Cross-Sectional Study. *PLoS One* 15 (4): eo231243. https://doi.org/10.1371/journal.pone.0231243.

Lown, E.A., and W.A. Vega. 2001. Intimate Partner Violence and Health: Self-Assessed Health, Chronic Health and Somatic Symptoms Among Mexican American Women. *Psychosomatic Medicine* 63: 352–360.

Marmot, M., S. Friel, R. Bell, T.A. Houweiling, and S. Taylor. 2008. Closing a Gap in a Generation: Health Equity Through Action on the Social Determinant of Health. *The Lancet* 372: 1661–1669.

Marshall, L.L. 1996. Psychological Abuse of Women: Six Distinct Clusters. *Journal of Family Violence* 11: 43–55.

Martin, S.L., K.L. Mackie, L.L. Kupper, P.A. Buescher, and K.E. Moracco. 2001. Physical Abuse of Women, During and After Pregnancy. *Journal of American Medical Association* 285: 1581–1584.

Phuangkhem, W. 2018. The Relationship Between Intimate Partner Violence and Quality of Life Among Thai Women: The Moderating Effects of Family Support and Friend Support. Ph.D. dissertation, Kent State University, College of Nursing.

Pico-Alfonso, M., B.A. Garcia-Lenares, N. Celda-Navarro, C. Blasco-Ros, E. Echeburua, and M. Martinez. 2006. The Impact of Physical, Psychological and Sexual Intimate Male Partner Violence on Women's Mental Health: Depressive Symptoms, Posttraumatic Stress Disorder, State Anxiety and Suicide. *Journal of Women's Health* 15 (5): 599–611.

Politzer, E., A. Shmueli, and S. Avni. 2019. The Economic Burden of Health Disparities Related to Socio-Economic Status in Israel. *Israeli Journal of Health Policy Research* 8 (1), 46: 1–16.

Raghupathi, V., and W. Raghupathi. 2020. The Influence of Education on Health: An Empirical Assessment of OECD Countries for the Period 1995–2015. *Archives of Public Health* 78 (20): 1–18.

Reardon, D.C., P.K. Coleman, and J. Cougle. 2004. Substance Use Associated with Prior History of Abortion and Unintended Birth: A National Cross-Sectional Cohort Study. *American Journal of Drug and Alcohol Abuse* 26: 369–383.

Ross, C.E., J. Mirowsky, and K. Goldsteen. 1990. The Impact of Family on Health. *Journal of Marriage and the Family* 52 (4): 1059–1078.

Ruiz-Pérez, I., J. Plazaola-Castaño, and M. Del Rio Lozano. 2007. Physical Health Consequences of Intimate Partner Violence in Spanish Women. *The European Journal of Public Health* 17 (5): 437–443.

Saltzman, L.E., C.H. Johnson, B.C. Gilbert, and M.M. Goodwin. 2003. Physical Abuse Around the Time of Pregnancy: An Examination of Prevalence and Risk Factors in 16 States. *Maternal and Child Health Journal* 7: 31–43.

Santelli, J.S., L. Robin, N.D. Brener, and R. Lowry. 2001. Timing of Alcohol and Other Drug Use and Sexual Risk Behaviors Among Unmarried Adolescents and Young Adults. *Family Planning Perspectives* 33 (5): 200–205.

Seeman, T. 1996. Social Ties and Health: The Benefits of Social Integration. *Annals of Epidemiology* 6 (5): 442–451.

Seepersad, R., and D. Williams. 2016. *Crime and Security in Trinidad and Tobago*. Kingston: Ian Randle Publishers.

Sheridan, D.J., and K.R. Nash. 2007. Acute Injury Patterns of Intimate Partner Violence Victims. *Trauma, Violence and Abuse* 8 (3): 281–289.

Siegrist, J. 2005. Social Reciprocity and Health: New Scientific Evidence and Policy Implications. *Psychoneuroendocrinology* 30: 1033–1038.

St. Bernard, Godfrey. 2003. *Major Trends Affecting Families in Central America and the Caribbean*. United Nations Division of Social Policy and Development, Department of Economic and Social Affairs Program on the Family.

Stidham Hall, K., C. Moreau, and J. Trussel. 2013. The Link Between Substance Use and Reproductive Health Service Utilization Among Young US Women. *Substance Use* 34 (3): 283–291.

Straight, E.S., and F. Harper. 2003. The Impact of Partner Psychological Abuse on Health, Behaviour and Health Status of College Women. *Journal of Interpersonal Violence* 18 (9): 1035–1054.

United Nations Development Programme. 2012. Caribbean Human Development Report: Human Development and the Shift to Better Citizen Security. UNDP, New York.

Wijma, B., B. Schei, K. Swahnberg, et al. 2003. Emotional, Physical and Sexual Abuse in Patients Visiting Gynaecology Clinics: A Cross-Sectional Study. *The Lancet* 361: 2107–2113.

World Health Organization. 2001. Putting Women First: Ethical and Safety Recommendations for Research on Domestic Violence Against Women. Department of Gender and Women's Health, Family and Community Health, WHO, Geneva Switzerland.

World Health Organization. 2010. Preventing Intimate Partner and Sexual Violence Against Women: Taking Action and Generating Evidence. Geneva Switzerland.

World Health Organization. 2011. Intimate Partner Violence During Pregnancy. Information Sheet. https://apps.who.int/iris/bitstream/handle/10665/70764/WHO_RHR_11.35_eng.pdf.

World Health Organization. 2019. Violence Against Women. Geneva Switzerland.

World Health Organization. 2020. Strengthening the Health System Response to Violence Against Women in Uganda: Lessons Learned from Adapting and Implementing WHO Guidelines and Tools. Geneva Switzerland.

Zajakova, A., and E. Lawrence. 2018. The Relationship Between Education and Health: Reducing Disparities Through a Contextual Approach. *Annual Review of Public Health* 39: 273–289.

Zellerer, E. 2000. Domestic Violence in Trinidad and Tobago: Some Comments. *Caribbean Journal of Criminology and Social Psychology* 5 (1 & 2): 209–227.
Zimmerman, E., and S.H. Woolf. 2014. Understanding the Relationship Between Education and Health. *National Academy of Medicine Perspectives*. Discussion Paper, National Academy of Medicine: Washington, DC. https://doi.org/10.31478/201406a.

CHAPTER 3

Older Adults and Intimate Partner Violence in Trinidad and Tobago: A View from Health Professionals

Akeem Modeste-James

Discussion

Little is known about the experiences of older adults in ongoing intimate partner violence (IPV) relationships and the effectiveness of how healthcare professionals respond in the small island state of Trinidad and Tobago. IPV can be defined as "behavior within an intimate relationship that causes physical, sexual or psychological harm, including acts of physical aggression, sexual coercion, psychological abuse and controlling behaviors by a current or former intimate partner, by a person who shares a child with the victim or by someone connected to the victim through domestic and financial means" (Centers for Disease Control and Prevention (CDC) 2015; World Health Organization (WHO) 2013).

A. Modeste-James (✉)
Graduate School of Social Work, University of Denver, Denver, CO, USA
e-mail: Akeem.Modeste-James@du.edu

A. M. Bissessar and C. Huggins (eds.), *Domestic Violence in the Anglophone Caribbean*,
https://doi.org/10.1007/978-3-030-88476-5_3

According to the CDC 2014, nearly 12 million intimate partner victimizations of women occur in the United States each year. The high rates of IPV have raised public awareness in addressing this social issue. However, certain populations such as older adults, seem to receive the least amount of attention. Most research focuses on women of childbearing age, while little attention is given to older victims and their unique service needs (Hightower et al. 2006; Mouton 2003). IPV in later life is an overlooked phenomenon that goes unnoticed (Dunlop et al. 2005; Phillips 2000). Resulting in further isolation of the older adult population, neglecting their need for resources and intervention.

Globally, the population of older adults 60 years and over will expand to nearly 2 billion by 2050 (Perel-Levin 2005). In the Caribbean, 17% of the population will be over 60 by 2050 (Rawlins and Alea 2014). The Caribbean is located between the North and South Americas with a population of 46 million people. It consists of thirty (30) territories including, thirteen (13) sovereign small developing states (World Population Review 2019). According to the WHO, the prevalence of abuse of older adults varies widely from 1 to 35%, which is shaped by the country's cultural backgrounds and definitions of abuse (Dong 2014). Globally, IPV in later life will become more pervasive if awareness is not heightened and social support standards strengthened, particularly in small island states. In economically resourceful countries such as Trinidad and Tobago, IPV still remains a "private sphere" matter (Lazarus-Black 2001). In this chapter, the emphasis is on the older adult population particularly those over 60 years. Furthermore, we will examine the experiences of older adults in ongoing IPV and the effectiveness of how healthcare professionals respond in the small island state of Trinidad and Tobago. Currently, there are no official studies in the Caribbean small island states examining experiences of older adults in ongoing IPV, nor an examination of the efficiency of the healthcare system to safeguard this population. Furthermore, the findings utilized in this chapter were taken from a previous study on older adults, conducted by the author, which was approved by The University of the West Indies at St. Augustine, Ethics Committee on human subjects.

Trinidad and Tobago

The Trinidad and Tobago population of 1,359,193 (World Populations Review 2019) is diverse with ethnicities (e.g. 35.43% African, 34.22% East Indian, 7.66% Mixed African and East Indian, and 15.16% Mixed) as well as, religions (e.g., Catholic, Hindu, Muslim; World Populations Report 2019). It has been an independent Republic since August 31, 1962 and is governed by an elected Prime Minister. Trinidad and Tobago have oil and gas resources with the economic means to sustain itself and an unemployment rate of 4% but a poverty rate of 20% (UNICEF 2013; Artana et al. 2009).

Older adults aged 60 years and over represent 13.4% or 177,676 persons of the national population. This figure is projected to grow to 30.1% in 2050 (Trinidad and Tobago Central Statistical Office 2011). This is significant because Trinidad and Tobago is a part of a select group of countries within the developing world to have an "ageing population", which is representative of the demographic trend within the Caribbean region (Rawlins and Alea 2014).

The Intersectionality of Intimate Partner Violence and Elder Abuse

Abuse of older adults sits awkwardly at the intersection of elder abuse and intimate partner violence, this has resulted in their needs being overlooked in intimate abusive relationships (Brandl 2005 as cited in Kilbane and Spira 2010). Indeed, Brandl and Cook-Daniels (2002) posit that abuse grown old covers both elder abuse and domestic violence. For example, women who experience long-standing domestic violence that transcends when the older adult turns 60 years of age now enters the realm of elder abuse. As a result, domestic violence in later life is treated as a subset of the larger elder abuse problem. Vinton (1991) indicated when working with older adults of domestic violence that the main question for service providers is whether it is elder abuse or domestic violence? There has been insufficient dialogue and ambiguity in distinguishing terms of knowledge between domestic violence and elder abuse (Montminy 2005).

Dynamics of Abuse in Later Life in Trinidad and Tobago

Abuse in later life refers to victims who are 60 years and over, who are in an ongoing relationship where there is an expectation of trust with the perpetrator who can be a spouse, intimate partner, adult child, family member, or caregiver (NCALL website 2011). It is difficult to ascertain the prevalence of IPV in later life, due to the fact that older adults' experiences are rarely included in research literature (Harbison 2008). Nevertheless, perpetrators are predominately male and victims are mostly female (CDC 2011). As IPV transcends through the stages of the life course often times the patterns of abuse changes in later life (Rennison and Rand 2003). For example, physical abuse declines in later life but it's often replaced with a new type, such as psychological/emotional abuse where the perpetrator uses a wide range of coercive tactics to main control and power in the relationship making the older adult feel insecure and unsure. Coercive tactics can include intimidation, isolation, threats, and physical violence (Stark 2010). For example, some abusers withheld money for food and basic essentials (Hightower et al. 2006).

Like younger victims of IPV, older victims are fearful of being harmed or even killed if they attempt to leave the abusive relationship (Abramson et al. 2011; Brandl et al. 2007). There are many factors at play that prevents an older adult from leaving the abusive situation. Perpetrators use coercive controlling behaviours to encourage the victim's dependency on them. For example, the victim may suffer from a serious or terminal illness and is dependent on the perpetrator for medical care. Older victims experiencing health challenges may have more limited options than younger healthy victims (Zink et al. 2003; Beaulaurier et al. 2005, 2007).

In Trinidad and Tobago, little is known about the dynamics of abuse in later life. As a result, it is difficult to identify the prevalence of IPV in later life, partly because older adults' experiences are rarely included in research studies (Harbison 2008). However, in analysing clinician's field notes it was discovered that in Trinidad and Tobago the Hindu Marriage Act allows fathers the decision-making power to marry off their daughters at age 14, notwithstanding that the legal cut-off age for girls in the general population which is 16; all boys have to be 18. One physician indicated that "*young East Indian girls when married to older men face a significant among of physical and verbal abuse where they are required emergency services for a broken rib cage or fracted arm. However, from my experience when the perpetrator declines in age the roles are reverse. The older victim may not receive physical abuse but would be a victim of neglect and verbal abuse*". One social worker confirmed that "*the wife was withholding the medication from her husband who was paralyzed from the waist down as revenge from what she endure in the past*".

Sugar Daddies

The term "sugar daddy" describes an older wealthy man who lavishes gifts on younger women in exchange for their company and/or sexual favours. The Caribbean region is no stranger to the sugar arrangement, however, it is known as a "transactional relationship". A transactional relationship can be defined as a deliberate exchange of sex for some form of "betterment", the relationship is not typically based on romance or love but it can be established. As a result, younger women are partnering with older men for a variety of reasons, including the payment of school fees, money, and to acquire material things. This type of relationship has become very common in today's society and is accepted and encouraged as a means of survival.

However, little is known about the intimate partner violence within the situation due to a lack of research in this area. An analysis of clinicians' field notes found that younger women would enter into intimate relationships with older men as a means of survival for financial gains. For example, "*a 68-year-old male retired School Principal has been divorced for 6 years and began an intimate relationship with a 34-year-old female. During the relationship the female was verbally abusive towards him and would accompany him to the bank to withdraw large sums of money such as $5000 which she stated was for the maintenance of the home. Luckily for him, his daughter was the co-signer on his bank account and began to intervene*".

Furthermore, it is important to note that older men have been marginalized in a system specifically designed for women. The construction of IPV as a gendered social problem portrays women as innocent victims whereby heterosexual men are presumed to be the perpetrators (Josolyne 2011). Dutton and White (2013) refer to these prejudices as the "gender paradigm" under which services are aimed at meeting the needs of female victims, as heterosexual male victims are impeded from reaching victim status (Josolyne 2011).

Cougars and Young Boys

Contrary to popular belief, intimacy does not decrease with age, as many older women have a desire for companionship and physical intimacy (Bulcroft and Bulcroft 1991; Bulcroft and O'Conner 1986) but social taboos often prevent people from acknowledging it. Society tends to view older women as asexual based on ageist attitudes, which view old age as a process of decline and deterioration (Jones and Powell 2006). Healthcare professionals also reported stereotypical beliefs thinking older women are asexual (Hinchliff and Gott 2011). Physical intimacy among older women continues to be a taboo topic as there is a misconception that sexual activities in later life are considered to be non-existent or associated with negative issues. However, this is far from the truth as single older women seek to explore new relationships (Davidson 2001) and continue sexual activity into later life (Lindau et al. 2007; Beckman et al. 2008).

Single heterosexual older women when seeking an intimate partner, seek a slightly younger man (Alterovitz and Mendelsohn 2009) because they prefer someone with whom they can have an active lifestyle and reduce risk of demanding caregiving roles. However, society does not look favourably upon these relationships as it's considered a mother and son relationship and most recently older women who seduce young men were being stereotyped as "cougars". While these mother/son relationships have become popular in the Caribbean, no research has been conducted to examine older women dating younger men and their experiences of IPV. However, interviews conducted with healthcare professionals (physicians and nurses) found that older women dating younger men were subjected to more financial abuse. They reported to have seen older women with injuries such as bruises, black eyes, lacerations, and broken bones if they do not give in to the demands of perpetrator for financial assistance. Furthermore, social workers also reported that while working with older adults, they have a fear when discussing finances. An example was given that an "*older woman was coerced to change her will and left her property and assets for boyfriend (a younger man)*". Financial abuse among older adults is a pervasive form of elder abuse internationally (Lachs and Berman 2011; Jackson and Hafemeister 2012; Mihaljcic and Lowndes 2013) and the most underreported.

Same-Sex Relationships and IPV

There is an emerging body of literature on same-sex couples and IPV (Donovan and Hester 2015; Donovan and Barnes 2017). However, there is a lack of research on older same-sex couples and IPV. Unfortunately, the life experiences of older same-sex individuals and IPV have long been silenced and ignored (Taranto 2015). IPV is more prevalent in same-sex relationships than in heterosexual relationships (Dunne 2014). Older same-sex couples have lifelong experiences of being denied rights and privileges throughout history (Watkins 2010). They have faced stigma, isolation, and unequal treatment. Older same-sex couples aged 65 and over lived through a historical period that distinguishes them from the younger generation as they faced more challenges. This cohort was labeled as the "preliberation" cohort as they lived their earlier years prior to the Stonewall rebellion of 1969, often considered the event that initiated gay civil rights (Kochman 1997; Morrow 2001).

Older gay and lesbian individuals discovered their sexual identity at a time when homosexuality was still considered illegal and deviant by healthcare professionals. For many years sodomy laws existed throughout the United States until some states repealed them in the 1960s and 1970s. However, three decades later sodomy laws still exist in most small island states in the Caribbean. In Trinidad and Tobago, same-sex relationships are still not regarded as the norm which may have contributed to the lack of research investigating the experiences of older same-sex relationships and IPV.

IPV is still considered a silent topic, which has forced not only women, but men that are in a same-sex violent relationship to feel afraid and to refuse to seek help (Baker et al. 2013). Due to the negative attitudes towards homosexuality many LGBT persons may internalize these negative attitudes and suffer in silence. Chan (2005) suggests that outing can be used by perpetrators as a tool for abuse, creating a barrier to help-seeking. In situations where the older lesbian or gay victim conceals their sexuality, in fear of societal stigma or other repercussions, the perpetrator may exploit this decision by threats of forced outing. The risk of exposure results in isolation and rejection from social support such as family and friends therefore, the older adults often succumb to their demands and remain in the abusive situation. Abusive partners rely on homophobia or heterosexism to control their victims this makes it difficult for older victims to seek help as they have been conditioned to believe that the police or the justice system will assist because the legal system is homophobic and does not understand lesbian or gay relationships or sexual practices because of heterosexism (Chan 2005). Analysing clinicians field notes, a social worker explains "*I don't have many LGBT older adults, however from the few older gay men I worked with explained he would have to continue to take the abuse because he can't afford for his relatives to know he's gay and hoping one day the abuse would stop*".

Most same-sex abusers use the tactic of fear to convince their victims that law enforcement or healthcare professionals will not believe that they are being abused as they may be too old to be abused. Victims often believe their abusers due to the past incidents of anti-LGBT bias at the hands of law enforcement and healthcare professionals where they experienced outright hostility and violence (National Senior Citizens Law Center 2011). Indeed, Brown (2008), states many older same-sex individuals may not report IPV for fear of discrimination and blame for abuse from their partner. Consequently, older victims of abuse are fearful to receive services that would improve their quality of life. Same-sex victims may face secondary victimization by governmental institutions which compounds their fear to leave the relationship (Rowlands 2006). As a result, many may develop psychiatric conditions and potential medical challenges (Mays and Cochran 2001). Trinidad and Tobago are considered a Christian society as a result, there are no laws or social policies that protect minority communities. Moreover, this type of IPV is even more dangerous in same-sex couples because this is not considered to be battery and the victim is not protected but blamed (Taranto 2015). Analysing clinicians' field notes, one physician indicated "*it's very sad that in 2020 we don't have any legislation to protect LGBTQIA individuals. They are people and deserve the same protection as anyone else*".

Same-sex couples continue to face discrimination and marginalization across the world. Abusive partners choose the weapons of power and control that often lead their older same-sex victims to be isolated and totally dependent on them. This method restricts outside intervention as the victims are already isolated from friends and family who may not accept or support their same-sex lifestyle.

Legislation and Interventions for IPV

In 1991, the small island state of Trinidad and Tobago, enacted legislation to protect women against abuse from an intimate partner violence (Lazarus-Black 2001). Since the inception of the Domestic Violence Act, there have been two amendments; one in 1999 and another in 2006. The Domestic Violence Act 2006 refers to domestic violence as a "physical, sexual, emotional or psychological or financial abuse committed by a person against a spouse, child, any other person who is a member of the household or dependent". The new amended act mandates that police officers are to intervene in domestic disputes and provide issuance of protection orders (Research Directorate, Immigration and Refugee Board of Canada, Ottawa 2008). While the domestic violence act does not specify the protection for older adults, there are additional legislation that protects all persons from abusive partners such as the Offences against the Person (Amendment) (Harassment) Act (Research Directorate, Immigration and Refugee Board of Canada, Ottawa 2008).

Victims of domestic violence, the main state agency which deals with incidents of domestic violence is the police. As first responders, they were encouraged to demonstrate empathy, provide information on order of protection and community base referrals such as hotlines, and non-governmental agencies. Nevertheless, for older adults especially older women they were reluctant to report intimate partner violence due to traditional ideals that domestic violence is considered a private family matter (Harbison 2008). Hightower and colleagues (2006) found that leaving the abusive situation was not considered an option for older women. Moreover, older women felt that domestic violence services were only for those who had experienced physical abuse and only for younger women (Beaulaurier et al. 2007; Dunlop et al. 2005). From analysing clinicians' fields notes some older adults in Trinidad and Tobago had a mistrust for the police and found that they were not helpful in domestic violence situations and would prefer to contact the National Domestic Violence Hotline (800-SAVE) where they could talk about their issues without fear or judgement from an active listener.

Domestic violence shelters in Trinidad and Tobago were designed to provide sanctuary for women who are in dangerous situations. The shelters provided an array of services including counselling services, legal advice as well as other services. Furthermore, the options for safe homes in Trinidad are limited, four shelters recently closed their door due to lack of funding and it is not known whether the other ten are fully functional (Trinidad and Tobago Guardian 2020). These shelters are run as charity organizations that receive a quarterly subvention from the government, as well as donations and funds from both private and cooperate enterprises. However, these funds are not enough for the sustainability of the organization and to meet the needs of the growing population. Furthermore, the safe houses have their own limitations, as boys above the age of twelve years are not.

Allowed and as a result, many women are unable to stay. Additionally, the shelters were not fit for older women as they were not equipped to facilitate caring for the aged and their specific needs such as assisting to bathe, eat, or even to take their medication. As a result, the lack of infrastructure may force older women to remain in the abusive situation.

Moreover, it is imperative to mention that research literature on domestic violence against older men are scarce (Allen-Collinson 2009). As a result, infrastructure for male victims of domestic violence is non-existent because often men are the recipients of legal intervention to reduce violence. Lambert (2010) conducted interviews with organizations who provided support services for male victims of domestic violence, he discovered that there was a shortage of help and support accessible to male victims.

In Trinidad and Tobago, there are no shelters for abused men. Allen-Collinson (2009) citing George (2003) posits that social exclusion, and the non-acceptance of male victimization prevents men from reporting violence in their intimate relationships. An interview with a physician who treated men who have experienced domestic violence revealed; "*Nobody believes men, the systems were designed to protect women not men*". The mistrust of the system is one reason why men refuse to seek to professional intervention.

Healthcare Professional

Healthcare professionals such as physicians, nurses, and social workers are on the frontline in free government healthcare facilities, to provide support and protection to older adults in order to improve their health and psychosocial situation (Olomi et al. 2019). Older adults see healthcare workers outside of the family more regularly than any other person. In the course of providing care management for chronic diseases to their older patients, these healthcare professionals are often faced with suspicions of abusing their patients, which they must take into consideration and make an assessment of the victim's physical, cognitive, and psychological well-being. Despite being strategically placed in these positions, when faced with situations of abuse, healthcare professionals are sometimes unable to differentiate between domestic violence or elder abuse when treating older adults. Hightower et al. (2002) and Zink et al. (2004) posit that older women, 50 years and over, suffer in silence as victims of domestic violence as healthcare professionals ignore their problems or understand the issue through the medical model. In Trinidad and Tobago, healthcare professionals are not mandated by law to specifically report abuse of older adults. Under the Constitution of the Republic of Trinidad and Tobago, older adults are not specifically recognized as a group. Nevertheless, healthcare professionals are mandated to report incidents of domestic violence however, the services provided to the needs of older adults are overlooked in a system designed to care for younger women. From analysing clinicians' field notes one physician stated, "*The protocols are different for IPV I would have to contact the police and fill out the medical report but for elder abuse I'm not too familiar with the protocols, procedures and policies that hospital has as it regards elder abuse, I just know if you do suspect a case, you refer them to the medical social worker. In the emergency department I most see physical abuse and most time the victims are reluctant to disclose I class it as elder abuse a refer for social intervention*".

Conclusion

In developing countries with an evolving infrastructure of government and social welfare systems, legislation should be explicit in addressing social problems such as IPV. It is important for legislation to be culturally relevant to the context, as well as progressive to handle issues as they evolve. As older victims of IPV seek out healthcare resources, hospital protocols should be clear and disseminated to all staff at all levels of the organization. There should be continuous training to ensure staff understand the expectations of the hospital as well as enhance practice within each discipline. There needs to be further training from the organization to ensure all disciplines are on the same accord when screening for IPV. There should also be more collaboration between agencies (i.e. police and healthcare facilities). As this is a small developing nation more collaboration is needed.

References

Abramson, B., M. Mansfield, and J. Raymond. 2011. Wisconsin's Individual-at-Risk Restraining Order: An Analysis of the First Thirty Months. *The Elder Law Journal* 18 (2): 247.

Allen-Collinson, J. 2009. A Marked Man: Female-Perpetrated Intimate Partner Abuse. *International Journal of Men's Health* 8 (1): 22–40.

Alterovitz, S.S., and G.A. Mendelsohn. 2009. Partner Preferences Across the Life Span: Online Dating by Older Adults. *Psychology and Aging* 24: 513–517.

Artana, D., S. Auguste, R. Moya, S. Sookram, and P. Watson. 2009. Trinidad and Tobago: Economic Growth in a Dual Economy. In *Growing Pains—Binding Constraints to Productive Investment in Latin America*, ed. M. Agosin, E. Fernandez-Arias, and F. Jaramillo, 365–415. Washington, DC: Industrial Development Bank.

Baker, N.L., J.D. Buick, S.R. Kim, S. Moniz, and K.L. Nava. 2013. Lessons from Examining LGBTQ+ Intimate Partner Violence. *Sex Roles: A Journal of Research* 69 (3–4): 182–192.

Beaulaurier, R.L., L.R. Seff, F.L. Newman, and B. Dunlop. 2007. External Barriers to Help Seeking for Older Women Who Experience Intimate Partner Violence. *Journal of Family Violence* 22: 747–755.

Beaulaurier, R.L., L.R. Seff, F.L. Newman, and B. Dunlop. 2005. Internal Barriers to Help Seeking for Middle-Aged and Older Women Who Experience Intimate Partner Violence. *Journal of Elder Abuse & Neglect* 17 (3): 53–74.

Beckman, N., M. Waern, and D. Gustafson. 2008. Secular Trends in Self-Reported Sexual Activity and Satisfaction in Swedish 70 Year Olds: Cross Sectional Survey of Four Populations, 1971–2001. *BMJ* 337: a279.

Brandl, B. 2005. Mandatory Reporting of Elder Abuse: Implications for Domestic Violence Advocates. http://www.ncall.us/docs/Mandatory_Reporting_EA.pdf.

Brandl, B., and L. Cook-Daniels. 2002. *Domestic Abuse in Later Life*. Washington, DC: National Resource Center on Domestic Violence.

Brandl, B., C.B. Dye.r, C.J. Heisler., L.A. Stiegel., and R.W. Thomas. 2007. Elder Abuse Detection and Intervention: A Collaborative Approach. New York, NY: Springer.

Brown, C. 2008. Gender-Role Implications on LGBTQ+ Intimate Partner Abuse. *Journal of Family Violence* 23 (6): 457–462.

Bulcroft, K., and M. O'Connor. 1986. The Importance of Dating Relationships on Quality of Life for Older Persons. *Family Relations* 35: 397–401.

Bulcroft, R.A., and K.A. Bulcroft. 1991. The Nature and Functions of Dating in Later Life. *Research on Aging* 13: 244–260.

Centers for Disease Control and Prevention. 2015. Intimate Partner Violence. http://www.cdc.gov/violenceprevention/intimatepartnerviolence/.

Centers for Disease Control. 2011. Understanding Intimate Partner Violence: Fact Sheet. http://www.cdc.gov/ViolencePrevention/pdf/IPV_factsheet-a.pdf.

Chan, C. 2005. IPV in LGBTQ+ Relationships. Domestic Violence and Family Violence Clearinghouse Website. http://www.adfvc.unsw.edu.au/PDF%20files/Gay_Lesbian.pdf. Accessed 2020.

Davidson, K. 2001. Late Life Widowhood, Selfishness, and New Partnership Choices: A Gendered Perspective. *Ageing & Society* 21: 297–317.

Domestic Violence Act. 2006. "Laws of Trinidad and Tobago." Ministry of the Attorney General and Legal Affairs. https://rgd.legalaffairs.gov.tt/laws2/alphabetical_list/lawspdfs/45.56.pdf. Accessed 2021.

Dong, Xinqi. 2014. Elder Abuse: Research, Practice and Health Policy: The 2012 GSA Maxwell Pollack Award Lecture. *The Gerontologist* 54: 153–162.

Donovan, C., and M. Hester. 2015. *Domestic Violence and Sexuality: What's Love Got to Do with It?* Bristol: Policy Press.

Donovan, C., and R. Barnes. 2017. Domestic Violence and Abuse in Lesbian, Gay, Bisexual and/or Transgender (LGB and/or T). *Sexualities* 22 (5–6): 741–750.

Dunlop, B.D., R.L. Beaulaurier, L.R. Seff, F.L. Newman, N. Malik, and M. Fuster. 2005. Domestic Violence Against Older Women: Final Technical Report. https://www.ojp.gov/pdffiles1/nij/grants/212349.pdf.

Dunne, N. 2014. IPV More Frequent for LGBTQ+ Couples. Northwestern News Letter, September 14.

Dutton, D.G., and K.R. White. 2013. Male Victims of Domestic Violence: New Male Studies. *An International Journal* 2 (1): 5–17.

George, M. 2003. Invisible Touch. *Aggression and Violent Behaviour* 8 (2003): 23–60.

Harbison, J. 2008. Stoic Heronines of Collaborators: Ageism, Feminism, and the Provision of Assistance to Abused Old Women. *Journal of Social Work Practice* 22: 221–234.

Hightower, J., M.J. Smith, and H. Hightower. 2002. *Silent and Invisible: What's Age Got to Do with It? A Handbook for Service Providers on Working with Abused Older Women in British Columbia and Yukon*. Vancouver: B.C./Yukon Society of Transition Houses.

Hightower, J., M.J. Smith, and H.C. Hightower. 2006. Hearing the Voices of Abuse Older Women. *Journal of Gerontological Social Work* 46 (3/4): 205–227.

Hinchliff, S., and M. Gott. 2011. Seeking Medical Help for Sexual Concerns in Mid and Later Life: A Review of the Literature. *Journal of Sex Research* 48 (2–3): 106–117.

Jackson, S.L., and T.L. Hafemeister. 2012. Pure Financial Exploitation (vs.) Hybrid Financial Exploitation Co-Occurring with Physical Abuse and/or Neglect. *Psychology of Violence* 2: 285–296.

Jones, H., and J.L. Powell. 2006. Old Age, Vulnerability and Sexual Violence: Implications for Knowledge and Practice. *International Nursing Review* 53: 211–216.

Josolyne, S. 2011. Men's Experiences of Violence and Abuse from a Female Intimate Partner: Power, Masculinity and Institutional Systems, October 11. http://www.dewar4research.org/DOCS/JosolyneSimonThesisWebVersion020512.pdf. Accessed Dec 2020.

Kilbane, T., and M. Spira. 2010. Domestic Violence or Elder Abuse? Why It Matters for Older Women. *Families in Society: The Journal of Contemporary Social Services* 91 (2): 165–170.

Kochman, A. 1997. Gay and Lesbian Elderly: Historical Overview and Implications for Social Work Practice. *Journal of Gay and Lesbian Social Services* 6 (1): 1–10.

Lachs, M., and J. Berman. 2011. Under the Radar. New York State Elder Abuse Prevalence Study. http://nyselderabuse.org/documents/ElderAbusePrevalenceStudy2011.pdf.

Lambert, K. 2010. 'Broken Men Break the Silence': Male Domestic Violence Victims and Their Struggle to Be Heard. Sheffield Hallam University.

Lazarus-Black, M. 2001. Law and the Pragmatics of Inclusion: Governing Domestic Violence in Trinidad and Tobago. *American Ethnologist* 28 (2): 388–416.

Lindau, S.T., L.P. Schumm, E.O. Laumann, W. Levinson, C. O'Muircheartaigh, and L. Waite. 2007. Sex, Health and Years of Sexually Active Life Gained Due to Good Health: Evidence from Two US Population Based Cross Sectional Surveys of Ageing. *British Medical Journal Advance Online Publication*. https://doi.org/10.1136/bmj.c810.

Mays, V., and S. Cochran. 2001. Mental Health Correlates of Perceived Discrimination Among Lesbian, Gay and Bisexual Adults in the United States. *American Journal of Public Health* 91 (11): 1869–1876.

Mihaljcic, T., and G. Lowndes. 2013. Individual and Community Attitudes Towards Financial Elder Abuse. *Journal of Elder Abuse & Neglect* 25: 183–203.

Montminy, L. 2005. Older Women's Experiences of Psychological Violence in Their Marital Relationships. *Journal of Gerontological Social Work* 46 (2): 3–22.

Morrow, D.F. 2001. Older Gays and Lesbians: Surviving a Generation of Hate and Violence. *Journal of Gay and Lesbian Social Service* 13 (1/2): 151–169.

Mouton, C.P. 2003. Intimate Partner Violence and Health Status Among Older Women. *Violence Against Women* 9 (12): 1465–1477.

National Senior Citizens Law Center. 2011. Protecting the Rights of Low Income Older Adults. http://justiceinaging.org/wp-content/uploads/2015/02/NSCLC-Annual-Rpt-2011-Final.pdf. Accessed 2021.

NCALL. 2011. www.ncall.us.

Olomi, Julie, Naomi Wright, Leslie Hasche, and Anne P. DePrince. 2019. After Older Adult Maltreatment: Service Needs and Barriers. *Journal of Gerontological Social Work* 62 (7): 749–761. https://doi.org/10.1080/01634372.2019.1668517.

Perel-Levin, S. 2005. Discussing Screening for Elder Abuse at Primary Health Care Level. http://www.who.int/ageing/publications/Discussing_Elder_Abuseweb.pdf. Accessed Dec 2020.

Phillips, L.R. 2000. Domestic Violence and Aging Women. *Geriatric Nursing* 21 (4): 188–193.

Rawlins, Joan M., and Nicole Alea. 2014. *Ageing in the Caribbean*. Florida: Lifegate Publishing.

Rennison, C., and M.R. Rand. 2003. Nonlethal Intimate Partner Violence Against Women: A Comparison of Three Age Cohorts. *Violence Against Women* 9 (12): 1417–1428.

Research Directorate, Immigration and Refugee Board of Canada, Ottawa. 2008. Trinidad and Tobago: Domestic Violence, Including Legislation, Services Available and Police Response to Complaints (2005–2008). https://www.refworld.org/docid/49b92b211e.html. Accessed Jan 2021.

Rowlands, J. 2006. *Domestic Abuse Among Gay and Bisexual Men: An Exploratory Study in South Wales*. Norwich: University of East Anglia.

Stark, E. 2010. Do Violent Acts Equal Abuse? Resolving the Gender Parity/Asymmetry Dilemma. *Sex Roles* 62: 201–211.

Taranto, A. (nd). 2015. LGBTQ+ Intimate Partner Violence: Current Barriers to Service & Future Goals for Community Agencies. Council on Crime and Justice. http://www.crimeandjustice.org/councilinfo.cfm?. Accessed January 2021

Trinidad and Tobago Guardian. 2020. Shelters Need $$ to Save Women's Lives, February 8. https://www.guardian.co.tt/article/shelters-need--to-save-womens-lives-6.2.1049895.202903fe9e. Accessed 2021.

Trinidad and Tobago Central Statistical Office. 2011. Trinidad and Tobago 2011 Populations and Housing Census Demographic Report. Trinidad: Ministry of Planning and Sustainable Development.

UNICEF. 2013. UNICEF at a Glance: Trinidad and Tobago. UNICEF. https://www.unicef.org/infobycountry/trinidad_tobago_statistics.html.

Vinton, L. 1991. Factors Associated with Refusing Services Among Maltreated Elderly. *Journal of Elder Abuse & Neglect* 3 (2): 89–102.

Watkins, T. 2010. Aging Issues Can Be Tougher on Gays, May 14. http://edition.cnn.com/2010/LIVING/wayoflife/03/17/gays.aging.problems/index.html. Accessed 2021.

World Health Organization. 2013. Global and Regional Estimates of Violence Against Women: Prevalence and Health Effects of Intimate Partner Violence and Non-Partner Sexual Violence. World Organization Press.

World Population Review. 2019. https://worldpopulationreview.com/countries/trinidad-and-tobago-population/. Accessed Apr 2020.

Zink, T., S. Regan, C.J. Jacobson, and S. Pabst. 2003. Cohort, Period, and Aging Effects: A Qualitative Study of Older Women's Reasons for Remaining in Abusive Relationships. *Violence against Women* 9 (12): 1429–1441.

Zink, T., C.J. Jr. Jacobson., S. Regan., and S. Pabst. 2004. Hidden Victims: The Healthcare Needs and Experiences of Older Women in Abusive Relationships. Journal of Women's Health 13 (8): 898–908.

CHAPTER 4

Financial Hardships of Domestic Violence Survivors in the Caribbean

Camille Huggins and Vidya Mungal-Bissessar

Discussion

When one tries to define domestic violence or intimate partner violence, the prevailing definition is physical or sexual abuse, perhaps because of the salacious nature of these acts. However, the silent and more detrimental form is financial abuse. Financial abuse occurs in 99% of all domestic violence situations. Financial abuse is behaviour that seeks to control a person's ability to acquire, use, or maintain economic resources, and threatens their self-sufficiency and financial autonomy (National Network to End Domestic Violence 2017). According to the Trinidad and Tobago Domestic Violence Act, financial abuse is a pattern of behaviour that exercises coercive control over or exploit a person's access to financial resources to ensure financial dependence.

C. Huggins (✉) · V. Mungal-Bissessar
University of the West Indies at St. Augustine, St. Augustine, Trinidad and Tobago
e-mail: Camille.huggins@sta.uwi.edu

A. M. Bissessar and C. Huggins (eds.), *Domestic Violence in the Anglophone Caribbean*,
https://doi.org/10.1007/978-3-030-88476-5_4

Globally, women disproportionately work in insecure, lower paid, part-time, and informal employment, with little income security and social protection, such as health insurance (UNWoman.org) and are more often in the position of being financially abused in intimate partner relationships. In Trinidad and Tobago, 60% of women participate in the workforce, most work in domestic and service industry earning 40% less than men, yet the burden of financially caring for children and the household disproportionately falls on women. This is due to normative Caribbean intimate relationships, such as common-law relationships (e.g. non-married living together), visiting relationships (e.g. living separately), and single-parent households (e.g. one parent handling all responsibilities, the other parent absent). As most households are matrifocal, whereas the mother handles most of the childrearing responsibility, the culture of these relationships gives legitimacy to the abdication of financial and emotional responsibility of the father (Blank 2013) leaving the women to maintain both roles as the mother and father.

In traditional heterosexual families with two married parents, men are expected to be the breadwinners, the providers, and the final authority of the home (Seegobin 1999). Women are expected to stay at home, be the homemaker, care for the children, and rely on the husband for financial support (Baboolal 2016). This concept is supported by Christian denominated countries and Indian traditional value systems, and it is seen as the highest status in society.

The woman is given the status of a wife, and the man has the power and privilege over the family and his word is to be obeyed.

Whatever the paradigm, within the heterosexual intimate relationship dynamic, women are in vulnerable positions to be financially disadvantaged. Women are socialized to be silenced and to be consistently treated unequally. Qin (2004), took a critical feministic approach, proposed that a woman's sense of self, grew out of a "gendered" culture that was grounded by unequal relations of power. Thornton (2015) called it the "inferiorization" of women throughout history made it difficult for women's voices to be respected and heard over the dominant patriarchal culture of men. Even if the woman is the breadwinner, she must take her earnings to provide for the family or give her earnings to her husband, so he can use it at his discretion. It is an ingrained concept of female children, that they are expected to adopt the responsibility of the family in a myriad of ways (Powell 1984). For example, if a woman remains single after a certain age, it is expected that she will remain as a spinster, and she will redistribute her income to care for her parents or her extended family. Whether she is single or married she is also expected to be a caregiver for parents, parent-in-laws, children, and husband, oftentimes leaving herself without. The women's role is to become the proverbial "doormat" of the family. These cultural norms become so ingrained that there is a lack of recognition that it is abuse.

Financial Abuse

Financial abuse is one of the most powerful methods of keeping a survivor trapped in an abusive relationship. Financial abuse occurs across all socio-economic, educational, and racial and ethnic groups, but it is quite pervasive for women living in poverty. Though financial abuse occurs in 99% of domestic violence cases, globally many do not recognize financial abuse as a form of domestic violence. Perhaps because this form of abuse is aligned within the power dynamics of the men and women. There are various forms of financial abuse including; forcing a partner to miss, leave, or be late for work, harassing a partner at work; controlling how money is spent; withholding money or basic living resources; giving an allowance, stealing money, credit, property, or identity from a partner, and/or forcing a partner to file fraudulent legal financial documents or overspend on credit cards. Survivors of domestic violence experience economic hardship throughout their lifetime.

For those who experience financial abuse, the short- and long-term effects can be devastating. In the United States, survivors of financial abuse lose a total of 8 million days of paid work each year, including unpaid sick leave and loss of job protections in order to recover from injury or to seek safety. Survivors of domestic violence experience insurmountable debt, sporadic employment histories, legal issues that make it difficult to gain independence and can possibly lead them and their children homeless. Overall, women caught in abusive relationships often find it difficult to leave because of financial entanglements and their partner's abuse with regards to the finances.

In industrialized countries, there are services to assist women in need such as; food assistance programmes, medical attention, housing, legal, and job protection. There are dedicated shelters and agencies to help women in need. Even with these services it still does not help survivors financially recover. In developing countries, the social service infrastructure is evolving.

Trinidad and Tobago

In the small island state of Trinidad and Tobago, with a population of 1.3 million people, there is a Domestic Violence Act, 1999, amended 2006, updated 2016, and on July 7, 2020 in the midst of the global pandemic COVID-19, the act was amended to include for emergency protection orders for the related matters. The Domestic Violence (Amendment) Act 2020, significantly expands the list of persons afforded protection under the law and cites a detailed description and definition of key instruments, beneficiaries, perpetrators, survivors, categories of relationships, and their participants which includes financial abuse.

The Trinidad and Tobago social safety net programmes for domestic violence survivors are provided through various agencies including; the Gender-Based Violence Unit of the Trinidad and Tobago Police Service and the Ministry's Social Welfare Division. These programmes include emergency lodging for survivors and their children, although it is not guaranteed as most places are already overwhelmed and lack sufficient space. There are also monetary grants to assist with living expenses. In order to qualify for any of the relief grants, the applicant must first pass the standard Means Test required. The formula used is **Net Income ≤ Poverty Line = Eligible Family**. Higher low income to middle-income survivors do not qualify.

The United Nations in their collaboration with the European Union, created a global enterprise called the Spotlight Initiative, to combat Domestic Violence. The initiative allocated fifty million Euros, 10% of which was allocated to the Caribbean region, four million Euros to Trinidad and Tobago. In May of 2020, the Prime Minister of Trinidad and Tobago and the Gender Affairs Division highlighted the plans the monetary contribution will cover including:

1. Adoption, implementation and/or the strengthening of family violence laws and policies.
2. Prevention measures encompassing youth and workplace initiatives to combat social norms and the culture of violence.
3. Enhanced capacity of institutions to foster an environment of gender equality, support survivors and reduce impunity for perpetrators.
4. Quality and accessible data to inform continuous improvements in programmes and services.

5. Improved service delivery for survivors through capacity building and the development of oversight and accountability mechanisms.
6. Empowerment of civil society and most notably women's rights and grassroots organisations to monitor and support responsive and survivor-centred services particularly for discriminated and marginalised populations.

   –Excerpted from looptt.com
   Alana Doodnath 2020.[1]

Currently in light of the COVID-19 pandemic, these initiatives have been slow to materialize. There has been the establishment of the Gender-Based Violence Unit in the Trinidad and Tobago Police Service, which its specific task is to address domestic violence cases and cases regarding violence against vulnerable populations. Statistics indicate that there has been a notable rise in the number of reported cases and charges laid against perpetrators since the inception of the unit.

Through the initiative, there has been an increase in psychosocial support services through the provision of domestic violence hotlines, counselling for physical and sexual abuse survivors. There has also been an increase in psycho-education classes regarding parenting skills and community peace initiatives. However, there has not been any real concentration on the financial costs and loss of these domestic violence survivors such as affordable housing, economic education, and greater job opportunities if survivors are to survive and thrive (VonDeLinde and Correia 2005).

Feminist Theory and Domestic Abuse

There is a myriad of feminist theories to explain women inequality in society. Some of the more predominant feminist theories were created by White middle-class women and they do not necessarily fit the complex environment that women of colour occupy. Although all feminist theories have common principles such as; discrimination on the basis of gender and sex, a personification of gender stereotypes, oppression of females, and structural and economic inequality. Women of colour (e.g. African, Indian, Indigenous, Spanish) who live in the Caribbean have competing identities that intersect to make their idea of feminism nuanced and multiplex.

Societies in the Caribbean that were created out of colonialism, enslavement, race, gender, sexuality, and the anti-imperial struggle; women movements have different connotations. In some aspects, men and women of the same colour were equal in their fight against oppression. Yet, women particularly Black women are subjugated and exploited by all men. Women living in Caribbean spaces, view feminism similar to racial discrimination and its resistance against imperial power. Therefore, incidents of domestic violence are not seen as an unique experience between a man and woman in an intimate relationship, but a reflection of a contemporary larger societal issue where both man and women are suppressed and the incident is apart of shared pain and anguish. The indelible remnant of colonialism remains. The post-colonial feminist theory must always take into account the textures of everyday life to understand race, gender, and sexuality (Piedalue and Rishi 2017).

To know how financial abuse is understood and experienced in a Caribbean context, a case study of one Caribbean woman was selected to examine domestic violence, specifically financial abuse. A life span interview method was used to guide the client through her childhood, adolescence, young adulthood, and marriage. This provides a background about normative cultural influences she was exposed to prior to getting married. The study will utilize the feminist theory through a Caribbean context to clarify the textures of everyday life as a Caribbean woman. There is also review of her experience with societal systems such as, the police and social services to understand the level of support she is afforded.

Methodology

A qualitative case study method was selected to examine a participant's understanding of financial abuse from a Caribbean context. A qualitative case study method (Stake 2005; Yin 2003) facilitates the exploration of a phenomenon through multiple facets. According to Yin (2003), a case study design should be considered when the focus of the study is to answer "why" questions. When behaviour cannot be manipulated and it is relevant to the phenomenon. The case study is a retrospective exploration of one woman's marriage and her experience of domestic violence. There is no inference by the researchers.

Researchers' Experience

All the authors have a minimum of three years' experience working with vulnerable women with children. One author worked in a single mother and child homeless shelter in New York City, USA and one author worked with the homeless population in San Fernando, Trinidad. One author was also the deputy mayor in Trinidad and Tobago and interacted with several women in domestic violence situations who were in need of various resources.

Recruitment

Due to COVID-19 and stay at home restrictions, recruitment was difficult. A case was referred from one of the researchers' work cases. The case was selected because of her account of financial abuse and willingness to participate in the study. Researchers offered counselling if the participant wanted it after the interview. Researchers also checked in post-interview for support.

Data Collection

Due to COVID-19 and the stay at home restrictions, the participant was met on Zoom in a teleconference format. Researchers interviewed her twice for 1.5 hours, the interviews usually took 45–50 minutes. All interviews were audio-taped and conducted by authors. To safeguard confidentiality, no identifying information was included in the interview material and tapes. Due to the intimate nature of the subject and the intricacies of the intimate relationship, the life review interview (Butler 1974) was the most appropriate format. Although life review is mostly used with older adults, it has also been used for people experiencing crisis (Butler 1974). The normal life review process is brought about in talking about their childhood, the relationship between the parents, and the family dynamics, her education, young adulthood, the courtship with her partner, the acts of violence, and the dynamics within the relationship. It is characterized by the progressive return to consciousness of past experiences, the resurgence of unresolved conflicts that can be looked at again (Butler 1974). It is a process whereby people can give meaning to their lives. The interview guide was done in a storytelling format with open-ended questions framed in everyday language that was broad enough to allow respondents to provide detailed stories, asking questions worded to elicit narratives that were complemented with probing questions (Buttina 2015; Riessman 2008).

The Case of Rose

Rose is a forty-seven-year-old woman of East Indian descent, who sits on the other side of a video screen, about to share her story of abuse, struggle, and survival, trying to present a composed and controlled picture. It does not take long into the interview before the shiver in her voice becomes a flood of tears rolling down her face. Her story maps the journey of a domestic abuse victim and survivor. It documents the transition from childhood to adolescence, young adulthood to middle age, and the lived experience of this woman and the cycle of abuse.

She grew up in rural Trinidad, Rose is the eldest of four children, three girls, and one boy. She tells of a mother who was a homemaker and housewife but grew dissatisfied with the humble and simple life provided by her hard-working husband. Her father earned his living to support his family as a taxi driver. Her father as the sole breadwinner, reinforced the notion that it was a male's role to provide and secure the needs of the family. She recalls a time during her younger years when she felt the family was happy and fulfilling. Issues began to arise as she got older and, in her words, her mother became unhappy with their lifestyle and as a result, there were behavioural changes to her "nice, loving and caring" father who following an episode of infidelity by her mother, became physically abusive.

Rose indicated as a teenager when the relationship between her parents deteriorated and her father left the home. Rose took on the role of provider for her entire family. Although Rose was intelligent enough to transition from a mediocre public school to a prestigious denominational school, she was not allowed to go any further than high school. Once she began to work, her mother would take her entire salary leaving her with just enough for transportation. Rose describes her sense of disappointment at having to work so hard and not have access to her own money. She grieved the lack of independence and autonomy that she had aspired to as a young adult. Her mother eventually left the home and Rose took up the responsibility of providing for, nurturing, and caring for her siblings and herself. She stated vehemently "If I am not doing something for someone else, I believe that I am doing nothing".

Rose got married to a young man from her neighbourhood at the age of twenty-six, they had dated for three years prior although she said she "knew him all her life". During their courtship, she was working and still assisting her siblings and supporting the home. Her new husband was a smoker and drinker and worked sporadically.

She went to live with his parents after the wedding. Early in the marriage, a pattern emerged where she had to account for her income to her husband. Rose stated she was expected to inform her husband about the value of her salary, when and how she would receive it, as well as how it was to be spent. While her husband refused to contribute to the household expenses even when he worked. This control became more intense and reached crisis level when she became pregnant and had to go on maternity leave. Rose found herself facing an escalation in abuse from verbal and emotional to physical. She describes an event when she was "choke slammed" against a wall while eight months pregnant. She was physically assaulted by her husband because he felt she had neglected her household responsibilities. He became enraged because she had responded to his complaints about chores being undone, she pointed out that he could do the chores because he was at home and unemployed at the time.

After the baby was born Rose's husband demanded that she stay at home to look after the baby, expressing the belief that she was now to become a homemaker and mother. Unfortunately, there was no corresponding change in his commitment of undertaking financial responsibilities. She felt like a burden whenever she made any requests even for basic necessities, so she began to do without more and more to avoid having to ask for things. Rose used this coping mechanism as a means of survival to avoid any explosive situations. She relates an incident when she was in urgent need of personal items and made repeated requests to her husband. He finally agreed after multiple refusals and took her to get the items and actually paid for them. Unfortunately, this was accompanied by a loud and public tirade at the store. She was so embarrassed that she refused to ask him for anything in the future. She also describes incidents when there was no formula, diapers, or money for food in the home because he refused to provide. She clandestinely got assistance from her sister and mother to ensure the baby had food. She was determined not to ask him for anything.

While noting, that he was not contributing financially to her or to the household, she did not perceive this as abuse at the time. Her definition of abuse was the derogatory and embarrassing verbal attacks, the physical attacks, but not her husband's refusal to provide monetary support for her and the home, even though during this time she was in dire need of financial aid. Rose stated, "I never went to the police for help because he never hit or beat to leave marks. I have no proof and what am I going to tell the police? I going to the police to tell them what? My husband cussing and quarrelling and mashing up the house?"

Rose thought of leaving her abusive situation when her baby was one year old. She was still unemployed as per his instructions. One time, the baby was ill and needed medication. Her husband was working and got paid, instead of getting the medications, he went to the bar and drank out all the money returning home drunk without the medications. She packed to leave but did not leave because she had no money and the only hope for the baby was for him to buy the medications.

This state of bankruptcy and risky financial dependence on her husband, left Rose with no choice but to return to work as the situation became untenable for her and her baby. In spite of his demands and awareness of the diminished resources, she faced a barrage of verbal and emotional abuse for her decision to return to work, not just from her husband but also his family.

The relationship between her and her in-laws became unbearable, so Rose asked if she could build a small living quarter on their land. Over the next few years, Rose took loans, worked overtime, and extra hours to pay for materials in order to construct a simple house. She also sacrificed to furnish the home.

Caught up in the maelstrom of a failing marriage along with daily physical, emotional, and mental abuse, Rose did not observe the effect it had on her daughter. One night, after a particularly bad fight between mother and father, Rose's eleven-year-old daughter went to her grandparents' home next door to escape. She made tea for her grandmother and herself and added a handful of her granny's dementia medications. She gave a cup to her grandmother, drank one herself, and went to bed.

The next morning, as Rose went next door to wake her daughter in preparation for school, she was alarmed and distressed because neither her mother-in-law nor her daughter would wake up. After getting medical treatment for both, Rose was devastated by her daughter's attempted suicide and the possible outcome. This episode gave Rose the motivation to leave the marriage, the home that she had financed, and all her hard-earned possessions. She left shortly after, taking with her a few pieces of clothing, her daughter, and the little savings she had been able to accumulate with great difficulty. She also took with her an enormous debt.

This was an extremely difficult time for Rose. She lived paycheck to paycheck and soon took on two additional jobs in order to service her debt and be able to support her and her daughter. The very little savings she had was quickly spent paying rent on the small unfurnished rental apartment. Furnishings were sparse and came by way of charitable individuals aware of her plight.

Rose went to the courts as a last resort to get her husband to assist in financial support for their child. With no money to pay an attorney and no knowledge of programmes or systems to guide her, Rose was left at the mercy of the court. Her husband in response to her application for maintenance for the daughter pleaded with the court and he was mandated to pay two hundred dollars a week. He was inconsistent in his payments and very often did not make his contribution. In addition to this, Rose never received any compensation for all of her investment in the building and furnishings they had acquired at her expense during the marriage. In fact, eight years later, she is still paying off the debts and loans incurred including, the maxed-out credit card he made her use.

During the course of the eight years since Rose so bravely and courageously tried to change her circumstances, things have not been easy. At the age of forty-four, while working three jobs she sacrificed to be able to go back to school and undertake accounting courses in an attempt to improve herself. Her life is still a financial struggle. She eats only one meal per day and limits her groceries to bare necessities in order to manage the cost of her and her daughter's studies.

COVID-19 has had a significant impact on Rose, as she lost one of her three jobs and was faced with reduced hours and salary cuts in the remaining two. This means that sometimes she is unable to pay all of her utility bills and is constantly negotiating with the relevant authorities. She sometimes gets minimal financial support from her sister.

Analysis

Culture-Caribbean Context

These early childhood experiences created a deep-rooted belief in Rose that there were preferred gender roles specifically as they related to financial matters (Linton and Lorde 2011). She witnessed that her father was the financial provider, and her mother was the homemaker. She recalled that she felt happiest with this family dynamic and her father was a loving man who took care of his family. She idolized her father and did not say anything negative about him. She did feel her mother was ungrateful and caused a lot of conflict in the home. Rose did not empathize with her mother and felt her grievances were unfounded and not in line with the accommodating nature of female gender roles. For Rose, observing the conflict between her parents, her perspective was formulated to always be aligned with, and empathic to the male gender.

When her father left the home, she did not blame him and felt he was justified due to her mother's behaviour. Rose promptly took on his responsibilities, because of her accommodating nature to be of support to the family. The ability to develop a healthy sense of self will vary from member to member of the family. This may explain the effects of the dysfunctional relationships that grew within the family during Rose's childhood and adolescence and their impact on her self-esteem and identity. She was forced to assume the role and function of her parents leaving behind an incomplete childhood (Murray 2006).

This role reversal between child and parent is described by the term parentification (Boszormenyi-Nagy and Spark 1973; Hooper et al. 2012; Garber 2011). The child takes on the role of caregiver and the parent looks to the child as a source of support. This can be emotional, physical, or financial and gets very little recognition. The child is forcibly thrust into adulthood and expected to behave in adult and mature ways while unprepared for this change.

Rose was the oldest child in an Indian Caribbean family. It was a traditional family with two married parents, her mother was a homemaker, and the father was the sole provider. The mother became indignant about her life circumstances and complained about it, disrupting the family dynamics and offending her father who became vengeful against the mother. This had a great impact on Rose and part of her identity was to do the opposite of her mother's behaviour and be accommodating in personality even to her own detriment. Rose had to step in and take over as the provider for the family when her father left and felt her role was to care for others. This pattern was again played out in her marriage where she was financially and physically abused.

The Meaning of Domestic Violence and Financial Abuse

Rose did not see her husband's unwillingness to contribute to the household and in caring for her or her child as abusive. The marriage which is considered a traditional high status within her culture, Rose became a wife and was relegated to a higher social status because of the marriage. Her husband fulfilled his role as the provider because she was living with his parents, he demanded that she did not work so she can become a homemaker and mother. With the marriage she had the title and role assignment but there was no clarity as to his and her role responsibilities. When she challenged him and stepped into the role of her mother, a complaining ungrateful wife she deservedly needed punishment. Challenges to the authority of the abuser and any attempt to change the accustomed role identity, may act as a catalyst or trigger for incidents of violence. This may be viewed as an undermining of the traditional hierarchy within the marriage and relationship and an attempt to strip the male partner of his power (Baboolal 2016; Jones et al. 2017). Henceforth, Rose decided that she would not complain to maintain her accommodating role as the good wife.

Rose was able to account for the financial abuse she endured from her husband, such as stopping her from working, making her accumulate debt, depraving her and her child of necessary goods, and making her account for where all of her money is spent. He stole from her and intimidated her to give him money. Rose's husband and her in-laws also blamed and shamed her when she decided to go back to work. One form of financial abuse is the exploitation of the survivor by generating debt and damaging their credit rating and reputation. The coercion to undertake loans and credit facilities through credit cards is a common practice in financial abuse (Sharpe-Jeffs 2015). However, according to Rose, those acts were not as harmful as his physical and verbal behaviours. Outward embarrassment and physical treatment were less tolerable than the insidious nature of financial abuse.

Lack of Services

Rose chose not to report any incidents of abuse to the police throughout her marriage. Wallace et al. (2019) propose that in Trinidad and Tobago, there is a distrust in police efficiency and effectiveness when dealing with issues of domestic abuse combined with little faith in the justice system, results in low reporting by survivors. They also found that in the cases of the East Indian community, cultural beliefs and systems contributed to low reporting.

Rose was supported sporadically by her mother and sister but was never encouraged to leave the marriage. In the Caribbean context which is an enmeshment of Christian principles, African traditions, and Indian cultural norms, leaving a marriage or divorce is not an option. Support systems often encourage the wife to stay and negotiate with the husband for better living conditions. It is the responsibility of the wife to maintain the marriage and obey the husband. Rose's family and her in-laws witnessed her struggling with her husband and marriage for years but she never mentioned that they encouraged her to leave. In some incidences, they agreed with the husband and his directives.

Even when Rose when to court and won maintenance for her daughter, there were no mechanisms in place for her to receive alimony or consistent maintenance.

Conclusion

Limitations

The limitations of the case study is that it is only of one survivor but similar stories can be heard from other survivors. Further research is needed to investigate the prevalence in the Caribbean. Sutton and Alvarez, 2016, articulate that while one in every three women in Latin America and the Caribbean region will experience Intimate Partner Violence in her lifetime, there is not enough research and statistics in the region. While there is focus on IPV in general, there is little or no disaggregation of information on the prevalence of financial abuse and its impact on Caribbean society. The scope of the studies is limited and often more characters are used in situating the region within an International context than detailed and focused region-specific research.

Although this chapter has focused on Rose and her story as the medium to discuss financial abuse and the hardships faced by survivors, it is important to acknowledge and not diminish the experiences of male survivors of Domestic violence. Very often, male survivors are viewed as weak and are faced with dismissal and disdain by authorities and the society as a whole. The subject of male victimhood in the context of domestic violence is taboo in Caribbean culture and Trinidad and Tobago is no exception (Wallace et al. 2019). According to some estimates, it is believed that at least one in six men will experience some form of domestic abuse in their lifetime (Melley 2018). This group of survivors should not be ignored and the reality of domestic violence is gender blind.

Implications

Although there have been significant strides regarding gender equality in the Caribbean over the past few decades, Rose's experience of sacrificing her education at the altar of female familial responsibility is far too common (Lacey et al. 2019). This is indicative of gender norms in the Caribbean that support assigned roles for men and women that are inherently gender-biased and places women in an unequal position (Singh 2018; Kanhai 2012). As previously alluded to, another key consideration is the way in which survivors of domestic violence perceive themselves. Perhaps it is important to first recognize and see themselves as survivors. Then and only then can they overcome the constructed reality of victimhood by changing their self-view, leading to success and recovery. The ability to become self-supporting and self-sustaining is crucial to breaking the cycle of abuse and to prevent recidivism, a return to the abusive relationship. The elimination of self-doubt and the proliferation of self-confidence can provide the impetus for continued growth and stability.

There is a definite increase in awareness regarding intimate partner violence and gender-based violence in the discourse surrounding domestic abuse in the Caribbean, little is discussed about financial abuse. Even more so during the COVID-19 pandemic, survivors are more vulnerable to financial abuse. Postmus et al. (2020) refer to financial or economic abuse as the "silent or hidden" side of Domestic violence. They argue that although financial abuse is considered by researchers and other stakeholders, more attention is given to physical abuse. They also posit that survivors themselves are not always aware of the impact of financial abuse because it may be hidden beneath the existing gender inequalities that affect women in most situations. Its impact is far-reaching and often extends long after the survivor has left the relationship.

Although the current legislation in Trinidad and Tobago addresses the issue of financial abuse in a fairly comprehensive way, the reality is that there is a dearth in data that would indicate if and how often the protection afforded by the act is utilized (Tisdale 2019; Tan 2019). Alongside legislation is the need for change in cultural norms and values that perpetuate violence against women and men. Equally important is the need for supporting systems and programmes that afford survivors the best options for financial and economic independence and autonomy. Very often, the focus is on convincing survivors to seek help and leave an abusive situation but not enough emphasis is placed on the question of what comes next.

In some developed countries, there are systems in place to provide financial education and support programmes for survivors. Opportunities to be educated about solutions, options, and strategies to reduce debt, improve credit health and future planning can make a significant difference for survivors. Also, the opportunity for housing programmes, employment, and skills training as well as food, bank, and child support would significantly increase the potential for resilience and success while reducing recidivism.[2]

The economic impact of the COVID-19 pandemic, effects external sources of support for domestic violence survivors. The availability of funding for state-sponsored programmes and infrastructure becomes severely constrained when there are so many responsibilities to be met by a severely reduced government budget. Non-Government Organizations and other civil society organizations provide significant and valuable support to aid survivors in finding safety. Funding for these organizations is sourced through a combination of philanthropic and charitable donations, combined (oftentimes) with government subsidies. Shrinking economies and economic hardship are not conducive to the longevity of such programmes.

Notes

1. From Alana Doodnath, 20 May 2020. Shelters ready soon for domestic violence victims, says OPM. http://www.looptt.com/content/shelters-homes-ready-soon-domestic-violence-victims-says-opm.
2. From Financial abuse: The ties that bind domestic violence victims, Stacey Tisdale, 25 October 2019. Financial abuse: The ties that bind domestic violence victims. *Business and Economy|Al Jazeera*.

References

Baboolal, Aneesa A. 2016. Indo-Caribbean Immigrant Perspectives on Intimate Partner Violence. *International Journal of Criminal Justice Sciences* 11 (2): 159–176.

Blank, Sharla. 2013. An Historical and Contemporary Overview of Gendered Caribbean Relations. *Journal of Arts and Humanities* 2 (4): 1–10.

Boszormenyi-Nagy, Ivan, and Geraldine M. Spark. 1973. *Invisible Loyalties: Reciprocity in Intergenerational Family Therapy*. Hagerstown, MD: American Medical Book Publisher, Harper & Row.

Butler, R. 1974. Successful aging and the role of the life review. *Symposium on Geriatric Medicine co-sponsored by the American Geriatrics Society and the Franklin Square Hospital*. Baltimore, MD, 2 March 1974. https://doi.org/10.1111/j.1532-5415.1974.tb04823.x.

Buttina, M. 2015. A narrative approach to qualitative inquiry. *Clinical Laboratory Science* 28 (3): 190–196.

Garber, Benjamin D. 2011. Parental Alienation and the Dynamics of the Enmeshed Parent–Child Dyad: Adultification, Parentification, and Infantilization. *Family Court Review* 49 (2): 322–335.

Hadeed, L. F. 2004. Domestic Violence in Trinidad and Tobago: Why Women Stay in Abusive Relationships: 1407–1407. https://www.vanessaprietolaw.com/4-reasons-why-victims-blame-themselves-for-domestic-violence/.

Hadeed, Linda, and Nabila El-Bassel. 2007. Typologies of Abuse Among Afro-Trinidadian Women. *Journal of Interpersonal Violence* 22: 479–497. https://doi.org/10.1177/0886260506297030.

Hadeed, Linda, and Yeon-Shim Lee. 2010. Intimate Partner Abuse and Women's Employment: A Study on Afro-Trinidadian Women. *Journal of Poverty* 14 (3): 285–307. https://doi.org/10.1080/10875549.2010.494948.

Hooper, Lisa M., Scyatta A. Wallace, Kirsten Doehler, and John Dantzler. 2012. Parentification, Ethnic Identity, and Psychological Health in Black and White American College Students: Implications of Family-of-Origin and Cultural Factors. *Journal of Comparative Family Studies* 43 (6): 811–835. http://www.jstor.org/stable/41756272. Accessed 8 May 2021.

Jones, Adele, Ena Trotman Jemmott, Hazel Da Breo, Tyrone Buckmire, Denise Tannis, Lee Rose, Francia Best, Debra Joseph, and Christian Moller. 2017. *Twenty-One Lessons: Preventing Domestic Violence in the Caribbean*.

Kanhai, Rosanne. 2012. Kamla at the Apex: Reflections on Indo-Caribbean Feminisms. CRGS, no. 6, ed. Gabrielle Hosein and Lisa Outar, 1–7. http://www2.sta.uwi.edu/crgs/march2013/journals/Kanhai.pdf.

Lacey, Krim K., Rohan D. Jeremiah, and Carolyn M. West. 2019. Domestic Violence Through a Caribbean Lens: Historical Context, Theories, Risks and Consequences. *Journal of Aggression, Maltreatment & Trauma*. https://doi.org/10.1080/10926771.2019.1660442.

Linton, Cheryl, and Troy Lorde. 2011. The Influence of Gender and Gender Role Attitudes on Domestic Violence Culpability Assignment in Barbados. https://www.cavehill.uwi.edu/salises/conferences/pastconferences/2009/lintoncheryl-domesticviolenceculpabillity.aspx.

Melley, James. 2018. BBC Victoria Derbyshire Programme Published 20 December 2018. https://www.bbc.com/news/uk-england-46623723.

Murray, Christine E. 2006. Controversy, Constraints, and Context: Understanding Family Violence Through Family Systems Theory. *The Family Journal* 14 (3): 234–239.

National Network to end domestic violence. 2017. Domestic Violence counts 12th Annual Census Report. https://www.nnedv.org.

Postmus, Judy L., Gretchen L. Hoge, Jan Breckenridge, Nicola Sharp-Jeffs, and Donna Chung. 2020. Economic Abuse as an Invisible Form of Domestic Violence: A Multicountry Review. *Trauma, Violence, & Abuse* 21 (2): 261–283. https://doi.org/10.1177/1524838018764160.

Powell, Dorian. 1984. The Role of Women in the Caribbean. *Social and Economic Studies* 33 (2): 97–122. http://www.jstor.org/stable/27862073. Accessed 5 May 2021.

Qin, Dongxiao. 2004. Toward a Critical Feminist Perspective of Culture and Self. *Feminism & Psychology* 14 (2): 297–312.

Riessman, C. K. 2008. *Narrative Methods for the Human Sciences*. Sage, London.

Seegobin, Winston. 1999. Important Considerations in Counseling Asian Indians. Faculty Publications—Grad School of Clinical Psychology. Paper 126. http://digitalcommons.georgefox.edu/gscp_fac/126.

Sharp-Jeffs, Nicola. 2015. A Review of Research and Policy on Financial Abuse Within Intimate Partner Relationships.

Singh, Felicia. 2018. Breaking Domestic Violence Silence in the Indo-Caribbean Community. https://browngirlmagazine.com/2018/01/breaking-the-taboo-of-talking-about-domestic-violence-in-the-indo-caribbean-community/

Stake, R. E., Denzin, Norman K. (Ed); Lincoln, Yvonna S. (Ed.). 2005. The Sage handbook of qualitative research (3rd ed.)., (pp. 443–466). Thousand Oaks, CA: Sage.

Sutton, Heather, and Lucciana Álvarez. 2016. How Safe Are Caribbean Homes for Women and Children? Attitudes toward Intimate Partner Violence and Corporal Punishment. https://publications.iadb.org/en/publication/12617/how-safe-are-caribbean-homes-women-and-children-attitudes-toward-intimate-partner.

Tan, Jennifer. 2019. 04:33 pm EDT Understanding the Financial Impact of Domestic Violence, May 24. https://www.forbes.com/sites/ellevate/2019/05/24/understanding-the-financial-impact-of-domestic-violence/?sh=82ffe0141d16.

Thornton, Karen Maria. 2015. Power, Privilege, and Patriarchy. PhD dissertation.

Tisdale, Stacey. 2019. Financial Abuse: The Ties That Bind Domestic Violence Victims. *Business and Economy|Al Jazeera*, October 25. https://www.aljazeera.com/economy/2019/10/25/financial-abuse-the-ties-that-bind-domestic-violence-victims/.

VonDeLinde, K. C., and A. Correia. 2005. Economic Education Programs for Battered Women: Lessons Learned from Two Settings. Building Comprehensive Solutions to Domestic Violence. Retrieved from http://new.vawnet.org/Assoc_Files_VAWnet/BCS18_EP.pdf https://vawnet.org/material/economic-education-programs-battered-women-lessons-learned-two-settings.

Wallace, Wendell C., Cherrie Gibson, Netty-Ann Gordon, Rennie Lakhan, Jinnalee Mahabir, and Cassandra Seetahal. 2019. Domestic Violence: Intimate Partner Violence Victimization Non-reporting to the Police in Trinidad and Tobago. *Justice Policy Journal* 16 (1): 1–30.

Yin, R. K. 2003. Case study research: Design and methods (3rd ed.). Thousand Oaks, CA: Sage.

AMY PIEDALUE AND SUSMITA RISHI Unsettling the South through Postcolonial Feminist Theory Feminist Studies 43, no. 3. © 2017 by Feminist Studies, Inc.

Qualitative Case Study Methodology: Study Design and Implementation for Novice Researchers Pamela Baxter McMaster University, baxterp@mcmaster.ca Susan Jack McMaster University, jacksm@mcmaster.ca

CHAPTER 5

The Challenges in Enforcing Domestic Violence Prescriptions in the Case of Trinidad and Tobago

Ann Marie Bissessar

Discussion

As Table 5.1 indicates, there were are a total of 5802 reported cases of domestic violence (according to different categories) during the period 2000–2005.[1] Prior to this, during the period 1995–1999, there were fifteen deaths as a result of domestic violence (Table 5.2).[2]

For the year 2018, there were over 1100 reported cases of domestic violence (or Intimate Partner Violence {IPV}) and over 143 women were killed by their partners in a country where the population is 1.3 million persons.[3] These statistics indicate that rather than a decrease in the number of cases over time,[4] that the incidents of domestic violence

A. M. Bissessar (✉)
The University of the West Indies at St. Augustine, St. Augustine, Trinidad and Tobago
e-mail: AnnMarie.Bissessar@sta.uwi.edu

A. M. Bissessar and C. Huggins (eds.), *Domestic Violence in the Anglophone Caribbean*,
https://doi.org/10.1007/978-3-030-88476-5_5

Table 5.1 Number of domestic violence cases reported by categories—2000–2005

Offences	*2000*	*2001*	*2002*	*2003*	*2004*	*2005*	*Total*	*% of total*
Murders/homicides	24	17	17	22	18	21	119	2.0
Sexual abuse	92	37	24	3	15	4	175	3.0
Wounding	48	42	37	9	29	7	172	3.0
Assault by beating	775	907	560	406	470	211	3329	57.4
Threats	214	217	133	227	245	50	1086	18.7
Verbal abuse	94	60	91	40	60	18	363	6.3
Emotional abuse	59	61	55	37	49	5	266	4.6
Malicious damage	0	2	0	5	10	1	18	0.3
Financial abuse	4	0	1	4	12	0	21	0.3
Child abuse	4	25	9	0	28	31	97	1.7
Breach of protection order	16	26	30	38	26	19	155	2.7
Total	1330	1394	957	791	962	367	5801	100

Table 5.2 Murders as a percentage of domestic violence, 1995–1999

Year	*Domestic violence*	*Non-domestic violence*	*Total*	*% domestic violence*
1995	22	99	121	18.18
1996	16	91	107	14.95
1997	12	89	101	11.88
1998	23	74	97	23.71
1999	15	77	92	16.30

Source Trinidad and Tobago Crime Report: 2006

are increasing. This chapter will accordingly examine the various prescriptions that have been introduced to minimize the incidents of domestic violence and then attempt to evaluate them.

A number of writers have attempted to define the causal factors leading to domestic violence. Madame Justice Desiree Bernard, for example, in her paper Confronting Gender-Based Violence in the Caribbean,[5] taking a feminist perspective, suggests that the rationale for this form of violence is rooted in the historical philosophy of women's subordination and inferiority to men. She contended that women were, and many still are, conditioned to believe in the superiority of their male partners in any relationship. She also touched on factors including low and moderate income and the pressures these place on families, as well as the impact, particularly in the context of the Caribbean, of drugs and alcohol. Others argue that conditions and experiences of diverse cultural groups, revealing a cultural or historical context of violence offers explanations for increased vulnerability for abuse, degrees of control, and barriers for receiving help.[6] Yet others suggest that gender role socialization, race, ethnicity, social class, and family structure are factors that also may lead to violence within homes.[7] This list of causal factors is certainly not limited.

Given the wide array of causal factors offered to explain the phenomenon of domestic violence or what has now been retermed intimate partner violence, a number of prescriptions have been advanced and instituted in countries around the world. This chapter will accordingly examine some of these measures introduced in Trinidad and Tobago—categorizing them as Regional Initiatives, National Initiatives, and Institutional Measures. At the same time, it will attempt an assessment of these prescriptions or remedies.

Regional Initiatives

The Government of Trinidad and Tobago has signed and ratified five major international human rights treaties to date. These include the International Covenant on Civil and Political Rights (ICCPR), the International Covenant on Economic Social and Cultural Rights (ICESCR), the International Convention on the Elimination of Racial Discrimination (ICERD), the Convention on the Elimination of Discrimination against Women (CEDAW), and the Convention on the Rights of the Child (CRC). Further to these on the 5 August 1996, The Government of Trinidad and Tobago ratified the Inter-American Convention on the Prevention, Punishment, and Eradication of Violence against women, referred to as "Convention of Belem do Para". This convention, at Article 7, (B) requires states or governments to apply due diligence to prevent, investigate and impose penalties for violence against women. Article 7, C–D also set out the differing requirements under the Convention as follows[8]:

©. States were also required to include in their domestic legislation penal, civil, administrative and any other type of provisions that may be needed to prevent, punish and eradicate violence against women and to adopt appropriate administrative measures where necessary;

D. adopt legal measures to require the perpetrator to refrain from harassing, intimidating or threatening the woman or using any method that harms or endangers her life or integrity, or damages her property;
E. take all appropriate measures, including legislative measures, to amend or repeal existing laws and regulations or to modify legal or customary practices which sustain the persistence and tolerance of violence against women;
F. establish fair and effective legal procedures for women who have been subjected to violence which include, among others, protective measures, a timely hearing and effective access to such procedures;
G. establish the necessary legal and administrative mechanisms to ensure that women subjected to violence have effective access to restitution, reparations or other just and effective remedies; and
H. adopt such legislative or other measures as may be necessary to give effect to this Convention. In other words Article 7 sets out the parameters for the establishment of appropriate legislation to minimize the occurrence of domestic violence.

Article 8, on the other hand, focused on measures such as awareness, observance of rights, modification of social and cultural patterns of conduct of men and women, and included the development of formal and informal education programmes appropriate to every level of the educational process. What was also stressed was that, in addition to sensitization and training of the wider citizenry, was the requirement to promote the education and training of all those involved in the administration of justice, police, and other law enforcement officers as well as other personnel responsible for implementing policies for the prevention, punishment, and eradication of violence against women. In addition, the Convention also included the requirement to provide appropriate specialized services for women who have been subjected to violence, through public and private sector agencies, including shelters, counselling services for all family members where appropriate, and care and custody of the affected children. The Convention also stressed the need to promote and support governmental and private sector education designed to raise the awareness of the public with respect to the problems of and remedies for violence against women; disadvantaged, affected by armed conflict, or deprived of their freedom.

Coming out of that Convention, all Parties to that Convention were required to submit national reports containing information on measures adopted to prevent and prohibit violence against women, and to assist women affected by violence, as well as on any difficulties they observe in applying those measures, and the factors that contribute to violence against women to the Inter-American Commission of Women. The Parties to this Convention could at the same time request the Inter-American Court of Human Rights advisory opinions on the interpretation of this convention. In examining the different measures suggested by the Convention, it is evident that in the case of Trinidad and Tobago, many of the recommendations were introduced. However, the extent to these measures have successfully been implemented is questionable given the rise in the number of cases over the years. The question, then, is to what extent are Conventions adhered to in words or are they merely at the level of intent?

Conventions, as we know are not binding to Parties but as Abbot and Snidal (2004),[9] observe sometimes states are unable to move directly to a cooperative solution because of informational, bargaining, and distribution problems that hamper collective action. They surmised, quite rightly, that states face uncertainties because of particular issues: the nature and capabilities of potential co-operators and the political reactions at home and abroad. In their article, they therefore recommended what they termed "pathways". According to them, the international agreements require that:

(a) The agreement include some substantive content governing the behaviour that needs to be modified;
(b) The agreement includes participation by at least some states whose behaviour is consequential for the issue;

Given these requirements, then, they suggest that states adopt a number of approaches. In the first case, they may manage the risk of such agreements by beginning with fairly shallow commitments and then deepen those commitments as they learn more about the problem, potential solutions, and the benefits of the cooperation. Second, they propose, that states gradually expand their scope which allows them to deal with certainty. They further suggest that states manage the risks of free-riding by beginning with strong, legalized agreements limited to core groups of members demonstrably committed to and capable of cooperation, then gradually adding members who can demonstrate similar levels of commitment and capability. Finally, states adopt detailed but non-binding instruments which allow them to address political uncertainties regarding how international agreements will be received domestically.

The analysis offered by Abbot and Snidal is to the point but to a large extent, addresses the question, as it relates to larger, more developed countries. In the case of ex-colonial, Small Island states such as Trinidad and Tobago, while no doubt a critical concern is the plurality of the population and a race-based two-party system of voting, other concerns centre around the vulnerability of the country and its exposures to climate change that bring about flooding, landslides, or intense dry seasons. Yet other challenges include the rising gap in the level of incomes, massive retrenchment by various private sector organizations, as well as scarcity of disposable income by the government. Thus, while in form, many of the proposed measures may be adopted, yet in many cases, the implementation of these measures will be severely limited. No doubt, however, the Government of Trinidad and Tobago, has to a large extent complied with many of the recommendations offered under the Convention, particularly at the legislative and institutional levels.

National Initiatives

A number of legislative measures have been introduced in the case of Trinidad and Tobago to address the issue of violence. These include:

(a) Children Act 2012 which came into force in 2015;
(b) Offences against the Person Act 1925;
(c) Sexual Offences Act 1986;
(d) Domestic Violence Act 1999;
(e) Trafficking in Persons Act 2011;
(f) Anti-Gang Act 2011;
(g) Anti-Terrorism Act 2005;
(h) Kidnapping Act 2003;

The objectives of the Domestic Violence Act of 1999 were to:

(a) Provide immediate injunctive relief to victims of domestic violence; and
(b) Ensure a prompt and just legal remedy for victims of domestic violence.

Persadie in a comprehensive thesis on the topic of Domestic Violence (2007)[10] has dissected the 1999 Act and exposed some of the weaknesses inherent in the legislation. One of the more pressing concerns, she argues is the "promptness" of the legal remedies. She notes that while women can in fact obtain immediate injunctive relief in the form of a protection order, this is unable to stop the abuser but may rather "inflame" the abuse. She contends, therefore, that the victim must have some refuge or her life would be in imminent danger. It is clear, however, that in looking at the establishment of centres, there are numerous shortcomings primarily because these centres are not Government-owned but run by private non-governmental organizations who are pressed for resources.

It was true that in 1987, The Shelter for Battered Women and Children was established as "a safe haven" for women and children who were victims of domestic violence. It operates a safe house granted to it by the Government of Trinidad and Tobago, providing accommodation for residents, staff quarters, a counselling room, children's activity room, and training room. As a registered charity, it is run by an Executive Committee of Volunteers. Although it receives an annual subvention from the Government as well as well-wishers, the funds generated are usually inadequate given the growing need and the extent of the services that the Shelter currently provides and wishes to provide to the victims.

The general lack of facilities and services in Trinidad and Tobago means that The Shelter is also regularly called upon to provide a safe house to persons from other Caribbean and foreign countries, such as Albania, Gambia, Colombia, the Dominican Republic, and Cuba. More recently, the facility has also been called upon to house victims of the growing problem of Human Trafficking in Trinidad and Tobago. In 2017, a bulletin from the Ministry of Gender advised that a further two (2) centres for victims of violence (women and children) were constructed and were expected to be operationalized in early 2018. In addition, it noted that additional facilities which were to serve as safe havens for victims of human trafficking and male victims of domestic violence have been identified for renovation and were expected to be completed later in 2018. However, as of the ending of 2019, no reports have been provided to advise whether these facilities have been established or at this time, functional.

While few statistics seem to be forthcoming of the number of women that are actually accommodated at the centres, what emerges is that it is usually a short-term arrangement of no more than three months. Further to this, children of a certain age and especially boys were not allowed at shelters[11] and some reports suggest that this can be a reason for women not staying. Additionally, places like Tobago are not considered to be well-serviced with shelters and counsellors. After an allocated time of three months, women may also have nowhere else to go and no income options, particularly if their partners were the main breadwinners.

In the Gender-Based Violence Study, also, a number of challenges with respect to the centres are highlighted. Included among them, are that service providers themselves express frustration with authorities who dismiss the severity of violence and they tend to focus on getting women to a point where they feel safe. In emphasizing healing, and recognizing that lifetime experiences of familial or sexual violence may have disempowered women, service providers use story-telling and sharing which is not focused on domestic violence, but rather on "whatever is hurting". Providers' time, the report observes, is also taken up with "begging and networking" in the effort to help survivors. However, their challenges are also related to follow-up. One source had this to say: "they never even keep coming back and checking on us. Survivors themselves do not always feel well looked after in the shelters."

As one explained in this report,

> *Most of the time it is people volunteering to just do something because they feel they doing something good, it is a good cause, but they come with their own biases and own problems and their own everything, so they not treating people humanly. I see children being abused because it may have orphans there and the adults are beating up children and, most of the time, the matron look up in the office or in her room or whatever and it is just like, survive, do what they say is the rules, it have different days you have to assist with cooking the food for everybody or whatever, and that is it.* (African-Trinidadian, 43 years old, tertiary school educated) Service providers also call for adequate training and constant re-training for police officers and for national sensitization on violence against women

Apart from the inability to provide long-term facilities to house the victims and children of domestic violence, the Act itself also comes up for scrutiny. The Judiciary of the Republic of Trinidad and Tobago's website (http://www.ttlawcourts.org/) indicates that applications for protection or restraining orders can be made before the local Clerk of the Peace of the District Magistrate Court in order to "[restrain] a person from engaging in abuse behavior of any type". The website also indicates that protection orders can be filed by:

- A spouse;
- a member of the spouse's household i.e. a child;
- a dependent;
- a parent or sibling of either the spouse or respondent of that sibling or parent who is not a member of the household;
- a person who has a child in common with the respondent;
- a person who is or has been in a visiting relationship with a person of the opposite sex for a period exceeding twelve months;
- A police officer, a probation officer or approved social worker on behalf of an alleged victim (ibid.).

The procedure to obtain a protection order is as follows:

1. The applicant goes to the court's registry at the respective Magistrate's court;
2. The applicant speaks to the Clerk of the Peace, who identifies the problem and determines whether it is a domestic violence matter or a matter for another court;
3. Applicant pays $3.00 [Trinidadian Dollars or C$0.48 (XE 18 July 2012)] in cash or the value of $3.00 in stamps for filing a domestic violence complaint;
4. The Clerk of the Peace then prepares the complaint and summons and at the same time fixes the date of hearing within seven days of filing of the application;
5. The applicant is required to sign the complaint;
6. The applicant takes the summons to be served on respondent to the police or may be served by the applicant or his/her agent (ibid.).

An examination of the various stages involved in making the complaint clearly is one that reflects the old bureaucratic administrative apparatus and neglects largely the complainant or the challenges in making these complaints. But more than lengthy bureaucracy is involved. According to Mills (1997), no matter how heinous the assault, the great majority of domestic violence victims have one characteristic in common: after making the initial report, they have neither the will nor the courage to assist prosecutors in holding the abusers criminally responsible[12] Mills, a state prosecutor based in the United States, observed that Prosecutors and the courts have taken a long time to accept that a domestic violence victim's "refusal to press charges" is the norm in domestic violence prosecutions. Indeed, prosecutors traditionally are reluctant to charge batterers because victims frequently change their minds and later drop the charges. Faced with having to testify in court, domestic violence victims, especially battered women, routinely either recant, minimize the abuse, or fail to appear.

No doubt, the considerations for the victims of domestic violence are numerous. For instance, the literature on domestic violence is limitless in trying to explain why women remain in abusive relations. Factors such as poverty, learned helpless, dependency, the question of custody for children are impacting factors. In the case of small countries such as Trinidad and Tobago, one can argue that the smallness of the society is one that creates the "stigma" of shame for the victim. Furthermore, victims, particularly those at the lower level income households have no means to support themselves or their children if they do seek to complain about their spouse. To a large extent, the refusal of the victim to proceed against their spouse/partner is supported by data from 2017/2018 Annual Report of the Judiciary of Trinidad and Tobago. The statistics indicate that a large percentage of those involved are either not ready to proceed or in 343 cases, both parties were absent. In other words, the cases would not be pursued nor is there a mechanism to follow-up to see how these matters were addressed or resolved (Table 5.3).

It appears as well that even with other remedies there have been some major gaps. In terms of the legislation, for instance, it again involves a number of lengthy procedures. These are accordingly raised under the sub-heads below[13]:

Table 5.3 Adjourments of DV cases

Adjourned for sentencing	*Adjourned for trial*	*Exhibits unus-able*	*Parties not ready to proceed*	*Both parties absent*	*Related to complainant*	*Related to witness*	*Application both sides*	*Total*
437	1041	0	144	343	559	4	430	2957

Source 2017–2018 Annual Report—Judiciary of Trinidad and Tobago: Amended Table 67 at page 80. http://www.ttlawcourts.org/annualreport2017/2017-2018%20Annual%20Report%20-%

Legislative Discretion to Grant Protection Orders

5. (1) *Where, on an application made by a person described in section 4, the Court determines, on a balance of probabilities, that domestic violence has occurred, it may issue a Protection Order containing any or all of the prohibitions or directions referred to in section 6.*

According to the argument advanced by Persaide (2007), the Court need not issue a protection order even where it determines that domestic violence has occurred. Rather, she suggests that the Court should adopt a pre-emptive approach to domestic violence given the recognition above of the "alarming frequency and deadly consequences" with which domestic violence occurs. Moreover, as Persadie notes, there appears to be a conflict between this section and subsection (2) (b) as they both seem to point to the need to prevent the abusive situation and should not be dealt with separately and neither should one be based on discretion. She suggests, that in order to avoid uncertainty in the exercise of any judicial discretion, the Domestic Violence Act should have clearly stated the circumstances under which domestic violence can be established on a balance of probabilities and yet no Protection Order is granted by the Court.

Persadie (2007) was also critical of the period of three years of a Protection Order. She asked what happens after three years or whatever timeframe the Magistrate sees fit. She questioned: Is it that the abuser is supposed to have been rehabilitated during this time? If the abuser was ordered to immediately vacate the place, will the abuser now be allowed to return to his home after all this time? If counselling is not ordered for the respondent and/or the applicant, the psychological fallout could serve to nullify the original effect and intent of the protection order.

Clearly, the Act of 1999, amended in 2004, has a number of "gaps" but there is evidence to suggest that some of the challenges are being addressed and the revision of the legislation is on the government's agenda. A number of institutional measures to support the legislation has been initiated to date and these are accordingly examined summarily below.

Institutional Measures[14]

(a) **The establishment of a Task Force**

The Institutional measures established by the Government of Trinidad and Tobago can be categorized into phases or action items. One of the first phase, for instance, was to establish the broader policies and to fill the gap in the existing legislation. In 1999, a Domestic Violence Task Force was established to elaborate a wholistic and multidisciplinary policy on domestic violence at the national level. The Task Force included representatives of the police, the judiciary, the Rape Crisis Centre, the Central Statistical Office, and the University of the West Indies. Its functions included deepening knowledge regarding the factors which contribute to domestic violence; develop the capacities of civil servants and civil society organizations; and develop innovative mechanism to measure the effectiveness and cost of interventions to prevent and respond to domestic violence in the country. At the end of 2019, however, it is not clear that major advances, apart from the 1999 Act, were chartered through the task force in the formulation and implementation of specific policies to address violence against women.

The establishment of the Task Force was a step in the right direction. Indeed, it was evident that the government was establishing what some writers (Rhodes and Marsh 1992)[15] refer to as a policy community. According to these authors, policy communities are based on major functional interests in and of government. It exists where there are effectively shared community views on the problem. These shared values and the frequency of the interactions thus facilitate the development of an exchange-based relationship between the policy actors. Later, Sabatier and Jenkins-Smith (1993) redefined the community terming it an advocacy coalition.[16] His broadening of the "community" was that the "group or membership" now comprised people from a variety of positions (elected and agency officials, interest group leaders, researchers) who share a particular belief system and who show a nontrivial degree of coordinated activity over time. According to Sabatier and Jenkins-Smith (1993), the glue that holds an advocacy coalition together is its members' shared beliefs over core policy matters. He argued that once formed, coalitions seek to translate their shared belief into public policies or programmes. It appeared that this was a useful intervention by the Government at that time since it led to the repeal of the 1992 Domestic Violence Legislation and its replacement with the Act of 1999 (further amended in 2006). However, follow-up action appear to be lacking.

(b) **Responsibility for Coordination**

In order for a policy to succeed, though, one organization should be accorded vested interest. In the case of Trinidad and Tobago, that organization is Gender and Child affairs, a Ministry which reports directly to the Prime Minister of the country. Apart from implementation of the Act and network coordination, Gender and Child Affairs have regular commemorative activities for the UN International Day for the Elimination of Violence against Women (25 November–10 December), International Women's Day (8 March), World Aids Day (1 December), and Human Rights Day (10 December) which invites the participation of primary and secondary school children. The National Children's Forum is an annual event where children are educated about their rights and their views are solicited via speeches and creative representations on issues affecting them. A Statement of Commitment is then developed featuring an action plan as promised by key stakeholders. Activities include: (a) Art/poetry/spoken word/essay competitions on the importance of ending violence against women. (b) Workshops, seminars, and panel discussions. (c) 5K Walk/Run on International Women's Day (which has become the signature event held by the Office of the Prime Minister (Gender and Child Affairs) in commemoration of this day. These take place annually. There is no information available on mechanisms and tools for implementation.

What also emerges at the national level, though, is that the Government has entered into a "policy-partnership" with major international organizations. The Office of the Prime Minister (Gender and Child Affairs) collaborates with several local, regional, and multilateral agencies to promote gender equity. Some of the key collaborative efforts with international organizations include:

(a) The Strengthening State Accountability and Community Action for Ending Gender-Based Violence project, done in collaboration with United Nations Women and the Government of Trinidad and Tobago, focuses on reducing violence against women. The main objective is to establish a National Action Plan for ending Gender-Based Violence (GBV);
(b) The Office of the Prime Minister (Gender and Child Affairs) collaborates with the Commonwealth Secretariat to strengthen the implementation of the Commonwealth Plan of Action on Gender Equality.
(c) The Women's City Centre project is a collaborative initiative with the Inter-American Development Bank that aims to provide integrated services for women.

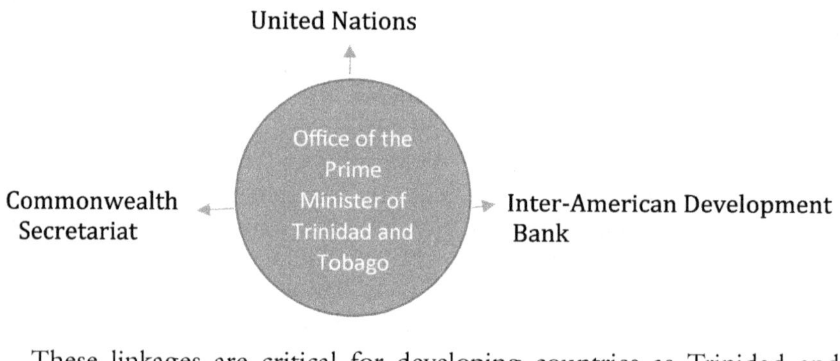

These linkages are critical for developing countries as Trinidad and Tobago particularly for support and resources as well as lessons that can be drawn from their experiences with other countries.

© Data Gathering

Further to these networks, The Government decided that another critical area that was lacking was data. Accordingly, The Central Registry on Domestic Violence was launched in April 2016. It is expected that data gathering and analysis will assist in obtaining the profiles of victims and perpetrators; allow for a deeper understanding of the incidence of Domestic Violence; identify groups at risk; and monitor the effectiveness of violence prevention and intervention activities.

A major source of data in the interim, though, was the National Domestic Violence Hotline. Launched in August 1996, in response to the escalating incidences of domestic violence, this service is a twenty-four (24) hour toll-free hotline service to persons experiencing or affected by domestic violence. The line operates seven days per week and can be accessed by phoning the number 800-SAVE (7283). The services provided by the hotline include safe and confidential listening; crisis intervention/counselling; referral to appropriate agencies, such as the police, shelters; and advocacy Data for the period 1 October 2005–30 September 2006 revealed that a total of 1867 clients benefited from the national domestic violence hotline, of which 1503 were female and 364 were male.

The Hotline provides listening, information, and referral services to victims and perpetrators of domestic violence. By 2006, the Hotline had received more than 13,000 calls related to domestic violence issues. The hotline is staffed by trained counsellors who are able to provide immediate crisis intervention assistance. Callers can be directly connected to get help in their areas, including emergency services and shelter as well as information and referrals, counselling and assistance in reporting abuse. The Hotline is structured to operate on a 24-hour basis, with eight active listeners rostered on three 8-hour shifts per day. The structure also provides for a Supervisor/Counsellor who manages the Hotline's daily operations and provides counselling services to some of the Hotline's clients. At present, the operations of the Hotline are managed and monitored by the non-governmental organization, Families in Action.

The data related to the activities of the hotline and presented in its 2010–2011 offer a useful snapshot of the main users of the service. A majority of users are female between the ages of 20 and 34 years old. 91% of the unemployed users are female and are primarily in common-law relationships (32%), or married (29%). Most of the cases relate to emotional, physical, or verbal abuse Interestingly, out of the 20,828 calls handled, 20% were referred by the hotline counsellor to the police, while 15% to the legal services, which seem relatively low. The data gathered by the service has also served to spearhead other initiatives and to inform national, regional, and global policy processes. These include the creation of the Male Support Programme, the policy roundtable on Domestic Violence data collection and multidisciplinary training for police officers and other service providers to victims and perpetrators of domestic violence.

(d) **The establishment of Drop-in Centres**

Apart from the Hotline, Drop-In Centres offer counselling services and "other forms of intervention to victims or perpetrators of domestic violence". The Drop-in Centres also refer victims to other agencies to "have their issues resolved". Drop-in Centres operate one day per week and services are provided on a walk-in basis. The government's web portal also indicates the names of the eight Drop-In Centres with their respective hours of operation: Manzanilla Community Centre, La Horqueta Regional Complex, Monroe Road Community Centre, Chaguanas Community Centre, Maloney Community Centre, Valencia Community Centre, Maracas Valley, and Penal Centre Community Centre. Each Centre is staffed by a trained social worker (contracted through the Domestic Violence Unit) who works as part of a service delivery team. In addition to Secretary/Warden or Manager of the Community Centre or Complex, a police officer; a representative from the Ministry of Community Development, Culture and Gender Affairs; and volunteers from within the community are also members of the team. At the outset, it appears that there are challenges with the Drop-in Centres. Firstly, the short duration during which the Centres operate will present challenges for those victims who are experiencing abuse and need to have counselling (face to face) immediately. Also, it would be useful to have received data which indicated whether persons within a village felt that there information would be kept in confidence if shared with a "volunteer" from the village. It is suggested that the NGOs in the country openly scoff at the Drop-In Centres and claim that these centres are largely non-functional. Further, the impressive description of Drop-In Centres with the high level of skilled staffing, it is contended only applies to one Drop-In Centre in Maloney in north Trinidad.

(e) **Enhancing the role of the Ministry of National Security**

Another support system that has been established within the Ministry of National Security is The Victim and Witness Support Unit (VWSU) which was established as part of reforms aiming at bridging the gap between the police and the victims and witnesses of crime. This Unit operates as a civilian unit within the Trinidad and Tobago Police Service (TTPS). Its main goals are to educate victims and witnesses and in this way prevent the risk of secondary victimization, collaborate with other agencies with the aim of enhancing existing victim support policies and programmes, develop a network system to harmonize governmental and non-governmental initiatives which promote victim and witness support, and to assist in promoting respect for the human dignity of victims through their interaction with all elements of the police service and by extension the criminal justice system. The VWSU offers holistic support to victims and witnesses of crime—persons who have reported a crime as well as those referred to the unit. Services include legal information by providing guidance on the criminal justice system, and information on the progress of investigations. Liaison services with other support agencies are also provided.

VWSU support officers are available in 10 different police stations throughout the country. The VWSU becomes involved in a case from the time a report is filed with the police. At this point, an investigator will be assigned to the case and make a referral to the unit. As a result of such referral, a victim and witness support officer will contact the informant or victims. One of the major gaps in addressing Domestic Violence occurs at the time of reporting. This is a crucial moment at which the victim may be either encouraged or discouraged to proceed. Many studies have reported dismissive and sometimes wholly inappropriate attitudes of police officers in receiving the report, notwithstanding their clear obligations under the Domestic Violence Act. During the consultations conducted as part of the elaboration of the National Gender Policy, it was revealed that the police had encouraged an abuser to inflict further violence on the victim because she had dared to report him. The dismissive attitude of police officers is exacerbated by the high level of victim recantation to initiate criminal proceedings, which appears to contribute to the frustration felt by the police in dealing with domestic violence. Many stakeholders have confirmed that the attitude of the police continues to constitute a serious concern. Police officers are still not sufficiently sensitized and will consider that only penetration constitutes sexual abuse, for instance. In some cases, the police officer knows the perpetrator, a relatively common occurrence in a small country such as Trinidad and Tobago, and will therefore not file the report.

To address this problem, a Domestic Violence Investigative and Procedural Manual for Police Officers in Trinidad and Tobago was prepared and accompanied by a series of training programmes targeting all police officers in the country. The manual provides examples of the type and evidence of abuse that may be reported under the legislation; explains who may apply for a protection order or who may be victims of domestic violence, how to handle the first interview in person or by telephone and how to prepare the domestic violence report; how to handle the situations on the scene of a domestic violence incident and how to collect the evidence at the scene. The manual specifically provides that interviews should be conducted privately and that a counsellor from the community policing section must be contacted. It recommends that the victim be immediately examined by a medical doctor, and that the accompanying police officer be a woman. The police officer is also expected to provide information to victims about relevant community and social services, such as shelters and legal aid, counselling, childcare, etc., and this first contact should constitute the starting point of an integrated response by the competent services.

While a number of reports examine the different kinds of training provided by police officers for victims of domestic violence, the statics provided by Thomas (2018)[17] suggests that the number of cases detected are low. For instance, she notes that a total of 1141 incidents were reported in 2016 of which a total of 293 were actually detected. In 2017, as well a total of 1075 cases were reported of which a mere 288 were detected. It can only be surmised the impact these statics would have on the confidence of the population (Table 5.4).

(f) The role of the Judiciary

Another major institution which assists persons who claim to be victims of domestic violence are the Courts. Victims of Gender-Based Violence may access legal aid through the Legal Aid Department and the Office of the Ombudsman. Also, access to courts and other "social interventions" are paid for by the state. In rural communities, the services provided by the ombudsperson are available on "specific days of the month". The Ministry of Legal Affairs indicates on its website that victims of domestic

Table 5.4 Reported domestic violence for the years January–December 2016 and January–November 2017

Offences	*Reported 2016*	*Detected 2016*	*Reported 2017*	*Detected 2017*
Homicide	35	17	43	25
Sexual abuse	5	2	2	1
Assault by beating	642	136	531	116
Breach of protection order	88	52	93	53
Child abuse and abandonment	3	1	5	1
Malicious damage	8	0	14	3
Psychological abuse	17	5	31	8
Threats	305	73	331	74
Verbal abuse	38	7	25	7
Total	1141	293	1075	288

Source Michelle A Thomas. 2018. Balancing the Domestic Violence Equation: Exploring Trinidadian Men's Perspective on Male Marginalization and Why Men Perpetrate Domestic Violence: https://nsuworks.nova.edu/cgi/viewcontent.cgi?article=1101&context=shss_dcar_etd

abuse may visit one of their nine offices to apply for legal aid. Before being referred to an attorney, the applicant must fill out an "enquiry for" and pay an initial fee of $10 Trinidadian Dollars. The legal aid office determines whether or not the applicant receives legal aid after reviewing a report submitted after investigating the case. The offices are located in Port of Spain, San Fernando, Sangre Grande, Arima, Couva, Debe, Siparia, Chaguanas, and Tobago. It also bears noting that according to several stakeholders, one of the main problems in the provision of legal aid is not related as such to resources but to the lack of trust that women have in legal professionals, whose integrity is not held in high regard, and they view legal aid as second class representation Legal aid is in principle available, particularly in domestic violence cases in civil proceedings. It is not clear whether women are sufficiently informed about the availability of legal aid before they apply for a protection order and it would be crucial to ensure that police officers, and other service providers who are in contact with a victim at the earliest stage provide that information. The attorneys who provide services under the legal aid scheme do not seem to receive specific training in this area, and may not be fully equipped to deal with an emotionally traumatized client. It appears that in many cases, legal aid will be provided at the first hearing before the court. It would be important to consider whether legal aid should not be made available from the very first contact with the police, so that advice could be provided at the earliest stage, to support the victim in seeking justice.

The judicial system in Trinidad and Tobago is based on British common law and is structured into three basic tiers, i.e. the Magistracy which consists of 13 Magisterial districts, with jurisdiction over less severe criminal and petty civil matters; the Supreme Court, which consists of the High Court and the Court of Appeal, with jurisdiction over civil and criminal matters and the Privy Council, which is the court of last resort, as in other countries of the English Caribbean. Sexual offences are indictable offences and are therefore first heard as preliminary enquiries in the Magistrate's Court. The Magistrate's Court also hears applications for protection order pursuant to the Domestic Violence Act.

To qualify to seek relief under the Domestic Violence Act, the applicant must be either married or previously married to the abusive person; have lived with or is living with a person of the opposite sex as husband or wife although not legally married to that person; have been in a visiting relationship with a person of the opposite sex for a period exceeding twelve months; or be a member of the household. The Magistrates' Court will grant the protection order on a balance of probabilities where it is satisfied that the respondent is engaging or has engaged in domestic violence against the applicant or is likely to engage in conduct that would constitute domestic violence. The court will consider the nature, history, or pattern of violence and whether a previous protection order or interim order has been issued; the need to protect the applicant and any other person for whose benefit the protection order has been granted from further domestic violence; the welfare of any child; the accommodation needs of the applicant and any other person; the hardship that may be caused as a result of making of the order; the income, assets and financial obligations of the respondent, the applicant and any other person affected by the order; the need to preserve and protect the institution of marriage and other relationships while affording protection and assistance to the family as a unit.

The proceedings in respect of an application for a protection order shall be held in camera unless the Court directs otherwise. The Protection order may be issued for the period deemed necessary by the Judge but shall not exceed two years. The judges in the Magistrates' Court may also issue an interim order on a temporary basis until a ruling on the Protection order is issued, and where it appears necessary and appropriate in order to ensure the safety and protection of the applicant. The interim order may apply for a maxim of 21 days. In case the protection order has been breached, the police may detain and arrest that person without warrant. Importantly, although legal aid may be available in principle, the law also provides that the applicant does not need an attorney to file her application.

For 2011–2012, 11,627 domestic violence cases were filed before the Magistrates' Court which constitutes around 10% of the total number of matters before the Magistrates' Court for that year, while 10,530 domestic violence cases were disposed of in the same year, meaning that there is a 0.91 disposed to file ratio applicable. The judiciary's annual report indicates that at the level of the Court of Appeal, out of 18 matters based on the Sexual Offences Act in 2011–2012, 12 took one to two years before being disposed of, four matters took between two to three years, and 2 took over six years. One needs to bear in mind that these periods of time apply for the proceedings before the Court of Appeal, and that the total of years a specific matter takes from the initial charges to final resolution will in all probability take twice as much or even more time. What is even more concerning is the number of cases that are not actively pursued as a result of one or more causes. For instance, as Table 5.5 indicates cases were not heard because of a number of reasons. Of this, 609 cases were postponed because the defendant was not served.

Further to this reasons for adjournments were presented in the Annual report of the Judiciary of Trinidad and Tobago (Table 66 page 79). In a total of 1597 cases, the Magistrate was unavailable (Table 5.6).

Table 5.5 Domestic violence cases not heard for period 2017–2018

Statement to be filed	*Awaiting report*	*Awaiting other reports*	*Reasons relating to attorney*	*Defendant not served*	*Reasons related to defendant*	*Interim order*	*All other reasons*	*Total*
23	97	118	116	609	1940	429	1326	4660

Taken from Annual Report of the Judiciary 2017–2018: Page 86 (Table 68)

Table 5.6 Reasons for adjournment of domestic violence cases

Not reachable	*Magistrate unavailable*	*Adjourned on behalf of magistrate*	*Adjourned for case notes*	*No reason given*	*Total*
6	1597	14	2	576	2188

Source Annual Report of the Judiciary of Trinidad and Tobago 2017–2018

Given these statistics, it is no wonder that in its *Annual Report 2012* for Trinidad and Tobago, Amnesty International reported that the conviction rate for sexual offences was only 3%. This very low figure also results according to Amnesty International from the fear of intimidation by the victim, the lack of support services, and the overwhelming distrust of the judicial system by the most vulnerable strands of the population. Another matter of concern is that the common law warning on corroboration, while no longer mandatory under Privy Council jurisprudence, is not strictly prohibited notwithstanding the fact that corroboration will notoriously be difficult to achieve in sexual offences cases, which usually are committed in the absence of witnesses.

The question of bias and of deep distrust of the judicial system and of legal professionals in general came up with some stakeholders going as far as concluding that the favoured approach was to avoid going through the judicial system and seek more pragmatic solutions to resolve individual situations instead. Among those women who decide to bring the matter before the courts, many eventually give up for a variety of reasons, not least, economic reasons, including their economic dependence on the perpetrator, lack of money for transportation, childcare arrangements, inflexible working hours, and as in all the other countries included in this study, the length of judicial proceedings. One woman had this to say:

> *The court system is designed to frustrate women, and I would go to court and go to court. Half of the time, I don't even know what going on, I have to ask people, and 'You could explain to me what going on?' People say, 'Well, it off because the police ain't come, what I go tell yuh, come back again.' And you just sit down there, sometimes you just sit down there until 12 o'clock, until the magistrate decide to call just to tell you, 'Well, okay, the officer not here, summons for the officer, come back so and so.' And, well you go back again, same thing. Some people would just not go, but I want justice, so I am going.* (Indo-Tobagonian, 41 years old, secondary school educated)"[18]

On the other hand, there is also an indication that judicial officers are not well equipped and prepared to handle cases of domestic violence, and deal with the victims with the required degree of sensitivity. On the occasion of the launch of the 16 days of activism against violence against women, the Chief Magistrate, Marcia Ayers-Caesar,[19] noted that judicial officers have to deal with victims of domestic violence who come to the court for help but do not have access to attorneys, adequate sources of income, access to counselling, functional extended families, or even a safe place to live, which can be a source of frustration. These remarks are borne out by earlier findings in an ethnographic study on the implementation of domestic violence legislation in Trinidad and Tobago, which found that officers of the court held "a physical, social, psychological or economic power over them", and that as a result, many victims did not feel at ease to speak freely, and "delegalized" the complaint, by their dismissiveness.

(g) The Establishment of a Family Court

In 2004, a Family court was established within the Magistracy and the High Court with jurisdiction in all family matters, including spousal abuse, divorce, and child maintenance. It still is at this time a pilot project based on alternative approaches that aim to improve services for citizens seeking assistance in dealing with family disputes. Some of the valuable innovations introduced by the Family Court have been a focus on user satisfaction through evaluation reports; the development of a unified office for both the High Court and Magistrate Court, and the availability for justice users of a "multi-door / one-shop court", which includes on site-availability of alternative dispute resolution, social work intervention, probation, and child and youth day care services. The philosophy behind the establishment of the Family Court was to promote a less adversarial approach to the resolution of family disputes. Judges sit together with the parties around a table rather than in a courtroom. While the Family Court is competent to hear domestic violence cases, an application for a protection order will only go before the Family Court if connected to other family proceedings. According to available data, domestic (violence) cases thus constitute only a relatively small proportion of the matters before the court, 237 over 2955 cases between February and July 2012, and 145 over 2476 from August 2011 to January 2012. If filed on its own, the matter will still be heard by the magistracy. This is unfortunate as it appears that the Family Court procedure is far more suitable to address these matters. One argument favouring, however, is that the adjudication of domestic violence cases by the Family Court is that one of its aims was to ensure the disposal of cases in a timely manner. The Rules of the Court specifically provide that before the High Court, all matters filed before it must lead to the first appearance before a judge within eight weeks of filing, a standard which was reached in 77% of cases in 2011/2012. Before the Magistrates' Court, the applicable deadline is of six weeks, a standard complied within 89% of cases in 2011/12.

Given that the Family Court enjoys a modern system of data collection, it is surprising that it does not offer information on the outcomes of applications filed before it, and on the reasons for dismissal. A common view among stakeholders was that overall, women who would apply for protection/restraining orders would generally succeed, and that the system worked fairly well at the level of the Family Court. This was not a unanimous view, however, and other stakeholders felt that the family court was also ineffective in addressing these types of cases. The UN Women research project Child Support, Poverty and Gender Equality in the Caribbean found that despite improvements in the justice sector, particularly through the pilot Family Court, delays; low levels of awards; noncompliance with court orders; limited avenues for enforcement of court awards and limited legal representation continued to persist. Another issue of concern related to the level of privacy afforded to applicants in these matters, which may affect women's willingness to pursue their cases. The study conducted for the purpose of the national gender policy noted in this respect that the situation is made worse due to the adversarial nature of the proceedings and the fact that many women have no legal representation.

According to stakeholders, the problem may be that there is no sufficient awareness as yet on the availability of legal aid, and of its importance. Another concern is that the referral may take too long while it is known that in SGBV cases, in its *Annual Report 2012* for Trinidad and Tobago, Amnesty International indicates that the under-reporting of cases of Gender-Based Violence is linked to "inadequate police training and the slowness of the justice system" (2012). Also, the US Department of State's *Country Reports* indicates that, according to local NGOs, violence against women is under-reported "partly due to perceived insensitivity on the part of police" (US 24 May 2012, Sec. 6).

(h) **Resources**

There is no separate itemization of Government allocation under Domestic Violence as this is lumped into the allocation dedicated to community development and social and cultural as well as recreational activities. During the period 1998–1999, a total of USD$13.4 million representing 7.7% of total sectoral allocations was budgeted to the Ministries of Social Development, Culture and Women's Affairs out of a total of USD$63.6 mn allocated to the development of social infrastructure. Funding was allocated to community centres, halfway houses, and rehabilitation centres, refurbishment of cultural centres and upgrading of the library services. There was no gender-specific expenditure except for USD$121,000 to complete training and outreach programmes in gender affairs and to purchase equipment and promotional materials.[20]

During the period 1999–2000, out of USD$113.7 million allocated to the development of social infrastructure, the Ministry of Culture and Gender Affairs was allocated USD$2.9 million, a mere 1% of total sectoral allocations, half of which was dedicated to the upgrade of library services. The remaining funding was dedicated to the establishment and continuation of refurbishment of cultural centres, training for museum staff, and the establishment of a Domestic Violence Unit. The government provided USD$167,000 for a Non-Traditional Training programme for women with an extra USD$357,000 coming from external sources. As of 2019–2020, the actual recurrent allocation to the Ministry of Social Development and Family Services was TT$26,541,000 MN much of which went to wages and office expenditure. The estimated allocation for 2020 was $27,188,247, a projected increase of $647,272 from 2019. When this amount is disaggregated, according to other special programmes including Senior Citizens Homes, Senior Citizens Centre, Social programme (Ageing), and Contribution to non-profit organizations, a total of $14,316,000 MN is projected. The breakdown indicates no proposed allocations for victims of domestic violence except for the Shelter.[21] Under the Development Programme, a mere TT$6,000,000 is proposed but again funding has been identified for socially displaced persons, street dwellers, and refurbishment of older persons' homes. The proposed budget for 2020 therefore is not reflective of any further remedies by way of institutional support or otherwise for the support of victims of domestic violence.

Conclusion

This chapter examined some of the remedies or prescriptions that have been introduced by the Government of Trinidad and Tobago to minimize the incidents of domestic violence. The chapter looked at the legislation as well as some of the institutions that have been established to assist victims of domestic violence. While some gaps have been identified in the literature, what emerges is that a number of the remedies recommended by the Inter-American Convention on the Prevention, Punishment, and Eradication of Violence against women, referred to as "Convention of Belem do Para" have been introduced. There were a number of weaknesses identified with many of the remedies proposed, such as the lengthy bureaucratic processes as well as the delays at the level of the Judiciary. It appears though that the major constraint facing Trinidad and Tobago is the lack of resources to improve systems of delivery as well as to allow for further sensitization of the various actors as well as the wider society. Indeed, while in 1999, some funding was allocated for the introduction and implementation of some parts of the 1999 Domestic Violence Act, in 2019/2020 resources seem to be directed at more pressing social problems such as ageing and youths. It is to be expected then that without necessary state intervention that the number of incidents of domestic violence will continue to increase.

Notes

1. https://sta.uwi.edu/nlc/2008/documents/papers/KAGittens-BaynesOrs.doc. An Economic Perspective with Implications for Trinidad and Tobago. By Karl Theodore, Christine Laptiste, Althea La Foucade, Charmaine Metivier.
2. Tables 1 and 2 were taken from https://sta.uwi.edu/nlc/2008/documents/papers/KAGittens-BaynesOrs.doc. An Economic Perspective with Implications for Trinidad and Tobago. By Karl Theodore, Christine Laptiste, Althea La Foucade, Charmaine Metivier.
3. See Domestic Violence at Crisis Level in TT, Melissa Doughty, NEWSDAY 20/3/2018.
4. Further to this, it is contended a large percentage of the incidents relating to DV is under-reported.

5. file:///C:/Users/Prof%20Bissessar/Documents/07-Confronting%20Gender-Based%20Violence%20%2029%2011%2006.pdf. Confronting Gender-Based Violence in the Caribbean.
6. A. Raj and J. Silverman. 2002. "Violence Against Immigrant Women: The Roles of Culture, Context, and Legal Immigrant Status on Intimate Partner Violence." *Violence Against Women* 8(3): 367–398.
7. G. D. Hill and E. M. Crawford. 1990. "Women, Race, and Crime." *Criminology* 28(4): 601–626.
8. Inter-American Convention on the Prevention, Punishment, and Eradication of Violence against Women (Convention of Belém do Pará), 1996.
9. Kenneth Wayne Abbott and Duncan Snidal. 2004. Pathways to International Cooperation. In *The Impact of International Law on International Cooperation: Theoretical Perspectives*, ed. Eyal Benvenisti and Moshe Hirsch, Copyright Cambridge University Press, 2004. Available at SSRN: https://ssrn.com/abstract=730908.
10. A Critical Analysis of the Efficacy of Law as a Tool to Achieve Gender Equality and to Address the Problem of Domestic Violence: The Case of Trinidad and Tobago by Natalie Renée Beulah Persadie. A thesis submitted to The University of Birmingham.

    For the degree of Doctor of Philosophy. Department of Political Science and International Studies School of Social Sciences University of Birmingham October 2007.
11. Gender-Based Violence in Trinidad and Tobago: A Qualitative Study. http://www.opm-gca.gov.tt/LinkClick.aspx?fileticket=ExJDa-bNLnw%3D&portalid=0.
12. Donna Mills. 1997. "Domestic Violence: The Case for Aggressive Prosecution." *UCLA Women's Law Journal* 7(2).
13. This portion is taken from Persaide's thesis (2007). Op cit.
14. A large percentage of the discussions that follow were taken from Legal Aid for Women Victims of Gender Violence in the Caribbean Identifying Gaps and Programmatic Responses; UNDP (2014).
15. Richard A.W. Rhodes and D. Marsh. 1992. "New Directions in the Study of Policy Network." *European Journal of Political Research* 21(1–2): 181–205 (May 2000).

16. P. A Sabatier and H. C. Jenkins-Smith (Eds.). 1993. *Policy Change and Learning: An Advocacy Coalition Approach*. Boulder, CO: Westview Press.
17. Source: Michelle A. Thomas. 2018. Balancing the Domestic Violence Equation: Exploring Trinidadian Men's Perspective on Male Marginalisation and Why Men Perpetrate Domestic Violence. https://nsuworks.nova.edu/cgi/viewcontent.cgi?article=1101&context=shss_dcar_etd.
18. Gender-Based Violence in Trinidad and Tobago: A Qualitative Study. http://www.opm-gca.gov.tt/LinkClick.aspx?fileticket=ExJDa-bNLnw%3D&portalid=0, p. 58.
19. https://ttwhistleblower.com/chiefmagistrate-speaks-please-help-women.
20. See Republic of Trinidad and Tobago, *Public Sector Investment Programme 2005* (Port of Spain, Trinidad: Ministry of Planning and Development and Ministry of Finance, 2004), p. 1. Republic of Trinidad and Tobago, *Public Sector Investment Programme 2002* (Port of Spain, Trinidad: Ministry of Finance, 2001), p. 3.
21. Republic of Trinidad and Tobago, Draft Estimates. Details of Estimates of Recurrent Expenditure for the Financial Year 2020, Prepared by the Government Printer, 2019, p. 405.

References

Abbott, Kenneth Wayne, and Duncan Snidal. 2004. Pathways to International Cooperation. In *The Impact of International Law on International Cooperation: Theoretical Perspectives*, ed. Eyal Benvenisti and Moshe Hirsch. Copyright Cambridge University Press. Available at SSRN: https://ssrn.com/abstract=730908.

Mills, Donna. 1997. Domestic Violence: The Case for Aggressive. *Prosecution UCLA Women's Law Journal* 7 (2).

Rhodes, Richard, and D. Marsh. 1992. New Directions in the Study of Policy Network. *European Journal of Political Research* 21 (1–2): 181–205 (May 2000).

Sabatier, P.A., and H.C. Jenkins-Smith (eds.). 1993. *Policy Change and Learning: An Advocacy Coalition Approach*. Boulder, CO: Westview Press.

Theodore, Karl, Christine Laptiste, Althea La Foucade, and Charmaine Metivier. An Economic Perspective with Implications for Trinidad and

Tobago. https://sta.uwi.edu/nlc/2008/documents/papers/KAGittens-BaynesOrs.doc.

Reports

Gender-Based Violence in Trinidad and Tobago: A Qualitative Study. http://www.opm-gca.gov.tt/LinkClick.aspx?fileticket=ExJDa-bNLnw%3D&portalid=0.

A Critical Analysis of the Efficacy of Law as a Tool to Achieve Gender Equality and to Address the Problem of Domestic Violence: The Case of Trinidad and Tobago by Natalie Renée Beulah Persadie. A thesis submitted to The University of Birmingham For the degree of Doctor of Philosophy. Department of Political Science and International Studies School of Social Sciences University of Birmingham October 2007.

Thomas, Michelle A. 2018. Balancing the Domestic Violence Equation: Exploring Trinidadian Men's Perspective on Male Marginalisation and Why Men Perpetrate Domestic Violence. https://nsuworks.nova.edu/cgi/viewcontent.cgi?article=1101&context=shss_dcar_etd.

Republic of Trinidad and Tobago, *Public Sector Investment Programme 2005* (Port of Spain, Trinidad: Ministry of Planning and Development and Ministry of Finance, 2004), p. 1. Republic of Trinidad and Tobago, *Public Sector Investment Programme 2002* (Port of Spain, Trinidad: Ministry of Finance, 2001).

Republic of Trinidad and Tobago, Draft Estimates. Details of Estimates of Recurrent Expenditure for the Financial Year 2020, Prepared by the Government Printer, 2019.

Legal Aid for Women Victims of Gender Violence in the Caribbean: Identifying Gaps and Programme Responses: UNDP 2014.

National Policy on Gender and Development *of the Republic of Trinidad and Tobago. Revised by the Gender Affairs Division* Ministry of Community Development, Culture and Gender Affairs, June 2009.

2017–2018 Annual Report—Judiciary of Trinidad and Tobago: Amended Table 67 at page 80. http://www.ttlawcourts.org/annualreport2017/2017-2018%20Annual%20Report%20-%.

Annual Report 2012 for Trinidad and Tobago, Amnesty International. https://www.amnesty.org/en/countries/americas/trinidad-and-tobago/.

UN Women research project Child Support, Poverty and Gender Equality in the Caribbean. https://caribbean.unwomen.org/en/materials/publications/2008/4/share-the-care-child-support-poverty-and-gender-equality-barbados-country-report.

Conventions

International Convention on Civil and Political Rights. Adopted and opened for signature, ratification and accession by General Assembly resolution 2200A (XXI) of 16 December 1966 entry into force 23 March 1976, in accordance with Article 49. https://www.ohchr.org/EN/ProfessionalInterest/Pages/CCPR.aspx.

International Covenant on Economic, Social and Cultural Rights Adopted and opened for signature, ratification and accession by General Assembly resolution 2200A (XXI) of 16 December 1966 entry into force 3 January 1976, in accordance with article 27. https://www.ohchr.org/en/professionalinterest/pages/cescr.aspx.

The International Convention on the Elimination of Racial Discrimination (ICERD), Adopted and opened for signature and ratification by General Assembly resolution 2106 (XX) of 21 December 1965 entry into force 4 January 1969, in accordance with Article 19. https://ohchr.org/EN/ProfessionalInterest/Pages/CERD.aspx.

The Convention on the Elimination of Discrimination against Women (CEDAW), Convention on the Elimination of All Forms of Discrimination against Women New York, 18 December 1979. https://www.ohchr.org/EN/ProfessionalInterest/Pages/CEDAW.aspx.

The Convention on the Rights of the Child (CRC). Adopted and opened for signature, ratification and accession by General Assembly resolution 44/25 of 20 November 1989 entry into force 2 September 1990, in accordance with article 49. https://www.ohchr.org/en/professionalinterest/pages/crc.aspx.

The Inter-American Convention on the Prevention, Punishment and Eradication of Violence against women, referred to as "Convention of Belem do Para". https://www.oas.org/juridico/english/treaties/a-61.html.

Acts of Parliament (Trinidad and Tobago)

CHILDREN'S AUTHORITY ACT CHAPTER 46:10. Act 64 of 2000

Amended by
8 of 2003
14 of 2008
12 of 2012

OFFENCES AGAINST THE PERSON ACT

CHAPTER 11:08

Act 11 of 1925 Amended by 2 of 1939 14 of 1939 28 of 1973 11 of 1979 19 of 1979 45 of 1979 3 of 1980 19 of 1985

SEXUAL OFFENCES ACT
CHAPTER 11:28
Act
27 of 1986
Amended by
20 of 1994
31 of 2000
LAWS OF TRINIDAD AND TOBAGO
CHAPTER 45:56
DOMESTIC VIOLENCE ACT
ACT
27 of 1999
Amended by
8 of 2006

TRAFFICKING IN PERSONS ACT
CHAPTER 12:10
ACT
14 of 2011
Amended by
12 of 2012

ANTI-TERRORISM ACT
CHAPTER 12:07
ACT
26 of 2005
Amended by
2 of 2010
16 of 2011
14 of 2012
15 of 2014

Act No. 13 of 2018
KIDNAPPING ACT CHAPTER 11:26
Act 21 of 2003 Amended by 9 of 2011

CHAPTER 6

A Prospective Legal Framework for Equitable Treatment of Domestic Violence Victims and Perpetrators in a Caribbean Context

Charmaine Pemberton and Avason Quinlan-Williams

Discussion

Gender-based violence is directed at an individual based on their gender and is disproportionately perpetrated by men against women. This is not limited to physical or sexual violence/abuse but includes psychological harm. Intimate partner violence captures aggressive acts between partners, casual intimate partners, or between former spouses. The law condemns any kind of violence, which reaches into other family relationships. These include sibling violence, violence, and abuse between close relatives such

C. Pemberton (✉) · A. Quinlan-Williams
Supreme Court of Trinidad and Tobago, Port of Spain, Trinidad and Tobago

A. Quinlan-Williams
e-mail: AQuinlan-Williams@ttlawcourts.org

A. M. Bissessar and C. Huggins (eds.), *Domestic Violence in the Anglophone Caribbean*,
https://doi.org/10.1007/978-3-030-88476-5_6

as uncles or aunts and the nieces and nephews, grandparents and grandchildren, adoptive parents and children, foster parents and children, and the stepparents and the stepchildren and their siblings. Any legislation therefore must reflect and encapsulate victims of domestic violence in the context of our Caribbean experience. C.L.R. James along with many Caribbean historians have recognized that Caribbean societies are unique in that they are always on a cusp, that is, they are constantly ready for "*the change*".[1] The law's response, then, to domestic violence must be multi-faceted in order for it to be comprehensible and effective in the society that it must serve. Laws and decision-making procedures must reflect our Caribbean realities.

Domestic violence legislation in the region is based on regional and international conventions and treaties. These conventions and treaties all recognize that violence against women is rooted in the historical relationship imbalance between men and women.[2] The conventions and the regional Charter are:

1. The Convention for the Elimination of All Forms of Discrimination against Women (CEDAW),
2. The Inter-American Convention on the Prevention, Punishment and Eradication of Violence against Women (The Belém do Pará Convention) and
3. The Charter of Civil Society for the Caribbean Community.

These conventions and the Charter cover physical, sexual, and psychological violence within households or domestic relationships. A summary of the various conventions and The Charter appear below.

1. CEDAW

This Convention treats domestic violence as a human rights violation. ARTICLE 5 mandates State Parties to take all appropriate measures, "*To modify the social and cultural patterns of conduct of men and women, with a view to achieving the elimination of prejudices and customary and all other practices which are based on the idea of the inferiority or the superiority of either of the sexes or on stereotyped roles for men and women*".[3]

2. BELÉM DO PARÁ

The theme of this Inter-American Convention is *violence against women*. Its Preamble recites,

- its abhorrence of violence against women and terms it, inter alia, as "*an offence against human dignity and a manifestation of the historically unequal power relations between women and men*";
- that violence against women "*pervades every sector of society regardless of class, race or ethnic group, income, culture, level of education, age or religion and strikes at its very foundations*";
- that the elimination of violence against women "*is essential for their individual and social development and their full and equal participation in all walks of life*"; and
- that the adoption of a convention on the prevention, punishment and eradication of all forms of violence against women within the framework of the Organization of American States is a positive contribution to protecting the rights of women and eliminating violence against them.

Article 7, in particular, enjoins states to inter alia, "*include in their domestic legislation, penal, civil administrative and any other type of provisions that may be needed to prevent, punish and eradicate violence against women...; take all appropriate measures, including legislative measures to amend or repeal existing laws and regulations or to modify legal or customary practices which sustain the persistence and tolerance of violence against women; adopt such legislative or other measures as may be necessary to give effect to the Convention*".[4]

3. THE CHARTER OF CIVIL SOCIETY FOR THE CARIBBEAN COMMUNITY

At Article XII (d), the Charter specifically provides for Women's Rights and that women, in particular, must be afforded *legal protection including just and effective remedies against domestic violence, sexual abuse and sexual harassment*.

Caribbean jurisdictions have for the most part adhered to their treaty obligations by incorporating these provisions into local legislation. Some of the features of existing legislation have shown a willingness on the part of Caribbean States to address frontally relationships and relational issues. The following illustrates this:

- the extensive definition of domestic violence;
- the wide range of victims who can apply for relief[5];
- the broad range of orders available to the aggrieved person;
- the imposition of criminal sanctions for breaches of the provisions, especially protection orders;
- specific mention in some jurisdictions of the powers and duties of police officers; and
- mandatory reporting of domestic violence especially when children are involved.

The Way Forward

While the Caribbean has seen an encouraging progressive domestic violence law environment in that the legislation provides comprehensive protection as outlined above, the scourge is still quite prevalent.[6] The World Health Organization (WHO) from as recent as 9 March 2021 commented, "*Over the past decade, violence against women has been endemic in every country and culture*".

Accordingly, the recommendation is that a more holistic approach as mandated by international law is necessary where there is an emphasis not just on law and policy but on changing the cultural and traditional norms underlying domestic violence. Thus, the response necessary to eliminate such violence[7] should take the form of legislative and policy measures coupled with extensive public education, all of which challenge historical discriminatory beliefs concerning victims.

Breaking the silence around domestic violence/abuse has everything to do with eliminating shame through public education and providing access to help.

Two issues that have emerged at the time of writing are Migration and the Pandemic.

Migration

The recent crisis in Venezuela presents a unique challenge for Caribbean countries in close proximity to that country (Trinidad and Tobago and Guyana). This is so because the most recent wave is humanitarian migrants fleeing economic and political instability. As of December 2020, it is estimated that since 2015, more than 5.4 million Venezuelans have fled to neighbouring countries (Atlantic Council). Of that number, as of June 2019, 24,000 have been registered officially in Trinidad and Tobago and 1827 were registered in Guyana—51% of whom were under the age of 18 and 25% were women.[8] There are reports of Venezuelans entering both countries illegally and this increases the risk of already vulnerable groups in Trinidad and Tobago and Guyana. In Trinidad and Tobago, 114 Venezuelan women and children have had to receive psychosocial support and counselling as survivors of trafficking and gender-based violence.[9] Studies published by the Family Violence Prevention Fund 2009, suggest that non-fatal intimate partner violence may be less prevalent among immigrant populations than the host country population. While this may be so, Alvarez et al. posit that domestic violence is more prevalent in migrant communities when the women work outside of the home. They no longer match the traditional gender roles of mother, wife, and domestic caregiver or conform to expected cultural norms. Further, the more the women themselves ascribed to traditional gender norms, the more likely they were to endure the abuse.[10]

The Pandemic

Worldwide, abuse and violence against women and children have been exacerbated during the COVID-19 Pandemic. Trinidad and Tobago are no different. Since the pandemic, reports of domestic violence increased sharply. In response, The Judiciary of Trinidad and Tobago introduced a Domestic Violence Hotline, which receives calls from victims. Table 6.1 shows the figures for reports received and cases filed as a follow up to these calls.

Legislative Action

C.L.R. James posited, "*Nobody knows what the Caribbean population is capable of. Nobody has even attempted to find out...*". Involvement of the people according to James "*will guarantee the success of what is proposed*".[11] For legislation to be effective, it ought to spring from the society that it is intended to regulate. Giving voice to those who are affected is one of the first steps to ascertain society's needs. This gives the

Table 6.1 Domestic violence hotline calls & emails received 2020 to 2021

Year	*Month*	*Total No. of Calls*	*Total DV Related Calls*	*Total Non DV Related Calls*	*Total No. of DVR Emails*
2020	April	275	226	48	–
	May	289	162	122	–
	June	322	181	140	7
	July	296	151	130	16
	August	223	152	71	15
	September	261	164	100	19
	October	298	220	127	62
	November	334	257	135	58
	December	280	220	110	36
2020 Total Calls		2578	1733	983	213
Year	*Month*	*Total No. of Calls*	*Total DV Related Calls*	*Total Non DV Related Calls*	*Total No. of DVR Emails*
2021	January	403	229	212	39
	February	378	214	134	31
	March	395	227	130	39
	April *(as at 19/04/21)*	205	153	79	28
2021 Total Calls		1381	823	555	137

opportunity to communicate those needs to the lawmakers. The overall needs for victims or perpetrators of domestic violence are safety and security—personal, emotional, and financial. It is important as well that the victim is assured that offenders will be held accountable. This is not without difficulty or challenges.

Legislation should cover both the systemic and structural aspects of a proposed regime. This must be evident in the context of domestic violence.

Legislative Structure

Proposals/Recommendations

- The name of the legislation should reflect the true nature and the scope of the mischief it is intended to cure. The legislation should reflect its true aims, to provide protection for victims of relationship abuse while at the same time making those who perpetrate abuse responsible.[12]

- The language used in drafting laws should be gender-sensitive/neutral.

  This dismantles the traditional view of the law, which is perpetrated by drafters and entrenched in all of the Interpretation Acts throughout the Caribbean where "*he*" includes "*she*". This type of interpretative rule does not take into account the many variants of description that now confront modern Caribbean societies.
- Definition of domestic violence/abuse—The mischief intended to be corrected must always be identified in clear terms. Grenada and St. Christopher and Nevis laws provide a model of a comprehensive definition as "*any controlling or abusive behaviour that harms the health, safety or well-being of a person or any child and includes but is not limited to the following*:

  (a) physical abuse or threats of physical abuse;
  (b) sexual abuse or threats of sexual abuse;
  (c) emotional, verbal or psychological abuse;
  (d) economic abuse;
  (e) intimidation;
  (f) harassment;
  (g) stalking;
  (h) damage to or destruction of property; or
  (i) entry into the applicant's residence without consent, where the parties do not share the same residence".[13]

Even so, it may be useful to look at Ghana,[14] which is conduct focused and details what types of conduct will constitute domestic violence. This includes "*sexual contact by a person aware of being infected with (HIV) or other sexually transmitted disease with another person without that person being given prior information of the infection*". This is extremely forward-thinking since HIV/AIDS is still, and despite best efforts, remains a taboo subject in the region. Prospective legislation in this area can break the silence. Further, in terms of psychological abuse, the Ghanaian legislation details the conduct that will be caught in the net as "*conduct that makes another person unhappy, miserable, humiliated, ridiculed, afraid, jittery or depressed or to feel inadequate or worthless*". The act may be a single act or a pattern of behaviour.

In the case of South Africa[15] on the other hand, the law frowns upon conduct described as "*the repeated exhibition of obsessive possessiveness or jealousy, which is such as to constitute a serious invasion of the complainant's privacy, liberty, integrity or security; (c) repeatedly sending, delivering or causing the delivery of letters, telegrams, packages, facsimiles, electronic mail or other objects to the complainant; (j) Any other controlling or abusive behaviour towards a complainant, where such conduct harms, or may cause imminent harm to, the safety, health or wellbeing of the complainant*".

In India,[16] the law recognizes that conduct considered unlawful under the Act includes "*verbal and emotional abuse...", including "insults, ridicule, humiliation, name calling and insults or ridicule especially with regard to not having a child or a male child*".

In New Zealand,[17] the concept of family violence was the mainstay of the legislation. The definition includes all we have discussed. It enfolds in the concept, "*a pattern of behaviour (done, for example, to isolate from family members or friends) that is made up of a number of acts that are all or any of physical abuse, sexual abuse, and psychological abuse, and that may have one or both of the following features*:

(a) *it is coercive or controlling (because it is done against the person to coerce or control, or with the effect of coercing or controlling, the person); and*
(b) *it causes the person, or may cause the person, cumulative harm*".

The legislators even recognize that violence against a person may be dowry related, "*(that is, violence that arises solely or in part from concerns about whether, how, or how much any gifts, goods, money, other property, or other benefits are—*

(a) *given to or for a party to a marriage or proposed marriage; and*
(b) *received by or for the other party to the marriage or proposed marriage)*".

In the Caribbean, many jurisdictions have special provisions with respect to children. Specific legislative provisions along those lines which provide, that "*A person psychologically abuses a child if that person—*

(a) *causes or allows the child to see or hear the physical, sexual, or psychological abuse of a person with whom the child has a family relationship; or*
(b) *puts the child, or allows the child to be put, at real risk of seeing or hearing that abuse occurring*".[18]

The province of Nunavut in Canada may be closest in description to any of the smaller islands in the Caribbean. Their Act explicitly states that any action taken in self-defence or in defence of another would not be considered family abuse, the term used to define the regime, "*if no more force than is reasonable in the circumstances...*" is used.[19] It is recommended that this may be incorporated in our region.

The above illustrates how each society recognizes that hitherto accepted conduct will now fall outside of the acceptable and legal codes of behaviour among persons. Caribbean societies may benefit from inclusion of provisions such as those highlighted above. Wide-ranging recognized behaviour expands the pie and will lend more certainty and clarity as to which acts constitute domestic violence/abuse. This will be helpful not only to the society as a whole but also to Judicial Officers who will have a definitive guide as to how to execute their duties especially in terms of how to fashion the relief granted to the parties.

Widening the Scope of Protected Persons

Any examination of legislation will reveal that most legislatures provide protection to persons in a wide range of relationships, with some countries providing protection to a wider range than others. In the main, it is fair to say that the legislation encapsulates the flavour of our Caribbean "domestic relationship". The categories covered by the legislation include the following:

(a) spouse/former spouse/co-habitant or former co-habitant
(b) relative of a co-habitant
(c) child
(d) reliant or dependent adult
(e) relative for instance, father, mother, grandparents, step parents, children, grandchildren, stepchildren, siblings, step or half, uncle, aunt, nephew, niece, cousin and all relatives by marriage

(f) fiancée
(g) a person in visiting and/or dating relationship
(h) member of the household
(i) person with a child in common with the alleged perpetrator[20]
(j) Adult in a residential institution.

The legislation in Nunavut Province uses umbrella terms to describe the relationships that are covered by it. They are spousal, intimate, family, and care. All of the relationships fall within one of those categories. In Yukon Province,[21] "*victim*" is used to describe "*persons who have been residing together or who are residing together in a family relationship, a spousal relationship or intimate relationship*"; "*intimate companions*" describe "*persons who have, or have had with each other a continuing relationship of intimate companionship*".

Notable Exceptions That Are Part of the Emerging Reality

LGBTQI Persons

In the Caribbean, the law does not recognize same-sex marriages or unions. The law does not provide protection from domestic violence to persons identifying as LGBTQI. In fact, the extent of protection in Grenada to persons in visiting relationships is limited to those between persons of the opposite sex. This shows a marked exclusion of persons identifying as LGBTQI.

Trinidad and Tobago now provide protection, though not explicitly in the following manner, "*dating relationship means where the parties do not live together in the same household, but may be engaged in romantic, intimate or sexual relations*",[22] leaving it to the judicial officer for interpretation. It is stressed that persons of the same sex who share a household are not protected.

In all of our constitutions, the fundamental rights to security of the person and protection of the law are guaranteed. We recommend that the law must provide for the protection for persons who are in same-sex relationships by adopting the formulation of "*intimate companion*" as provided for in Yukon.

Domestic Workers

Workers in the care economy, domestic workers provide personal and household care. While they are not recognized as "members of the same household",[23] the nature of their work involves caring for families, loved ones, and homes. The International Labour Organisation (ILO) stated that the COVID-19 Pandemic has accentuated their continued vulnerabilities especially when it comes to violence/abuse at the hands of householders.[24] We recommend that domestic workers ought to benefit from the protection of the law and have equal access to justice. This applies whether they "live-in" or not.[25]

We suggest that any prospective legislation contains specific protection for persons identifying as LGBTQI and for domestic workers.

Types of Relief/Orders Made

- Only some countries enable the court to make an order for compensation consequent upon domestic violence. The countries that do not should provide such compensation for victims of domestic violence from the abuser.
- Since it has been recognized that domestic violence is a form of discrimination that affects women disproportionately to men, it is not an unreasonable assertion that when children are involved it affects women even more. Legislation should provide that when a woman secures a protection order, that order should be automatically referable and applicable to the child.[26]

In the OECS and Trinidad and Tobago, the legislation provides a wide range of orders. The court can make prohibitory orders, for example, prohibiting the perpetrator from committing any act of domestic violence, entering the residence of the victim, entering a shared household, entering the place of employment or education and enlisting the help of any person to commit an act of domestic violence. Orders can also be made, in which the court directs that,

- the victim occupy the household to the exclusion of the perpetrator;
- that the victim be deemed the tenant of the household to the exclusion of the perpetrator;

- any or all of the conditions of an order be applied for the benefit of a child;
- the perpetrator pay monetary compensation to the victim for loss caused by the perpetrator;
- the perpetrator make or continue to make rent or mortgage payments; and
- the victim or perpetrator or both and/or child attend counselling or therapy.

Additionally, the court can accept an undertaking from the perpetrator not to engage in acts that constitute domestic violence.

In Nunavut, the province is not widely serviced by judicial officers and many hearings are not in person. The Act states that a justice of the peace may grant emergency protection orders and community intervention orders upon stated criteria. This may be a worthwhile step for smaller and not well-resourced territories.

Orders can be interim or final. The duration of final orders varies. In Montserrat, Trinidad and Tobago, St. Christopher, Nevis, and Grenada, the protection order is only in force for three (3) years. However, in St. Vincent and the Grenadines, St. Lucia, Antigua, and Barbuda, and Dominica, it remains in effect unless varied or discharged by the Court. Every society must look carefully at its environment to determine whether they should adopt provisions for permanent orders in their legislation.

- The law should also expressly provide that if the conduct complained of amounts to criminal conduct the criminal law will apply. The Act in Ghana specifically provides for this.[27]
- In the OECS and Trinidad and Tobago, a breach of a protection order constitutes a criminal offence punishable by fine and/or imprisonment.

Responsibility of Employers to Domestic Violence Victims

- There should be provisions mandating employers of domestic violence victims, to give the employee time off to go for medical care, counselling, and court hearings.

- As part of their health and safety training, employers should be mandated to create and implement a policy governing domestic violence and provide training in this regard to employees.
- Employers must not discriminate against victims of domestic violence when they are recruiting, disciplining, or terminating employees.

Migrants

Studies also show that over half of physically abused women in migrant populations do not seek help from formal services in the host country. This suggests severe underreporting of domestic and gender-based violence by migrant women. Reasons for underreporting include limited language proficiency since women who could not speak the language of the host country proficiently or at all were less likely to report incidences of domestic or gender-based violence. Disparities in economic and social resources present another reason why migrant women may not report domestic or gender-bases violence. This is particularly acute when the victim does not have legal status in the host country or where there are economic imbalances between the perpetrator and victim. In addition, this is exacerbated when the victims are afraid that they would lose custody of their children. Social isolation and ignorance of legal rights also contribute to underreporting. When the perpetrator of violence/abuse is a member of the victim's social circle or migrant community, often the community pressures the victim to remain silent. Further, a victim will not make a report if they fear that they or their dependents will be deported (*op. cit. # 1*).

Illegal migrants may hesitate to seek legal redress for fear of adverse consequences and lack of knowledge or trust in the justice system. Immigrant women experiencing intimate partner or gender-based violence need innovative interventions to help end abuse since many immigrant women view domestic violence as normal. It is important that legislation makes specific provisions for the appropriate and sensitive treatment of them.

Systemic Recommendations

- In the Caribbean, courts grant orders. In most jurisdictions that is the province of the Parish Court Judge, the District Court Judge, or the Magistrate. There may be occasions when a judicial officer may not be present or available, especially when there is need for an emergency protection order. In Nunavut, a justice of the peace may issue such an order upon stated criteria. Another type of order, the community intervention order, can be made either by Justices of the Peace or by Community workers who are not lawyers. In communities that are not serviced by many qualified lawyers or by judicial officers, this route to justice is well worth investigation.
- While most countries make provision for privacy of domestic violence victims during the hearing and reporting of the case, the law should provide for privacy during the reporting and investigation of a complaint of domestic violence.
- Legal Aid schemes should be available to victims of domestic violence. There is an established authority in Trinidad and Tobago, to aid persons who cannot afford legal representation.[28] In jurisdictions where no such scheme exists, the relevant professional associations should be encouraged to set up pro bono services to victims and perpetrators.
- The regional and national Bar Associations could partner with The American Bar Association in one of its Advocacy Initiatives, a global consortium "*Women and Girls Empowered*" part of the ABA "*Rule of Law*" initiative programme that is established to "*prevent gender based violence and support economic empowerment*". The International and National or local or regional Associations of Women Judges have made and continue to make major contributions in that there are standing committees which continually provide training and access to necessary resources to all concerned.
- The countries that do not set out the duties and powers of the police should do so.
- The law should make clear the significance of counselling and or therapy to the final disposition of the matter.
- The law should make provision for rehabilitation orders and in particular make provision for Court annexed Batterer Intervention and Compliance programmes.

Management of Domestic Violence Cases in the Traditional Court System

Perhaps the biggest change to the regime is the recognition that judicial skills, while aimed at truth in fact-finding are essentially management skills, based on the acronym ICEE—impartiality, competence, efficiency, and effectiveness. Worldwide judicial reform in procedure and practice embrace case management and case flow management principles. Domestic violence hearings have not escaped that approach. In fact, judicial officers, court staff, and attorneys-at-law should all engage in the process management when hearing or handling domestic violence cases.

The Caribbean has largely adopted this approach to adjudication with the objective of ensuring procedural fairness, access to justice, and enhancing public trust and confidence in the administration of justice. These in turn ensure that the victim's and perpetrator's constitutional rights and necessarily the human rights to safety and security of the person or the right to a fair hearing before an independent and impartial tribunal are observed in reality. We would proffer that case management and case flow management rules be introduced to support the new regime and that there be extensive training of all persons involved in the delivery of justice. This training should have as main components, communication skills, and strategies, how to make effective orders, arriving at difficult decisions, and overall timetabling, scheduling, and conduct of meaningful hearings such as monitoring and compliance hearings.[29]

Judicial officers should be encouraged to use ADR methods as part of their case management. Bernard JCCJ opined[30] that in cases when the victim is overwhelmed with the prospect of testifying against the perpetrator or when economic realities will not happily reside with a term of imprisonment for the perpetrator, the court should "*be empowered to order mediation with therapeutic treatment and counselling for both abuser and abused aimed at fostering respect and tolerance of another's point of view... Very rarely, if at all are abusers or the abused encouraged by court officials to engage in counselling or mediation before or after trials. Cases are dealt with in a cold and impersonal manner, in a system which is punitive rather than rehabilitative. ... [R]ehabilitation must be considered in certain circumstances and situations as a viable alternative*".

Some Suggested Details of Procedural Changes

There are material provisions that should form part of the practice and procedure of domestic violence law as follows:

- Protection orders should be allowed to be introduced as a material fact in family law proceedings like custody, maintenance, and property settlement;
- The law should provide that there should be no adverse inference against the victim of domestic violence from the delay in reporting the matter.

These may be included as part of the law that will ensure the proper enforcement of the domestic violence regime.

Structural Recommendations

- ESTABLISHMENT OF A DOMESTIC VIOLENCE/FAMILY ABUSE SPECIALIST COURT

  Establishing a Domestic Violence/Family Abuse Specialist Court within the Family and Children Division will provide the hub where a victim and perpetrator can access all the services required during a domestic violence matter. This will include stakeholders such as the police, judges, magistrates, lawyers, medical practitioners, and social workers.

  It can be introduced using a specially designed courtroom. This may not require new staff but can use present staff and resources from various government bodies who will receive specialist training and be assigned to the court.

  Training will be necessary and a Batterer Programme can be added as an adjunct to the court.

  This will allow for effective and expeditious hearing and disposition of domestic violence matters. Appeal Court Judges who have specialist training and interests should be assigned to hear those appeals, which should be automatically expedited.
- THERAPEUTIC COURTS

  The establishment of Therapeutic Courts will certainly enhance this regime by combating recidivism and the revolving door syndrome. Therapeutic courts are no strangers to the Caribbean legal landscape, for instance, Drug Treatment Courts operate in both Jamaica and Trinidad and Tobago.

One of its main features is the team approach used to deal with these matters. Another feature is that the perpetrator must agree to take part in the court-driven programme. Victims may be encouraged to participate.

In that regard, there is a directed treatment and rehabilitation programme that, although judge driven, comprises a multidisciplinary team of social services agencies, medical personnel, addiction or anger therapists, and non-governmental organizations, to assist the judicial officer.

Some of the issues that can be addressed as part of the rehabilitation include dealing with personal problems and accepting responsibility for actions, while producing attitudinal change.

These courts can also address both the victim's and perpetrator's needs for concrete reintegration into society such as proper housing, literacy, and employment. It is an opportunity as well for the system to address both victim and perpetrator psychological issues, such as ostracism and/or expulsion from communities as they try to reintegrate into their communities. This is especially useful when dealing with children and young adults who have been exposed to violence and/or abuse.

This early interventionist and non-adversarial approach may well redound to the benefit of not only the perpetrators and the family unit, but also society as a whole.

It is necessary to note that judicial decisions are made in court in the presence and hearing of all concerned parties, where possible. They need not be in the same physical space as technological advances may facilitate virtual hearings.

To ensure success it is critical to keep data and statistics so as to carefully evaluate the impact of the law on domestic violence control and the impact of the court on the individual.

There are ethical issues that would arise for both defence counsel and the claimant's counsel with both never losing sight of the duty to act in the best interests of the client. If children are involved then the focus is on the best interests of the child. If the elderly are involved then the interests of the elderly must be taken into account. In this environment, the report from the probation officer or social worker is crucial as these may form the bases of fashioning the remedies or penalties that fit the circumstances of the case.

Adjuncts of the Legal Environment

Law is only part of the transformation. A change in the policy and cultural norms of society is also necessary to provide a comprehensive and effective treatment of domestic violence. The State must allocate adequate resources geared towards the prevention of domestic violence. In this regard, the following are recommendations:

- Establish a specialized unit within police services in the region to treat with domestic violence matters. A good model is the Gender-Based Violence Unit in the Trinidad and Tobago Police Service.
- Create a manual of standard operating procedures to be used for investigating domestic violence matters.
- Training for officers expected to execute duties in the unit. These officers should be carefully selected.
- In Antigua and Barbuda, St. Vincent and the Grenadines, and St. Lucia, police officers' duties and powers should be provided for in legislation.[31] These duties include,
    - to respond to every complaint or report alleging domestic violence,
    - to make detailed records of every complaint or report alleging domestic violence,
    - to provide the person making the complaint or report with a copy of the record,
    - to investigate every complaint or report alleging domestic violence and
    - to assist the victim where the police officer enters on the premises.

In Grenada, Montserrat, St. Christopher, and Nevis, officers have a duty to inform the victim of his or her rights under the Act.

In Trinidad and Tobago, any police officer may apply for a protection order on behalf of a victim.[32] In Australia, the police officer may apply for a temporary protection order as well as issue a protection notice.[33] Caribbean jurisdictions may well consider this provision.

In Trinidad and Tobago, police officers above the rank of Inspector are justices of the peace. We suggest that they have the jurisdiction to grant emergency or temporary protection orders. This too, is a worthwhile provision for inclusion.

Judicial Officers and Court Staff

- Judiciaries through their Judicial Education Institutes or other continuing education initiatives should construct a gender equality protocol for judicial officers, similar to the one launched in 2018 in Trinidad and Tobago. The protocol should be subject to systematic review and update. Judicial officers and staff should be mandated to attend training on a regular basis.
- Create a standard operating procedure manual for use in domestic violence matters for court staff, and providers of adjunct services, such as social, health workers and probation officers. Again, mandatory periodic training is necessary.

Wider Societal Recommendations

- There should be a change in the education curriculum to bring awareness of the gender roles of boys and girls from an early age and to denounce violence against boys and girls. This will go a long way in seeking to erode long-entrenched unequal power relations between men and women and the culture of domestic violence being a private matter.
- There should be a greater emphasis in schools, on conflict management and resolution.
- Expose students and young adults to the basic elements of emotional intelligence.
- There should be widespread awareness campaigns, which include sensitizing the media that violence against women is wrong and that women have rights if they are subjected to violence.
- Encourage the media to inform on the scourge of domestic violence and where to access necessary assistance.
- The State should increase its collection and publication of statistical data on the incidence of domestic violence;

- The State should provide shelters and financial support to domestic violence victims and support non-governmental organizations, which provide these services.
- Citizens should hold their Members of Parliament accountable. They should insist that the State actively monitors the implementation and effectiveness of laws concerning domestic violence beyond laying Annual Reports in Parliament.

Migrants

With respect to migrant women, innovative interventions should be centred on awareness campaigns that educate immigrant women about their legal rights and create awareness about domestic and gender-based violence. The response should be culturally appropriate and involve working with both partners in the relationship given the pre-eminence of family.[34]

If these measures are implemented, effectively and cumulatively, the incidence of domestic violence is more than likely to decrease exponentially.

Conclusion

It is hoped that these transformative measures will result in,

- alleviating the deep cultural disease of unequal gender power relations,
- modification of traditional and legal practices which sustain the power imbalances,
- the active holistic approach to fulfilling our treaty obligations and
- producing attitudinal changes and behaviours that propagate and sustain cultures of violence.

Acknowledgements The Authors gratefully acknowledge the sterling contributions of, Ms. Candace Layers, Ms. Romela Ramberran, and Ms. Koya Ryan, Judicial Research Counsel, Supreme Court of Judicature of Trinidad and Tobago.

Notes

1. "*The Birth of a Nation*" C.L.R. James in "*Contemporary Caribbean: A Sociological Reader*", Edited by Dr. Susan Craig, vol. 1, pages 3–35 (1981, The College Press, Maracas Trinidad and Tobago West Indies).
2. The scourge of domestic violence has not escaped consideration by the United Nations. The Sustainable Goals for Development at Goal #5 deals with Gender Equality, which necessarily imports State recognition of challenges posed by gender based violence. UN observers remarked that one in five women and girls including 19% of women and girls aged 15–49 have experienced physical and/or sexual violence by an intimate partner within the last twelve months (as at December 2020).

   Goal # 16 deals with providing access to justice for all and building effective, accountable and inclusive institutions.
3. CEDAW, Article 5 (a).
4. See Candace Layers "*Domestic Violence Laws in the OECS and Trinidad and Tobago—An evaluation of their Compliance with International Conventions and Charters—Recommendations for Effective Measures to Reduce Domestic Violence*" (Unpublished 2021).
5. Desiree Bernard JCCJ opened a segment in her treatise "*Reflections and Opinions*" (Hansib Publications Limited 2018) with this thought, "*the highest incidents of violence perpetrated against women occurs in the home and within the bosom of the family*". We have to agree this statement sadly, but with one change—the violence that we see today, is perpetrated against family members simpliciter. The law as it has expanded who can be victims of domestic violence and what constitutes violence itself recognizes this.
6. https://blogs.worldbank.org/latinamerica/casting-light-shadow-pandemic-caribbean-violence-against-women.
7. https://www.ohchr.org/EN/HRBodies/CEDAW/Pages/Recommendations.aspx and https://www.un.org/womenwatch/daw/egm/vaw_legislation_2008/vaw_legislation_2008.htm.
8. Caribbean Coordination Platform for Refugees and Migrants from Venezuela (R4V) (2019), "*Caribbean Sub-Region Refugees & Migrants Response Plan: Summary Figures*".

9. *Ibid.*
10. *Op. cit.* #1.
11. *Op. cit.* #3.
12. See for instance the title of the Act in Trinidad and Tobago, "*The Domestic Violence Act*".
13. Section 2 of the Domestic Violence Act, Grenada (Act 19 of 2010) and St. Christopher and Nevis (Act 22 of 2014), *op. cit.* #6.
14. See Romela Ramberran, "*A Comparative Study of Domestic and Intimate Partner Violence Legislation in the Commonwealth*" (Unpublished 2021).
15. *Ibid.*
16. *Ibid.*
17. *Ibid.*
18. *Ibid.*
19. *Ibid.*
20. This is the standard in Trinidad and Tobago and is replicated throughout the Caribbean with some additions. In Montserrat, persons who have shared parental responsibility for a child whether or not at the same time are included. In some jurisdictions, relationship by blood is specifically provided for in the legislation, as in Dominica and Grenada.
21. *Op. cit.* #17.
22. *Op. cit.* #6.
23. Domestic Violence (Amendment) Act 2020, Section 3(l) (Trinidad and Tobago).
24. https://www.ilo.org/global/topics/domestic-workers/lang-en, accessed on: June 30, 2021.
25. https://www.cnn.com/2021/06/23/asia/singapore-court-domesticworker-killing-int/-hnk/index.html, accessed on: June 23, 2021 (This article highlights the plight of domestic workers in South East Asia but can be applied to anywhere in the Caribbean).
26. See Trinidad and Tobago's Domestic Violence (Amendment) Act 2020, Section 6A, where once a Protection Order is granted it automatically applies to the child.
27. *Op. cit.* #17.
28. Legal Aid and Advice Act Chap 7:07, Section 16A (Trinidad and Tobago).
29. Adapted from "The Spotlight Initiative". This is a global, multi-year partnership between the European Union and the United

Nations to eliminate all forms of violence against women and girls (https://www.spotlightinitiative.org).

30. *Op. cit.* #7, p. 335.
31. The duties and powers of police officers are set out in the Dominica, Montserrat, Trinidad and Tobago, St. Christopher and Nevis and Grenada legislation.
32. *Op. cit.* #6.
33. *Op. cit.* #17.
34. *Op. cit.* #1.

Reference

James, C.L.R. 1981. The Birth of a Nation. In *Contemporary Caribbean: A Sociological Reader*, ed. Dr. Susan Craig, vol. 1, 3–35. Maracas, Trinidad and Tobago West Indies: The College Press.

CHAPTER 7

A Sociological Perspective of Men's Underreporting of Domestic Violence and a Lack of Appropriate Interventions in the Caribbean

Camille Tamara Cummings

Discussion

Domestic violence is defined as the "intentional use of physical force or power, threatened or actual, against oneself, another person, or against a group or community that either results in or has a high likelihood of resulting in injury, death, psychological harm, maldevelopment or deprivation" (WHO 1996). Alternately, Lawrence (2003) defined domestic violence as verbal, sexual, and emotional intimidation. The definition of domestic violence extends the problem to the family home and includes other interactions such as elderly abuse, sibling abuse, child abuse, and

C. T. Cummings (✉)
The University of the West Indies, St. Augustine, Trinidad and Tobago

A. M. Bissessar and C. Huggins (eds.), *Domestic Violence in the Anglophone Caribbean*,
https://doi.org/10.1007/978-3-030-88476-5_7

parental abuse. It also recognizes that both men and women have the propensity for violence (see Dutton 2008).

There is a common social perception of domestic violence that illustrates a one-sided picture of men as perpetrators and women as victims. Studies such as McFeely et al. (2013) and Smith (2012) have demonstrated that although domestic violence can be perpetuated and experienced by any group, women's experience of domestic violence as victims is considerably more documented than men's experience. However, there is growing evidence of men as victims of domestic violence. The UNODC (2013) report indicated that of the men who were killed in Grenada, 12% were killed as a result of domestic violence. The report also indicated that of the men that were killed through violence, 7% of men in Jamaica and 4% of men in Trinidad and Tobago were killed as a result of domestic violence. The statistics, on the other hand, do not show the extent of men's experience with domestic violence as victims since it is grossly underreported in the Caribbean and requires further in-depth research for more accurate data on male domestic violence victimization.

Data relating to domestic violence has largely focused on women as the victims and men as the perpetrators (Barber 2008). This is supported by the fact that as Barber (2008) described, men are apprehensive to report incidents of domestic violence victimization because of fear of ridicule, embarrassment, and a lack of appropriate male-centred support services. As a result of the aforementioned experiences and feelings, male victims of domestic violence may not have their health and social care needs appropriately met (Du Plat-Jones 2006).

This paper discusses specifically men's experience of domestic violence at the hands of their female partner in an intimate heterosexual relationship. Data presented within the existing literature illustrate that men did experience domestic violence, predominantly physical and psychological violence. However, it is observed that the prevalence rates for male domestic violence victimization is still significantly underreported in the literature particularly for the Caribbean.

The paper also discusses interventions for men and highlights the fact that the majority of domestic violence services are designed to assist mostly women and children. A sociological perspective is applied to the discussion to explain why men underreport domestic violence and why there is a lack of appropriate interventions to assist them. Recommendations are made in terms of research, intervention, and service provision.

Therefore this paper focuses primarily on (1) men's experience with domestic violence, (2) the Caribbean context, (3) men's disclosure of domestic violence, (4) men's disclosure of domestic violence in the Caribbean, (5) interventions for men who are victims of domestic violence, (6) interventions for men in the Caribbean, (7) sociological perspective, and (8) recommendations.

Men's Experience with Domestic Violence

Kolbe and Büttner (2020) conducted a retrospective analysis of domestic violence data through a comprehensive review of publications that focused on the nature of domestic violence, the type of perpetrators and victims as well as the injuries sustained. Through their research, they found a prevalence rate of 3.4–20.3% for male victims of domestic violence who had experienced particularly physical abuse. The authors concluded that the prevalence of domestic violence against men has not been extensively studied to date. Schlack et al. (2013) compared men and women's domestic violence victimization and looked specifically at physical abuse over a 12-month period. The study found of those that participated in the German Health Interview and Examination Survey, 0.9% of men had been victims of physical abuse compared to 1.2% of women victims, which demonstrated a very small significant difference of 0.3% between the two sexes.

Studies such as Afifi et al. (2009) and Carbone-López et al. (2006) demonstrated a prevalence rate between 3.4 and 20.3% for physical violence against men, while Lövestad and Gunilla (2012) and Umubyeyi et al. (2014) reported that between 7.3 and 37% suffered psychological violence and other studies such as Tjaden and Thoennes (2000) and Mechem et al. (1999) showed that between 0.2 and 7% men reported experiencing sexual violence. Forensic medical studies that focused on domestic violence, for example, Thureau et al. (2015) and Carmo et al. (2011) demonstrated that between 53.8 and 85% of men reported minor injuries during a violent episode with their female partner. In their retrospective data analysis, Thureau et al. (2015) further demonstrated that 9% of men experienced domestic violence on numerous occasions, 70% of men had suffered psychological violence, 10% of men had been strangulated by their partner, and weapons were used against 33% of men in the study, all by their female partner.

However, there continues to be a lack of sound measure for the prevalence of domestic violence perpetration against men (Alhabib et al. 2010). Although there is some data that illustrates the existence of female-perpetrated domestic violence against men in intimate relationships, there remains uncertainty as to the prevalence of such violent relationships (Hines and Douglas 2010).

The Caribbean Context

In the Caribbean, domestic violence has become prevalent over time with studies such as Krug et al. (2002) and Fritz (2000) highlighting an increase in incidence rates ranging from 16 to 69%. Quantitative data on domestic violence particularly domestic violence against men are limited in the Caribbean in comparison to qualitative data which demonstrate more evidence that the phenomenon is escalating, becoming more pervasive and grave (CAREC 2006; Le Franc and Rock 2003; Clarke 1998; Gopaul et al. 1996; Danns and Persad 1989). It has therefore become critical to ascertain a clearer understanding of the characteristics, prevalence, and causes of domestic violence against men in the Caribbean.

A global study conducted by UNODC (2011) on homicide examined statistics in five Caribbean countries: Bahamas, Grenada, Jamaica, St. Vincent and Trinidad and Tobago. The report acknowledged that, half of all female victims were killed by a family member and that 80% of the perpetrators were men. Statistics from a follow-up UNODC report showed that 12% of men who were killed in Grenada were as a result of domestic violence (UNODC 2013). The aforementioned figures highlight the fact that there is still limited research on men and domestic violence in the Caribbean.

According to van Wijk (2012), while there have been some efforts to identify male domestic violence victimization incidence rates in the Caribbean, only domestic violence against women and children has been studied and that "virtually nothing is known about domestic violence against men in the Caribbean, or its consequences". Due to the lack of empirical studies on male domestic violence victimization in the region, there is an inaccurate perception that the phenomenon only affects women and children in Caribbean societies. For example, A 2018 UNDOC study on gender-related homicide of women and girls showed that in Guyana, 85% of women that were killed were murdered by an intimate partner or family-related homicide. The figure was slightly higher in

Jamaica where 90% of domestic violence-related homicide victims were women. In Trinidad and Tobago, nearly one-third of female homicides were domestic violence and family-related, according to the study. There were no comparative data for men in these countries.

Men's Disclosure of Domestic Violence

According to Kaura and Lohman (2007), the majority of research within both the medical and social sciences literature has been limited to samples of women. Male victims have not been researched as comprehensively as shelter populations of battered women (Hines et al. 2007). A myriad of studies has discussed several factors and causal variables pertaining to the disclosure of domestic violence and barriers to women's help-seeking more than studies that have actually discussed men's disclosure and the challenges to their help-seeking. For example, studies such as Barrett and Pierre (2011), which examined the role of socio-demographic factors and violence characteristics in influencing women's use of informal and formal supports in response to domestic violence victimization.

In addition, other studies such as Ellsberg et al. (2008) and Bonomi et al. (2006) formed part of a growing body of research suggesting that a substantial proportion of women who experienced domestic violence victimization often present with physical and mental health problems, including depression, post-traumatic stress disorder (PTSD), and suicidality to name a few. However, in comparison, there is insufficient data on male victims in this area. The unreported numbers of men who are victims of domestic violence and the health problems they suffer from as a consequence, are likely to be much higher in view of such a low willingness to report domestic violence victimization (Carmo et al. 2011).

Discussion of women's disclosure of domestic violence, both in general and specific contexts, raises questions about the underreporting of men's experience with domestic violence. In fact, societal attitudes towards male victimization have had a significant impact on men's underreporting as victims of domestic violence. For example, Bates' (2020) study findings demonstrated that the attitudes towards male victims of domestic violence impacted on their help-seeking behaviour. The men in the sample from Bates' study indicated that "they felt that society did not believe them" or "perceived them as either weak or abusers".

Similarly, other studies have pointed to the fact that male victims of domestic violence homicides are more likely to be identified as "previous abusers" than female victims of domestic violence homicides (see Jurik and Winn 1990). Additional studies suggest that the abuse experienced by male victims at the hands of their female partners is contextually different than that experienced by female victims of male partners (see Pence and Dasgupta 2006). In other words, just as male victims differ, so do females convicted of abusing male partners (see Miller and Meloy 2006). This demonstrates a disparity in men's and women's context as it relates to abuse, homicides, and convictions.

According to Hogan et al. (2012), there is a lack of recognition within society that men can be affected by domestic violence. Men are apprehensive to discuss and disclose their experiences of domestic violence because they tend to feel shame and emasculation (McCarrick 2015). In fact, McCarrick (2015) further elucidated that when men speak out about domestic violence victimization, they are viewed as "the minority man". The concept of the "minority man" is further discussed by Hester (2013) who explains that media coverage of domestic violence places quite an emphasis on female victims, with very little mention of male victims, only to state that "men are in the minority".

Men's Disclosure of Domestic Violence in the Caribbean

In the Caribbean, there is insufficient data on men's disclosure of domestic violence. In comparison to women, a modicum of information exists about men's experience with domestic violence as victims. According to Joseph-Edwards and Wallace (2020), in Trinidad and Tobago, a common perception is that domestic violence is a heteronormative[1] and gendered experience and that men are unlikely victims of domestic violence. The authors further argued that discourses and research on the island are based on stereotypical views of what the victims and abusers look like (ibid.).

One of the issues in the Caribbean region is there is a tendency towards what Elam (2016) describes as "putting the needs, wants, and desires of women ahead of all others" also known as gynocentrism.[2] This "gynocentrism" underpins institutions and by extension the wider society, hence the lack of understanding of and adequate attention to men's experience with domestic violence as victims and the rationales behind their apprehension to disclose victimization on the part of policymakers and organizations created to treat with domestic violence as a whole.

Men presenting at institutions, organizations, police stations, and even counselling services to report domestic violence victimization or the behaviour of their female perpetrator do not fit the dominant discourse of male-perpetrated domestic violence in the Caribbean. According to Archer (2000), there tends to be an assumption that the consequences for male victims of female-perpetrated domestic violence against men are less severe. However male underreporting of injuries sustained from female partners suggests difficulties in establishing sufficient data (Randle and Graham 2011).

Male victims of domestic violence are often reluctant to disclose or even admit their victimization due to fear of ridicule, embarrassment, stigmatization, and negative treatment towards them. One of the few studies conducted in the Caribbean by Joseph-Edwards and Wallace (2020) found that, in Trinidad and Tobago, men were reluctant to admit to being victims of domestic violence. The main theme that emanated from their qualitative study was "embarrassment". According to the researchers, "the male victims of domestic violence were mortified and embarrassed to disclose their victimization to individuals within their social support system as well as to the police and other state agencies for fear of emasculation or being viewed as "less than manly" (p. 19).

In another study conducted in Trinidad and Tobago by Wallace et al. (2019), it was highlighted that the main barrier to reporting domestic violence victimization to the police was embarrassment. A key research finding in the study was that males were nine times more likely than females to not report their domestic victimization to the police (ibid.). This similarly applies to reporting by males in other countries, given the particular social shame and humiliation, even punishment attached to being a male victim of domestic violence (George 1994, 2002).

While there are data on the percentage of men who reported domestic violence victimization to law enforcement in comparison to women, there is a lack of data in Trinidad and Tobago and the wider Caribbean to show the accurate percentage of men that present themselves at domestic violence shelters, hotlines, the police, or other existing intervention services.

Interventions for Men Who Are Victims of Domestic Violence

Traditional programmes were not essentially designed to assist men who are victims of domestic violence. These programmes tended to be based on the Duluth model, which according to Archer (2002), failed to address the lack of sex-differences in intimate partner violence in western countries. Programmes based on the Duluth model neither took into account women's propensity for verbal aggression towards their male partners (see Stockdale et al. 2013) nor did they consider physical aggression and control by women towards their male partners (see Bair-Merritt et al. 2010; Bates and Graham-Kevan 2016; Straus and Gozjolko 2016) as well as men's victimization (see Hines and Douglas 2010).

Extensive research has focused on the barriers surrounding female victims' reporting of domestic violence and their help-seeking behaviour (e.g. Gondolf 1998; Hutchison and Hirschel 1998; Kaukinen et al. 2013). However, limited research has focused on men's experiences of help-seeking as a result of female-perpetrated domestic violence (McCart et al. 2010). The narrative that has emerged from the literature on this topic to date, reflects a depiction of complexity, reinforced by internal and external barriers including shame, embarrassment, and a lack of awareness of or access to support services (Douglas and Hines 2011; Tsui et al. 2010).

Qualitative research studies found that interventions for men experiencing domestic violence victimization are not always able to provide them the services that they need and that many men are actually turned away or not encouraged to access such services (Hines et al. 2007; Cook 2009). According to Addis and Mahalik (2003), men are not likely to seek help for problems that the wider society perceives as non-normative or based on social norms surrounding masculinity, that men should be able to solve or control themselves. The barriers to appropriate interventions for men are further exacerbated by gender stereotypical roles in heterosexual relationships as well as domestic violence being perceived more as a "women's issue" than a human issue (Sweeney 2007; Walker and Browne 1985).

Studies such as Cook (2009) demonstrated apparent challenges men faced when they sought help from existing hotlines, programmes, and even law enforcement. Cook's study indicated that when calling domestic violence hotlines, the men in the sample reported that the hotline workers advised that they only helped women. The men also reported that when they sought help, it was either inferred or explicitly stated that they (men) must have been the actual instigators of the domestic violence, or they were ridiculed. In fact, the men Cook's study admitted that they were referred to batterers' programmes instead of receiving the help that they required. Interestingly, some men reported that when they called the police during an incident in which their female partners were violent, the police sometimes did not respond to their emergency. This highlights a clear gender bias, discrimination, and stereotypical behaviour towards male victims of domestic violence.

Within the judicial system, studies such as (Migliaccio 2002) and (Cook 2009) documented that some men reported experiencing gender-stereotyped treatment. These studies indicated that where evidence was corroborated that their female partners were violent and that the men were not, they (men) reportedly lost custody of their children, were blocked from seeing their children, or were falsely accused by their partners of domestic violence and even abusing their children. Consequently, violence perpetrated by women against their male partners tends to be considered to be less serious, trivialized, or even considered humorous (Pagelow and Pagelow 1984; Saunders 2002).

Interventions for Men in the Caribbean

Through the works of CEDAW,[3] major efforts have been made in bringing domestic violence to the forefront and calling for change across the globe, including the Caribbean region. However, the regional response has been primarily towards women. Significant gains have been made in elevating societal consciousness regarding violence against women and girls and this could be gauged from the formulation of a myriad of responses from Caribbean organizations, NGOs, and governments to regional and international statements on the issue.

Clarke (1998) pointed out that within the Caribbean, domestic violence has been the most fundamental issue on which women's organizations have fought to eliminate gender discrimination and gender inequality. The governmental response in the Caribbean concentrated on legal reform, following the extended guidelines from the international instruments such as CEDAW, which addressed violence against women. National collaborative efforts on the part of advocacy groups and diverse women's organizations resulted in removing the shrouds of privacy that relegates domestic violence to the private sphere and highlighting it as a public and therefore political issue (ibid.). In addition, women's organizations worked together to demand state action, particularly in the area of legislative reform to create laws criminalizing domestic violence (Gibbons 2013).

Different Caribbean countries have developed national organizations to treat domestic violence, which have targeted mostly women. One such country is Jamaica, which has over seven national domestic violence agencies, most of which provide services mainly for women. The very use of the word "women" in the title clearly illustrates this. For example, "Women Inc.", "Bureau of Women's Affairs" and "Women's Resource and Outreach Centre" to name a few. Similarly, in Grenada, two out of its four national domestic violence agencies are called "Grenada National Organization of Women" and "Cedars Home for Abused Women". On the other hand, agencies in Trinidad and Tobago have what appears to be gender-neutral names, for example, "Coalition Against Domestic Violence" and "Organization for Battered and Abused Individuals". However, these organizations have historically tailored and provided services aimed at mostly women and children.

Consistent monitoring and evaluation are not often conducted to determine the effectiveness of intervention programmes in the field of domestic violence even for women and much less for men. Limited measures in this field have created conflicts between research and practice. In addition, the urgency of the problem which is often highlighted by the media and the need for services lead to governments to promise programmes and approaches which tend to be implemented in an ad hoc manner and subsequently lack empirical evidence of effectiveness.

Sociological Perspectives

There is a sociological significance of domestic violence. Sociological theory has been effective in analysing societal conflict and violence but it has also been applied to the study of domestic violence to help us understand the specifics of interpersonal violence particularly in intimate relationships. This paper discusses the application of symbolic interaction perspective as well as concepts of hegemonic masculinities, gender stereotypes, gender roles, and gender bias in relation to explaining why men underreport domestic violence and why there is a lack of appropriate interventions to assist them.

Symbolic Interaction

Symbolic interactionism in general acknowledges both social agency and the social forces shaping and constraining social action, so that social behaviour is theorized as both structurally constrained and actively constructed (Allen-Collinson and Hockey 2007). Symbolic interactionism, with its interest in the social actor, meanings, context, and everyday experience, offers a powerful lens through which to view domestic violence particularly from the perspective of the male victim including their reasons for not reporting domestic violence victimization as well as the barriers they face to help-seeking.

Symbolic interactionism explains that people look to one another to support their self-concept (Johnson 1986). This theoretical perspective originates from Charles Cooley who discussed the concept of "looking glass self" and explains that through role-taking, individuals develop a sense of self. In other words, support and appraisals from others influence both people's identity and self-esteem. Stryker (1980) further elucidates that the development of self is an ongoing process, which changes as people's social experience changes. Therefore, the way male victims of domestic violence are perceived and appraised by other members of society including law enforcement and those that provide intervention services may influence their own identity and self-esteem as males in society as well as influence the appropriate action taken on the part of service providers to assist the male victim.

Furthermore, the behaviour of law enforcement, domestic violence hotline operators, other support services as well as members of the wider society may reinforce an already low sense of self-worth from the domestic violence situation. This can be used to further explain the gross underreporting of domestic violence victimization on the part of male victims.

Symbolic interactionism sensitizes us to the male victim's difficulty in determining an appropriate course of action for themselves when their sense of self is weak as a result of being invalidated by others when they do seek help. From a symbolic interactionist perspective and based on the report of men's experiences when they seek help from previous studies, intervention services tend not to support male victims of domestic violence in restructuring their sense of self as well as recognizing their competencies on which to rebuild their self-esteem.

Hegemonic Masculinities

Historically, domestic violence has been conceptualized as a gendered problem of men's violence towards women, based on a model of male patriarchy. Within this paradigm, "victims" are considered female, and "perpetrators" are considered male. Male domestic violence victimization challenges prevailing societal norms of masculinity and manhood. Like male sexual victimization, male domestic violence victimization is not taken seriously in support services and even policy and practice.

Male victims of domestic violence tend to be relegated in the gender hierarchy. Gender expectations, hegemonic masculinities, and sexism exist in all societies, state, and voluntary agencies. Caribbean societies are no exception. With specific reference to the Caribbean, Johnson (1996) discussed the historical impact of White hegemonic masculinity of slave owners and the implications for the importance, which Caribbean males attach to the exercise of power and control over women. Parry (1996) pointed to ethnographic research carried out in Jamaica, Dominica, and Guyana which demonstrated that "manhood" is proven by sexual prowess that is usually measured in terms of numbers of concurrent female sexual partners. Secondary proof of "manhood" according to Parry (1996) resides in numbers of offspring whether inside or outside of a steady relationship. Men as victims of domestic violence in the Caribbean therefore, are not consistent proof of this constructed "manhood" in Caribbean societies.

Just as male rape victims embody subordinate masculinities, so do male domestic violence victims who are also marginalized and stigmatized as "abnormal" or "deviant". They are classified as the "other" for challenging and contradicting hegemonic masculinity thereby disrupting the gender order of men (Javaid 2017). According to Connell and Messerschmidt (2005), the requirements of contemporary "hegemonic masculinity" strongly censure male victimization by women, so that any admission of being abused is tantamount to admitting that one is not a "real man".

Men's attitudes towards seeking help is strongly associated with adherence to social norms and ideologies surrounding masculinity (Addis and Mahalik 2003; Berger et al. 2013). Such norms endorse being apathetic, self-reliant, emotionally inexpressive, and in control of one's self and situation (Nam et al. 2010), values which men perceive as being inconsistent with help-seeking behaviour. Nam et al. (2010) further identified that gender is a significant predictor of attitudes towards help-seeking behaviour, with women more likely to hold positive attitudes towards help-seeking than men.

The admission of a need for help, dependence on others, and the stigma associated with help-seeking may result in some men perceiving help-seeking as a failure to adhere to internalized standards of masculinity (Vogel et al. 2011; Nam et al. 2010). However, the nature and manner in which help is offered to male victims of domestic violence may influence men's openness to seek help (Berger et al. 2013), with some evidence suggesting that men react more positively to intervention or support services that emphasize on self-autonomy and self-reliance (ibid.).

Self-perception and societal perception of masculinity are also important factors in reporting domestic violence, help-seeking, and the lack of appropriate interventions that provide specific support for male victims (see Huntley et al. 2019). A study of male victims by Gadd et al. (2002), for example, found that few men reported their experiences of domestic violence to the police for fear of disbelief and lack of proper service provision.

Gender Stereotypes

According to Dutton and White (2013) "the stereotype invoked when one mentions 'domestic violence' is of a bullying, domineering man who is hyper-reactive to jealousy and has a drinking problem. He threatens, assaults and verbally intimidates a non-violent woman-victim" (p. 6). The more prominent image that is featured is one of an aggressive male perpetrator and their victimized female partner (ibid.). This view highlights the influence of gender stereotypes within mainstream society, as well as media coverage and an emphasis within domestic violence research placed more on female than on male survivors. McCarrick (2015) further argues that gender-role stereotypes have been found to influence practitioners, criminal justice officers and the public's perceptions of the severity of domestic violence against men which in turn affect their help-seeking behaviour as well as the services that are provided for them.

The predominant societal belief of what it means to be male or female is influenced by gender stereotypes. Addis and Mahalik (2003) referred to the emotional stoicism and toughness that is applauded as a positive aspect of masculinity. Males reporting domestic violence victimization or engaging in help-seeking behaviour is not consistent with the aforementioned toughness Addis and Mahalik (2003) described and such men are not applauded and are in fact stigmatized as being "less masculine".

Steinmetz (1978) highlighted the culturally prescribed norms to gender, making reference to comics in which husbands deviate from their norm of being strong, assertive, and intelligent, thus making their wives justified in chastising them for not living up to their ascribed gender role. Historically, gender-role stereotypes are so entrenched that when men and women deviate from them, there have been consequences. Similarly, the aforementioned literature in this paper, points to the fact that men who report domestic violence victimization or seek help have been made into the objects of ridicule and scorn.

The emphasis upon female survivors within the academic literature and the media is indicative of decades of campaigning for women's rights to support in domestic violence situations. However, Pizzey et al. (2000) describe what they call the "ultrafeminists" who aspired to define women as a victim group oppressed by men. This has contributed significantly to the negative gender stereotypes faced by males particularly when they present themselves as victims and not perpetrators. Despite the growing body of research challenging this perspective and suggesting more equality between men and women in their propensity for violence, services, and treatment programmes particularly in the Caribbean continue to be influenced by the traditional gender paradigm, thus according to Hammon (2016) neglecting men and women whose experiences do not fit this dominant discourse.

Gender Roles and Role Conflict

A consistent agreement within the literature is that male domestic violence victimization is severely underreported. Brown (2004) suggested that commonly held beliefs about social gender roles are another reason for the underreporting. As O'Neil (2008) explained, seeking help for any type of issue, might threaten the socially conceived gender-role standards that exist for men. The very idea of therapy seems to go against male gender-role norms that have been set in place (ibid.).

In society, men have been socialized to be powerful, independent, and always in control congruent with their male gender roles. During the socialization process, men learn to be emotionally restrictive and exhibit that they are capable of solving their own problems rather than complaining to others. If men were to seek help it is perceived to be discordant with their male gender roles, which may have negative societal consequences. It is in this context men experience what is referred to as "gender-role conflict". Gender-role conflict (GRC) according to O'Neil (2008) is "a psychological state in which socialized gender roles have negative consequences for the person or others". O'Neil further explained that gender-role conflict stems from gender-role socialization in that the strict gender-roles men subscribe to prohibit them from acting in a way that is incongruent with their thoughts and feelings which in turn, creates a significant strain in their lives. This can be used to explain why men are apprehensive to report domestic violence victimization.

Also, men's experience of domestic violence, the way they are treated by intervention services as well as their unwillingness to report, represent two of the three categories of contexts in which gender-role conflict occurs. These contexts as explained by O'Neil (2008) are described as (1) Intrapersonal GRC which is the internal experiencing gender-role devaluations, restrictions, and violations and (2) GRC experienced from others occurs when an individual is devalued, restricted, or violated by someone else. Men can experience intrapersonal GRC as a result of domestic violence victimization and they can also experience GRC experienced from others when they are devalued, restricted, or violated by law enforcement, social support services, or any other available interventions from which seek help.

Gender Bias

Gender biases may be highly influential in affecting people's perceptions of the severity of domestic violence particularly when men are victims. For example, Taylor and Sorenson (2005) found that acts were more likely to be perceived as abusive if they were perpetrated by males rather than by females. In addition, qualitative research that examined the experiences of counsellors working with male survivors of female-perpetrated domestic violence (Hogan et al. 2012) also reported a lack of recognition within society that men can also be affected by domestic violence.

Follingstad et al. (2004) further highlighted that this gender bias is also true of service providers such as counsellors and psychologists, who judged husband's behaviours as more psychologically abusive and severe than the wife's use of the same action. Explicit and implicit gender biases, coupled with gender stereotypes and gender-role expectations about domestic violence, are still embedded in our culture and can affect the way society and intervention services respond to male victims. The aforementioned literature has demonstrated that there is a disparity in the way male and female victims are treated with respect to the same issue of domestic violence victimization.

With respect to social services and law enforcement, these gender biases may affect how police officers as well as other service providers perceive domestic violence incidents, which may prevent them from effectively providing appropriate intervention. These explicit and implicit gender biases can also affect the choices men themselves make with regard to their help-seeking behaviour. This is supported by findings from Corbally (2015) who found that the men in the study who had children, reported that they received gender-biased treatment from social services and the bias and consequently the negative experiences they encountered resulted in the men giving up on future help-seeking.

Gender bias is also evident in the lack of appropriate interventions for male victims in comparison to the many interventions and supports available to female victims (Choi and An 2016). There are few data available to describe the experiences of male domestic violence victims particularly in the Caribbean. If there are services available, there are very few opportunities, spaces, or professionals trained to work with specifically males when it involves domestic violence (ibid.).

Conclusion and Recommendations

Historically, the women's liberation movement which began in the 1960s and progressed throughout the 1970s and 1980s, highlighted the issue of domestic violence and influenced the development of domestic violence programmes to address the needs of female survivors, who, according to what the current data show, still represent the majority of victims seeking services today. Subsequent violence against women and domestic violence movements have operated on a gender binary with men as perpetrators and women as victims. However, this has created a female-centred approach to advocacy that only addresses the needs of one group of survivors and largely fails to acknowledge and address the other group of survivors, which are male.

Addressing this stigmatized topic in an open and supportive way is a mandatory prerequisite to identifying male victims of domestic violence in any practice. More training measures for service providers as well as law enforcement should be made available in order to raise awareness of the issues facing male victims. Using a trauma-informed approach allows for a more gender-inclusive approach (e.g. Dutton 2010; Hamel 2007) to research and intervention. It will also shift the focus from preconceived gender attributions to the merit of individual cases.

Further understanding of this topic is warranted through extensive and updated research particularly in the Caribbean. This would therefore lead to a much-enhanced understanding of male domestic violence victimization in the region, demystify socially constructed myths surrounding masculinity and domestic violence victimization, and the development of gender-specific interventions which would be beneficial to males (Gadd et al. 2003). Such research may lead to the development of theory and practice, which may inform practitioners' work with male victims (Hogan et al. 2012; Migliaccio 2002).

What is needed specifically in Caribbean societies such as Trinidad and Tobago and others in the region to debunk notions of domestic violence victimization as a male-perpetrated phenomenon, are studies that clearly articulate the nature and extent of male victimization and its disclosure (Joseph-Edwards and Wallace 2020). Our understanding of domestic violence victimization should not be influenced by gender bias or stereotypes and neither should gender disparities continue to be perpetuated as a result of these biases and stereotypes. Many requests have been made in the past for a more gender-inclusive approach to the measurement of domestic violence in order to facilitate both genders in reporting their experiences (Esquivel-Santoveña and Dixon 2012).

What is also needed in the region currently, are more detailed descriptions of intervention goals for male victims of domestic violence, the strategies used to achieve these specific intervention goals, institutional barriers to recognition and service implementation, and hypothesized outcomes that could serve as a basis for further research and improvements in service efforts for men experiencing domestic violence victimization. Updated and rigorous research would be particularly useful in the development of training efforts for both service providers and law enforcement.

The role of the media has been highlighted with regards to perpetuating gender stereotypes and negatively impacting men's help-seeking experiences as well as their willingness to report their victimization and seek further help. More media coverage addressing the specific experiences of men is needed in order to educate society about this issue.

Encouraging awareness of the plight of male survivors may persuade more men to report domestic violence victimization and make them feel assured that they will be taken seriously and treated with empathy, respect, and dignity regardless of their gender-role expectations.

Intervention services should be tailored specifically to support men and this should receive considerable funding similar to interventions that were developed to support women. Services geared towards males would allow a safe space for men to disclose their issues and process their feelings that are deemed incongruent with their gender roles. This would also eliminate the gender biases inherent in generic services. In order for such interventions services to be developed and receive the necessary funding, the public needs to be more sensitized to the issue of male domestic violence victimization. By providing the appropriate interventions where men have the experience of being heard and validated rather than stigmatized and chastised, the issue of domestic violence would be addressed in a wholistic manner, which would consequently be beneficial to the wider society.

From a symbolic interactionist perspective, intervention services must be developed with the purpose of supporting men's efforts in restructuring their sense of self. For example, recalling positive identities prior to domestic violence victimization, recapturing lost social identities as a result of the way they are treated by institutions and the wider society due to the social perception of being a male victim of domestic violence and recognizing individual competencies on which to rebuild self-esteem that is not connected to traditional masculinity constructs, gender stereotypes, and gender-role expectations.

Funding remains a critical issue for victim services even for women. The bulk of public funding comes from governments who have the power to prioritize resource allocation. Countries are experiencing major shifts in their political and economic climates coupled with the current global COVID-19 pandemic which is also having a significant impact on Caribbean countries. Major cuts to public expenditure are inevitable and the future of establishing appropriate interventions specifically for men and securing funding for such interventions remain austere during the pandemic. However, there should be increasing and continued advocacy for separate services for men and women as provision of generic services for men and women as a homogenous group will be neither appropriate nor effective.

Notes

1. The belief that heterosexuality is the default, preferred, or normal mode of sexual orientation (Harris and White 2018).
2. Gynocentrism is a dominant or exclusive focus on women in theory or practice; or to the advocacy of this (Oxford English Dictionary 2009).
3. Convention on the Elimination of all forms of Discrimination against Women.

References

Addis, M.E., and J.R. Mahalik. 2003. Men, Masculinity, and the Contexts of Help Seeking. *American Psychologist* 58 (1): 5–14.

Afifi, T.O., H. MacMillan, B.J. Cox, and G.J.G. Asmundson. 2009. Mental Health Correlates of Intimate Partner Violence in Marital Relationships in a Nationally Representative Sample of Males and Females. *Journal of Interpersonal Violence* 24 (8): 1398–1417.

Alhabib, S., U. Nur, and R. Jones. 2010. Domestic Violence Against Women: Systematic Review of Prevalence Studies. *Journal of Family Violence* 25 (4): 369–382.

Allen-Collinson, J., and J. Hockey. 2007. Working Out' Identity: Distance Runners and the Management of Disrupted Identity. *Leisure Studies* 26 (4): 381–398.

Archer, J. 2000. Sex Differences in Aggression Between Heterosexual Partners: A Meta-Analytic Review. *Psychological Bulletin* 126 (5): 651–680.

Archer, J. 2002. Sex Differences in Physically Aggressive Acts Between Heterosexual Partners: A Meta-Analytic Review. *Aggression and Violent Behavior* 7 (4): 313–351.

Bair-Merritt, M.H., S. Shea Crowne, D.A. Thompson, E. Sibinga, M. Trent, and J. Campbell. 2010. Why Do Women Use Intimate Partner Violence? A Systematic Review of Women's Motivations. *Trauma, Violence and Abuse* 11 (4): 178–189.

Barber, C.F. 2008. Domestic Violence Against Men. *Nursing Standards* 22 (51): 35–39.

Barrett, B.J., and M.S. Pierre. 2011. Variations in Women's Help Seeking in Response to Intimate Partner Violence: Findings from a Canadian Population-Based Study. *Violence Against Women* 17 (1): 47–70.

Bates, E.A. 2020. "No One Would Ever Believe Me": An Exploration of the Impact of Intimate Partner Violence Victimization on Men. *Psychology of Men & Masculinities* 21 (4): 497–507.

Bates, E.A., and N. Graham-Kevan. 2016. Is the Presence of Control Related to Help-Seeking Behavior? A Test of Johnson's Assumptions Regarding Sex-Differences and the Role of Control in Intimate Partner Violence. *Partner Abuse* 7 (1): 3–25.

Berger, J.L., M.E. Addis, J.D. Green, C. Mackowiak, and V. Goldberg. 2013. Men's Reactions to Mental Health Labels, Forms of Help-Seeking, and Sources of Help-Seeking Advice. *Psychology of Men and Masculinity* 14 (4): 433–443.

Bonomi, A.E., R.S. Thompson, M. Anderson, R.J. Reid, D. Carrell, A. Dimer, and E.R. Rivara. 2006. Intimate Partner Violence and Women's Physical, Mental, and Social Functioning. *American Journal of Preventive Medicine* 30 (6): 458–466.

Brown, G. 2004. Gender as a Factor in the Response of the Law-Enforcement System to Violence Against Partners. *Sexuality and Culture* 8: 3–139.

Carbone-López, K., C. Kruttschnitt, and R. Macmillan. 2006. Patterns of Intimate Partner Violence and Their Associations with Physical Health, Psychological Distress, and Substance Use. *Public Health Reports* 121 (4): 382–392.

Caribbean Community Secretariat (CAREC). 2006. *Report of the Caribbean Commission on Health and Development*. Kingston, Jamaica: Ian Randle Publishers.

Carmo, R., A. Grams, and T. Magalhães. 2011. Men as Victims of Intimate Partner Violence. *Journal of Forensic and Legal Medicine* 18 (8): 355–359.

Choi, Y.J., and S. An. 2016. Interventions to Improve Responses of Helping Professionals to Intimate Partner Violence: A Quick Scoping Review. *Research on Social Work Practice* 26 (1): 101–127.

Clarke, R. 1998. *Violence Against Women in the Caribbean: State and Non-state Responses*. New York: United Nations Development Fund for Women.

Connell, R.W., and J.W. Messerschmidt. 2005. Hegemonic Masculinity: Rethinking the Concept. *Gender and Society* 19 (6): 829–859.

Cook, P.W. 2009. *Abused Men: The Hidden Side of Domestic Violence*, 2nd ed. Westport: Praeger.

Corbally, M. 2015. Accounting for Intimate Partner Violence: A Biographical Analysis of Narrative Strategies Used by Men Experiencing IPV from Their Female Partners. *Journal of Interpersonal Violence* 30 (17): 3112–3132.

Danns, G., and B. Parsad. 1989. *Domestic Violence and Marital Relationships in the Caribbean: A Guyana Case Study*. Georgetown: University of Guyana, Women's Study Unit.

Douglas, E.M., and D.A. Hines. 2011. The Helpseeking Experiences of Men Who Sustain Intimate Partner Violence: An Overlooked Population and Implications for Practice. *Journal of Family Violence* 26 (6): 473–485.

Du Plat-Jones, Joanne. 2006. Domestic Violence: The Role of Health Professionals. *Nursing Standard* 21 (14–16): 44–48.

Dutton, D.G. 2008. My Back Pages: Reflections on Thirty Years of Domestic Violence Research. *Trauma, Violence and Abuse* 9 (3): 131–143.

Dutton, D.G. 2010. The Gender Paradigm and the Architecture of Anti-Science. *Partner Abuse* 1: 5–25.

Dutton, D.G., and K.R. White. 2013. Male Victims of Domestic Violence. *New Male Studies: An International Journal* 2 (1): 5–17.

Elam, P. 2016. *Gynocentrism: The Root of Feminism* [Speech]. The International Conference on Men's Issues, Excel London, UK.

Ellsberg, M., H. Jansen, L. Heise, C.H. Watts, and C. Garcia-Moreno. 2008. Intimate Partner Violence and Womens Physical and Mental Health in the WHO Multi-Country Study on Women's Health and Domestic Violence: An Observational Study. *The Lancet* 371 (9619): 1165–1172.

Esquivel-Santoveña, E.E., and L. Dixon. 2012. Investigating the True Rate of Physical Intimate Partner Violence: A Review of Nationally Representative Surveys. *Aggression and Violent Behavior* 17 (3): 208–219.

Follingstad, D., D.D. DeHart, and E. Green. 2004. Psychologists' Judgments of Psychologically Aggressive Actions When Perpetrated by a Husband Versus a Wife. *Violence and Victims* 19 (4, September): 435–452.

Fritz, G.K. 2000. Domestic Violence Hurts Children as Well as Adults. *Brown University Child and Adolescent Behaviour Letter* 16 (7): 8.

Gadd, D., S. Farrall, D. Dallimore, and N. Lombard. 2003. Male Victims of Domestic Violence. *Criminal Justice Matters* 53: 16–17.

Gadd, D., S. Farrall, N. Lombard, and D. Dallimore. 2002. *Domestic Abuse Against Men in Scotland*. Edinburgh: Scottish Executive.

George, M.J. 1994. Riding the Donkey Backwards: Men as the Unacceptable Victims of Marital Violence. *Journal of Men's Studies* 3 (2): 137–159.

George, M.J. 2002. Skimmington Revisited. *Journal of Men's Studies* 10 (2): 111–127.

Gibbons, A.Y. 2013. The Commonwealth Caribbean: Family Policy in the Caribbean Community (CARICOM). In *Handbook of Family Policies Across the Globe*, ed. M. Robila, 405–425. New York, NY: Springer.

Gondolf, E.W. 1998. The Victims of Court-Ordered Batterers: Their Victimization, Help-Seeking, and Perceptions. *Violence Against Women* 4 (6): 569–676.

Gopaul, R., P. Morgan, and R. Reddock. 1996. *Women, Family and Family Violence in the Caribbean: The Historical and Contemporary Experience with Special Reference to Trinidad and Tobago.* Kingston and St. Augustine:

Caribbean Community Secretariat; University of the West Indies, Centre for Gender and Development Studies.

Hamel, J. 2007. Toward a Gender-Inclusive Conception of Intimate Partner Violence Research and Theory: Part 1-Traditional Perspectives. *International Journal of Men's Health* 6 (1): 36.

Hammon, A.M. 2016. Women's Experiences of Engaging in Intimate Partner Violence in Heterosexual Relationships: An Interpretative Phenomenological Analysis. Professional Doctoral thesis. University of East London Psychology. https://doi.org/10.15123/PUB.5842.

Harris, J., and White, V. 2018. *A Dictionary of Social Work and Social Care*, 2nd ed. Oxford University Press. https://doi.org/10.1093/acref/9780198796688.001.000.

Hester, M. 2013. Who Does What to Whom? Gender and Domestic Violence Perpetrators: Gender and Domestic Violence Perpetrators in English Police Records. *European Journal of Criminology* 10 (5): 623–637.

Hines, D., J. Brown, and E. Dunning. 2007. Characteristics of Callers to the Domestic Abuse Helpline for Men. *Journal of Family Violence* 22 (2): 63–72.

Hines, D.A., and E.M. Douglas. 2010. Intimate Terrorism by Women Towards Men: Does It Exist? *Journal of Aggression, Conflict and Peace Research* 2 (3): 36–56.

Hogan, K.F., J.R. Hegarty, T. Ward, and L.J. Dodd. 2012. Counsellors' Experiences of Working with Male Victims of Female-Perpetrated Domestic Abuse. *Counselling and Psychotherapy Research* 12 (1): 44–52.

Huntley, A.L., L. Potter, E. Williamson, A. Malpass, E. Szilassy, and G. Feder. 2019. Help Seeking by Male Victims of Domestic Violence and Abuse (DVA): A Systematic Review and Qualitative Evidence Synthesis. *British Medical Journal Open* 9 (6): 1–13.

Hutchison, I.W., and J.D. Hirschel. 1998. Abused Women: Help-Seeking Strategies and Police Utilization. *Violence Against Women* 4 (4): 436–456.

Javaid, A. 2017. The Unknown Victims: Hegemonic Masculinity, Masculinities, and Male Sexual Victimisation. *Sociological Research Online* 22 (1, February): 28–47.

Johnson, D. 1986. Using Sociology to Analyze Human and Organizational Problems: A Humanistic Perspective to Link Theory and Practice. *Clinical Sociology Review* 4: 57–70.

Johnson, U. 1996. The Reconstruction of Masculinity: Breaking the Link Between Maleness and Violence. Presented at The University of the West Indies Centre for Gender and Development Studies, St. Augustine, Conference on *The Construction of Caribbean Masculinity: Towards a Research Agenda*, January 11–13.

Joseph-Edwards, A., and W.C. Wallace. 2020. Suffering in Silence, Shame, Seclusion, and Invisibility: Men as Victims of Female Perpetrated Domestic

Violence in Trinidad and Tobago. *Journal of Family Issues* 42 (8, September): 1805–1830.

Jurik, N., and R. Winn. 1990. Gender and Homicide: A Comparison of Men and Women Who Kill. *Violence and Victims* 5 (4, Winter): 227–242, NCJ 130043.

Kaukinen, C.E., S. Meyer, and C. Akers. 2013. Status Compatibility and Help-Seeking Behaviors Among Female Intimate Partner Violence Victims. *Journal of Interpersonal Violence* 28 (3): 577–601.

Kaura, S.A., and B.J. Lohman. 2007. Dating Violence Victimization, Relationship Satisfaction, Mental Health Problems, and Acceptability of Violence: A Comparison of Men and Women. *Journal of Family Violence* 22: 367–381.

Kolbe, V., and A. Büttner. 2020. Domestic Violence Against Men-Prevalence and Risk Factors. *Deutsches Arzteblatt International* 117 (31–32): 534–541.

Krug, E.G., J. Mercy, L. Dahlberg, A. Zwi, and R. Lozano (eds.). 2002. *World Report on Violence and Health*. Geneva: World Health Organization.

Lawrence, S. 2003. Domestic Violence and Men. *Nursing Standards* 17 (40): 41–43.

Le Franc, E.R., and L. Rock. 2003. *Domestic Violence in Barbados: Changing Interpersonal Relationship Dynamics*. Christ Church, Barbados: United Nations Development Fund for Women.

Lövestad, S., and K. Gunilla. 2012. Men's and Women's Exposure and Perpetration of Partner Violence: An Epidemiological Study from Sweden. *BMC Public Health* 12: 945.

McCarrick, J. 2015. New Voices: The "Minority" Man? *The Psychologist* 28: 376–379.

McCart, M.R., D.W. Smith, and G.K. Sawyer. 2010. Help Seeking Among Victims of Crime: A Review of the Empirical Literature. *Journal of Traumatic Stress* 23 (2): 198–206.

McFeely, C., N. Whiting, N. Lombard, and M. McGowan. 2013. Domestic Abuse and Gender Inequality: An Overview of the Current Debate. Retrieved from https://www.era.lib.ed.ac.uk/handle/1842/8769, 2021.

Mechem, C.C., F.S. Shofer, S.S. Reinhard, S. Hornig, and E. Datner. 1999. History of Domestic Violence Among Male Patients Presenting to an Urban Emergency Department. *Journal of the Society for Academic Emergency Medicine* 6 (8): 786–791.

Migliaccio, T.A. 2002. Abused Husbands: A Narrative Analysis. *Journal of Family Issues* 23 (1): 26–52.

Miller, S., and M. Meloy. 2006. Women's Use of Force: Voices of Women Arrested for Domestic Violence. *Violence Against Women* 12 (1, January): 89–115, NCJ 212762.

Nam, S.K., H.J. Chu, M.K. Lee, J.H. Lee, N. Kim, and S.M. Lee. 2010. A Meta-Analysis of Gender Differences in Attitudes Toward Seeking Professional Psychological Help. *Journal of American College Health* 59: 110–116.

O'Neil, J.M. 2008. Summarizing 25 Years of Research on Men's Gender Role Conflict Using the Gender Role Conflict Scale New Research Paradigms and Clinical Implications. *The Counseling Psychologist* 36 (3): 358–445.

Oxford English Dictionary Version 4.0. 2009. Oxford University Presss, ISBN 9780199563838.

Pagelow, M.D., and L.W. Pagelow. 1984. *Family Violence*. New York: ABC-CLIO.

Parry, Odette. 1996. In One Ear and Out the Other: Unmasking Masculinities in the Caribbean Classroom. *Sociological Research Online* 1 (2, July): 10–22.

Pence, E., and S. Dasgupta. 2006. *Re-Examining 'Battering': Are All Acts of Violence Against Intimate Partners the Same?* Final Report to Office on Violence Against Women, U.S. Department of Justice, Grant Number 1998-WR-VX-K001, June. Duluth, MN: Praxis International.

Pizzey, E., J.R. Shackleton, and P. Urwin (eds.). 2000. *Women or Men—Who Are the Victims?* London: Institute for the Study of Civil Society.

Randle, A.A., and C.A. Graham. 2011. A Review of the Evidence on the Effects of Intimate Partner Violence on Men. *Psychology of Men and Masculinity* 12 (2): 97–111.

Saunders, D.G. 2002. Are Physical Assaults by Wives and Girlfriends a Major Social Problem? A Review of the Literature. *Violence Against Women* 8 (12): 1424–1448.

Schlack, R., J. Rüdel, A. Karger, and H. Hölling. 2013. Physical and Psychological Violence Perpetration and Violent Victimization in the German Adult Population: Results of the German Health Interview and Examination Survey for Adults (DEGS1). *Bundesgesundheitsblatt, Gesundheitsforschung, Gesundheitsschutz* 56 (5–6): 755–764.

Smith, D. 2012. *A New Response to Youth Crime*. New York: Routledge.

Steinmetz, S. 1978. The Battered Husband Syndrome. *Victimology* 2: 499–509.

Stockdale, L., S. Tackett, and S.M. Coyne. 2013. Sex Differences in Verbal Aggression Use in Romantic Relationships: A Meta-Analytic Study and Review. *Journal of Aggression, Conflict and Peace Research* 5 (3): 167–178.

Straus, M.A., and K.L. Gozjolko. 2016. Concordance Between Partners in "Intimate Terrorism": A Comparison of Two Typologies. *Aggression and Violent Behavior* 29: 55–60.

Stryker, S. 1980. *Symbolic Interactionism*. Menlo Park, CA: Benjamin/Cummings.

Sweeney, K. 2007. *Restrictions of Race, Class, and Gender Norms on Ability to Attain Preferred Gender Roles*. Conference Papers—American Sociological Association.

Taylor, C.A., and S.B. Sorenson. 2005. Community-Based Norms About Intimate Partner Violence: Putting Attributions of Fault and Responsibility into Context. Retrieved April 19, 2021, from http://repository.upenn.edu/spp_papers/76.

Thureau, S., I. Le Blanc-Louvry, S. Thureau, C. Gricourt, and B. Proust. 2015. Conjugal Violence: A Comparison of Violence Against Men by Women and Women by Men. *Journal of Forensic Legal Medicine* 31: 42–46.

Tjaden, P., and N. Thoennes. 2000. Prevalence and Consequences of Male-to-Female and Female-to-Male Intimate Partner Violence as Measured by the National Violence Against Women Survey. *Violence Against Women* 6: 142–161.

Tsui, V., M. Cheung, and P. Leung. 2010. Help-Seeking Among Male Victims of Partner Abuse: Men's Hard Times. *Journal of Community Psychology* 38 (6): 769–780.

Umubyeyi, Aline, et al. 2014. Women Are Considerably More Exposed to Intimate Partner Violence Than Men in Rwanda: Results from a Population-Based, Cross-Sectional Study. *BMC Women's Health* 14: 99.

UNODC. 2011. *Global Study on Homicide: United Nations Office on Drugs and Crime*. Retrieved April 18, 2021, from http://www.unodc.org/gsh/en/data.html.

UNODC. 2013. Retrieved April 30, 2015, from Male and Female Homicide Victims Killed by Intimate Partner or Family Members as Percentage of Total Homicide Victims, Time Series 2005–2012.

UNODC. 2018. *Global Study on Homicide: Gender-Related Killing of Women and Girls*. Retrieved from https://www.unodc.org/documents/data-andanalysis/GSH2018/gsh18_Genderrelated_killing_of_women_and_girls.pdf.

van Wijk, N.P.L. 2012. *Domestic Violence by and Against Men and Women in Curaçao: A Caribbean Study*. Reprografie Vrije Universiteit.

Vogel, D.L., S.R. Heimerdinger-Edwards, J.H. Hammer, and A. Hubbard. 2011. "Boys Don't Cry": Examination of the Links Between Endorse-ment of Masculine Norms, Self-Stigma, and Help-Seeking Attitudes for Men from Diverse Backgrounds. *Journal of Counseling Psychology* 58: 368–382.

Walker, L.E.A., and A. Browne. 1985. Gender and Victimization by Intimates. *Journal of Personality* 53 (2): 179.

Wallace, W.C., C. Gibson, N. Gordon, R. Lakhan, J. Mahabir, and C. Seetahal. 2019. Domestic Violence: Intimate Partner Violence Victimization Non-Reporting to the Police in Trinidad and Tobago. *Justice Policy Journal* 16 (1): 1–30.

World Health Organization. 1996. *WHO Global Consultation on Violence and Health. Violence: A Public Health*. Geneva. Retrieved from http://www.who.int/violenceprevention/approach/definition/en, 2021.

CHAPTER 8

The Use of the Social-Ecological Model of Intervention for Addressing Domestic Violence in Trinidad and Tobago

Cheryl-Ann Sarita Boodram

Discussion

Domestic violence refers to the "physical, social and emotional abuse and acts of aggression within relationships that are considered as family connections or akin to family connections" (Gibbons 2015, p. 2). According to Wallace et al. (2019, p. 2):

> In Trinidad and Tobago, DV (Domestic Violence) is a term that has traditionally been used to describe the violence that occur between individuals with all forms of familial relationships, including persons in intimate relationships. According to Trinidad and Tobago's Domestic Violence Act,

C.-A. S. Boodram (✉)
Faculty of Social Sciences, University of the West Indies, St. Augustine, Trinidad and Tobago
e-mail: CherylAnn.Boodram@sta.uwi.edu

A. M. Bissessar and C. Huggins (eds.), *Domestic Violence in the Anglophone Caribbean*,
https://doi.org/10.1007/978-3-030-88476-5_8

> Chapter 45:56, Act 27 of 1999 as amended by Act #8 of 2006, DV refers to the 'physical, sexual, emotional or psychological or financial abuse committed by a person against a spouse, child, any other person who is a member of the household or dependent.'

Many authors have used the term "domestic violence" and "intimate partner violence" interchangeably, which is helpful in the Caribbean context, as doing so broadens the concept of domestic violence to include violence in same-sex relationships and the pervasive Caribbean family structure of "common-law" relationships referring to intimate partners living together.

There is a lack of data detailing the extent of the occurrences of domestic violence in Trinidad and Tobago. However, a report by Pemberton and Joseph (2018) noted that one in three women has experienced domestic violence in Trinidad and Tobago. The report also highlights data from the Crime and Problem Analysis Branch of the Trinidad and Tobago Police Service which revealed that 15,000 reports of domestic violence were made between 2010 and 2016. 72% of these reports were related to women and there were 181 domestic violence-related deaths, with 58% of these deaths being women.

Many have surmised that the nature of violence is rooted in the cultural and historical background of the islands (Gibbons 2015). The history of the Caribbean, deep-rooted in violence from the early recorded history of violence against indigenous peoples to slavery and indentureship and then the harsh realities of colonialism from European countries such as Great Britain, France, and Spain have been entrenched in the collective memory of Caribbean people. The lasting impressions have shaped behaviours and been normalized in ways that both men and women have somewhat tolerated its manifestations especially when manifested in the context of intimate partner relationships.

Domestic violence is fuelled by the dynamic interplay of cultural, economic, social, and political factors (Sutton and Alvarez 2016). Therefore, addressing domestic violence requires, first, a multi-textual understanding of the accepted norms and attitudes which fuel domestic violence and second, an approach to addressing the issues using multiple strategies and modalities. This is particularly crucial as cultural tolerance of domestic violence can result in intergenerational transmission of violence against women, which indicates the need to shape attitudes and practices that will prevent this onward transmission of these acceptances to young people and subsequently future generations.

Literature on intimate partner abuse/domestic violence intervention throughout the world has mainly focused on the provision of support to the survivor or victim or services that are implemented separately (e.g. Hester et al. 2005; Guedes et al. 2016; Richard et al. 2018). According to Richard et al. (2018, p. 8), interventions have been implemented separately but reports found that there may be overlapping risk factors which existing community, social, and cultural norms that support power imbalances.

While these interventions have supported the victims by providing protection and medical, legal, and psychosocial care, there is a need to consider the issue of domestic violence as a public health issue which ultimately requires interventions throughout society to ensure the social and cultural factors which perpetuate unhealthy power imbalances between men and women are not accepted.

Traditional models of domestic violence interventions in Trinidad and Tobago have often focused on empowering victims with knowledge and skills to cope with violence. However, literature has documented the role that community and family beliefs in the play in both exacerbating as well as mitigating violence against women. Therefore, efforts targeting only the victim herself do not address the broader context of women's lives. This context calls for domestic violence prevention programmes, which focus on breaking the social, cultural, and historical systems that support violence against women within communities.

Though the author recognizes the occurrences of males as victims of domestic violence, this chapter focuses on the value of social-ecological interventions in mitigating the incidents of violence against women and provides discussion for implementing such action. The choice to focus on domestic violence situations against women is based on the prevalence of the phenomenon in the Caribbean. According to Sutton and Alvarez (2016, p. 6), "Although little is known about the prevalence of intimate partner violence across the sub region, there is evidence of acceptance of violence and traditional gender norms, which are often linked to higher levels of violence against women in societies". The chapter argues that a social-ecological model has the potential for disrupting traditions of abuse at the individual, family, community, and societal levels.

A Social-Ecological Model (SEM) of Domestic Violence

The Social-Ecological Model was created by Urie Bronfenbrenner (1994) to demonstrate how behaviours of individuals were shaped by the dynamic interplay between an individual and environmental factors. Tekkas Kerman and Betrus (2020, p. 2) described the SEM as a "theory-based framework for understanding the interactive effects of individual and environmental factors that influence attitudes and behaviours". Heise (2011) later applied the SEM model to understand the root causes and possible interventions for intimate partner violence.

The SEM is a four-dimensional framework, which allows for organizing the risks and protective factors that an individual is exposed to which produces behaviours. These four dimensions can be visualized as a pattern or concentric circles which start inward with the individual (intrapersonal) and extends to outward circles that include the relational dimension (relationships), the community, and the society. The SEM acknowledges that people are both influenced by and influence their environment (Golden and Earp 2012).

The ecological framework posits that there is no singular factor that can explain why some people or groups are at higher risk of being victims or perpetrators of domestic violence, while others may not be as susceptible. The framework views domestic violence as the result of interactions among factors along the four dimensions (Fig. 8.1).

The Use of the Social-Ecological Model in Understanding Domestic Violence

The Individual Level

Persons may be at greater risk of domestic violence because of individual and personal level factors. These risk factors include age, level of education, income or means of earning an income, or history of abuse. Younger age has been a consistent risk factor for being both perpetrator and victim of violence against women (Tekkas Kerman and Betrus 2020). Literature also shows that women with lower levels of education are at greater risk for experiencing violence (Abramsky et al. 2011).

A 2018 Report on Gender-Based Violence in Trinidad and Tobago,[1] commissioned by UNWomen and the Government of Trinidad and Tobago shows that "Some of the most consistent factors associated with

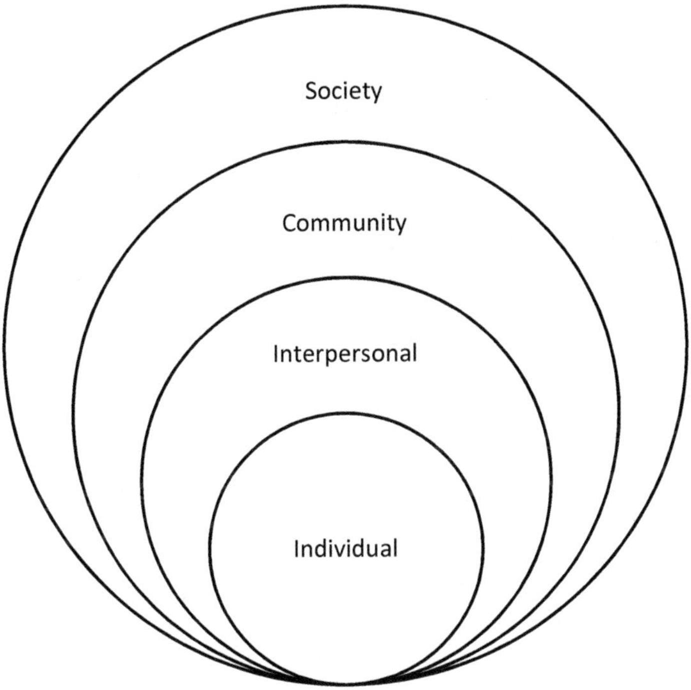

Fig. 8.1 The social-ecological model

men's increased likelihood of committing intimate partner violence are young age, low levels of education, witnessing or experiencing violence as a child, harmful use of drugs and alcohol and acceptance of violence as a strategy for control" (p. 22). The report also noted that "substance abuse is also cited as a factor turning men from being non-violent to violent" (Hosein et al., p. 24).

In a study conducted by Hadeed (2007), women's economic situation was also connected to why women stay in abusive relationships. The financial security of women was also seen as a risk factor which contributed to the reason for non-reporting of domestic violence to police (Wallace et al. 2019).

Personal Relationships (Relational)

The second level within the SEM refers to the relational factors which represent direct interaction with others such as social support, peers, and family (Cramer and Kapusta 2017). The individual's personal relationships may increase an individual's risk of domestic violence. Personal relationships such as family, friends, and peers may influence the risk of becoming a perpetrator of domestic violence. For example, violent friends may encourage a person to participate in violent acts. Therefore, prevention approaches must involve programmes designed to reach persons within the relational dimension.

Relational factors which contribute to domestic violence include conflict in relationships, economic stress on women, and the ideas of male dominance in the household. According to the 2018 Report on Gender-Based Violence in Trinidad and Tobago, "male dominance can be associated with behaviours such as sexual violence and controlling behaviours including accusation, threats, and stalking" (Hosein et al. 2018, p. 27).

The Community Context

Cramer and Kapusta (2017, p. 1756) define community-level influences as "those circumscribed to a certain region like neighbourhood centres, schools, workplaces and healthcare providers". Risk factors here may include the nature of the community in which an individual resides, such as rural vs. urban. Community perceptions and tolerance of violence against women is also a significant risk factor for both victims and perpetrators of domestic violence.

A study by Bott et al. (2012) showed that Caribbean adults were likely to tolerate domestic violence against a woman if she neglected the household chores or if she was unfaithful. The survey also indicated that people living in a rural community had a higher tolerance for intimate partner violence.

Societal Factors

Societal factors influence whether violence is encouraged or inhibited. According to Cramer and Kapusta (2017, p. 1756), "Societal factors concern larger scale issues such as social and cultural norms, policies, and other guiding rules or laws". Tekkas Kerman and Betrus (2020) argue that these include economic and social policies that perpetuate inequalities between people as well as social and cultural norms which reinforce messages of male dominance over women. Sukhu (2013) contends that in Trinidad and Tobago, an integral component of men's violence against women are beliefs around masculinity and gender identity. The Report on Violence against Women in Trinidad and Tobago (2018, p. 35) contends that "Gender ideologies have shaped women and men's understanding of power, thus normalizing toxic masculinity as an expression of manhood. Men have to be able to show that they are 'handling' their women rather than being controlled by women."

Another important risk factor which influences both the victim and perpetrator, is the influence of religion on the views of men and women. A Report on Violence against Women in Trinidad and Tobago (2018) explains that in some cases, religious organizations reinforce patriarchal gender ideologies which can result in minimizing the concern of violence against women which can lead to women staying in abusive relationships or non-reporting to the police.

The policing systems and cultural beliefs of some police officers are also risk factors for domestic violence. Johnson and Boodram (2019) claim that the absence of risk assessments and the pervasive patriarchal cultural notions of some of the police officers impedes women's reporting of domestic violence. In a study by Wallace et al. (2019) which examined intimate partner violence victimization and non-reporting to the police in Trinidad and Tobago, the authors concluded that one of the main barriers to reporting domestic violence victimization to the police was embarrassment/shame. Another conclusion of the study was that persons chose not to report incidences of domestic violence because of the lack of trust and confidence in the police.

The popular culture and messages contained in the lyrics of popular music in Trinidad and Tobago also promote tolerance of violence against women. According to Johnson (2017, p. 20), "Caribbean masculinity is also tied to what is known as a 'macho' man ... This type of man and behaviour is sung about in calypsos that praise them and support their behaviour. These songs also construct gender identities, suggesting roles and behaviours for males and females in relationships". Here, Johnson connects the societal perception of the dominance of the man and masculinity with the popular music in the Caribbean.

The ecological framework considers the interface between factors at the different dimensions with equal significance as those within a single level. This framework is also relevant in developing multitiered ecological strategies to mitigate the number of domestic violence situations in Trinidad and Tobago.

A Case Study

The following case represents the true experience of a woman, now in her forties, who has given permission for the story to be told to illustrate the application of the social-ecological model to the issue of domestic violence. The name of the owner of the story has been altered to protect her identity.

Carmel, a Case Study

Carmel was an eight-year-old girl who lived in an extended family, with her mother, sister, aunts, and grandfather in a rural village in Trinidad. Her mother, Shanti, and father, Deo, were never married, and her father lived with his own wife and children about twenty minutes away from Carmel's family house. Her mother worked in a laundry, ironing clothes for a living that contributed to the financial upkeep of the household. Intermittently, her father would give her mother some money that she used to augment her small pay. The relationship between her mother and father was sometimes tenuous, as her father often accused her mother of being unfaithful, and if he saw her in public with her friends, would often follow her.

One day, her father, who drove a panel van that accommodated passengers, was hired to transport villagers on an excursion to the beach. Carmel was excited, and on the day, she remembered her mother preparing food for the much-anticipated trip.

The journey to the beach was eventful. The villagers in the van drank lots of alcohol, played loud Indian music, and got up every so often to dance with each other, even while they were on the road. She remembered the music lyrics that promoted messages that men should be wary of women. By the time the excursion reached the beach, many were drunk. Carmel remembered also seeing her father drinking alcohol on the way, even though he was driving. On the beach, there was much merriment, with villagers playing cricket, dancing, drinking alcohol, and bathing in the sea waters. She could sense that her mother was becoming upset because of her father's drinking. Her mother mentioned her feelings to her father once or twice. On the way home, there was tension in the vehicle, as Carmel could sense her father was getting angry with her mother. His friends who were also in the vehicle, she listened to a conversation that encouraged her father to "hit her a slap", referring to her mother. As they approached the village, others in the vehicle, including some of the women, were taking her father's side in the argument—admonishing her mother to stop complaining because he was just enjoying himself drinking.

Just before reaching the village, her father pulled the vehicle over to a stop, came to the side where her mother was sitting, and slapped, cuffed, and kicked her, in full view of the passengers in the vehicle. Her father shouted "Woman! Know your place! I am the man!" Carmel heard one woman say "it good for her, she must know her place". The men in the vehicle also applauded her father's actions, saying they thought it took him long enough to correct Shanti. Carmel vowed that if a man ever hit her when she was older, she would kill him. She had seen many men beat women in her village and knew that even if you call the police, the response to the victim was always that they did not interfere in "man and woman" business.

The above case study of Carmel details the dynamic interplay of the four dimensions of the social-ecological model in domestic violence in Trinidad and Tobago. Using the social-ecological model as a framework of analysis, the case shows the multiple factors which contribute towards domestic violence.

At the intrapersonal level, Deo's problems with alcohol distorted his thinking and increased the risk of him responding in an aggressive manner to Shanti. At the relational level, Deo's male friends from the village instigated that he should handle the conflict using violence against Carmel's mother. There is also evidence of male domination, as Deo would accuse Shanti of infidelity and maintain stalking behaviours. The women in the vehicle who supported the use of aggression and justified Deo's action, also demonstrated how culturally there was some level of tolerance or acceptance for domestic violence. The village excursion, a culturally celebrated recreational activity in rural communities in Trinidad and Tobago, created a risky setting, with the high use of alcohol and music lyrics that glorified violence against women. Carmel's own reaction to the violence, her desire to "kill" anyone who hits her also demonstrates the potential of this situation to contribute to intergenerational violence.

The Social-Ecological Model Approach Towards Ending Domestic Violence

Individual Level Prevention Strategies

Prevention strategies that target change and support along the individual dimension of the social-ecological model should focus on changing attitudes, beliefs, and behaviours which support domestic violence. This requires that the mindset of men and boys which perpetuate the social norms and power imbalance that promote domestic violence against women, be changed. In the case study, Deo repeated messages that promoted the subordination of women. His use of alcohol also presented a risk for aggressive behaviour. Thus, the social-ecological approach is important for addressing several things, firstly the need for a programmatic intervention that challenges the gender-power imbalances and the personal belief that men hold on the subordination of women and secondly, the need to educate on the connections between alcohol use and domestic violence.

The financial situation of Shanti represents a risk factor which made her vulnerable to domestic violence. Thus, intervention at the individual level must also focus on promoting social and economic empowerment of women and girls.

Relational Strategies

In the case study, Carmel mentions the trigger to the violence was one of conflict. Thus intervention in domestic violence situations must also include widespread training in communication and conflict management skills. There is also a need to alter the shared beliefs that reinforce messages that denigrate women and tolerate violence against women. This should be targeted to peer groups, in a context that will promote men-talk in a space where men feel free to talk about the views they hold about women and violence. In the Caribbean, men-centric spaces such as barbershops or the popular 'Sunday sweat' sporting activity that many Trinidad and Tobago men engage in on Sunday afternoons can be used as conducive environments to unpack messages that promote male dominance. At the same time, it is crucial to also engage women in these conversations that empower them or address their own tolerance of violence against women, and these can be situated in spaces such as the beauty salons. Peers such as friends, family members, and schoolmates can challenge messages that promote social norms that accept violence and gender stereotypes.

Community Level Strategies

The case of Carmel highlights key community risk factors for domestic violence in Trinidad and Tobago. Firstly, the response by other men who reinforced gender stereotypes to Carmel's father and justified his violence against Shanti. Secondly, the community tolerance of violence, which reinforced social norms that accept violence and as a means of resolving conflict. Therefore, community-based programming is needed to transform the existing gender norms that perpetuate violence against women.

Community and societal interventions are crucial in changing toxic gender norms and attitudes that tolerate violence. This approach calls for the use of interventions that engage a wide array of stakeholders along all the social-ecological dimensions. Some approaches to community and societal interventions include community partnering and community intervention.

Participatory models of intervention for addressing social gender norms in communities play an essential role in changing maladaptive thoughts and behaviours held by community members. Participatory models advocate for collaboration with trusted community influencers who are keen to participate and inclusion of persons that represent the different circles of influence in the community. These members of the community are seen as experts who inform the design and implementation of community action.

Community partnering uses a whole-of-society approach which builds networks of partners or stakeholders which plan and implement domestic violence programming. The entire process centres on high collaboration with stakeholders, including the business sector, school, formal and informal community groups, and religious organizations. Partnering must target the involvement of NGOs, youth groups, community-based organizations, the business community, and all other major stakeholders including mental health services, shelters, and social services.

Community partnering efforts must recognize the importance of and involve all community members as this creates a sense of ownership of the project and supports change at the community level.

Community Intervention

Community intervention should focus on expanding women's knowledge of resources which are available to them in communities and ensuring ease of access for women utilize such services when they are in need. These services should be private and confidential.

Capacity-building programming should also be integrated to ensure that the efforts to transform communities are sustainable. The establishment of technical advisory committees and task forces can assist in both designing and implementing community-based initiatives. Examples of community intervention are peer mediation and education training, support groups, community-based police sensitivity training, and workshops with religious leaders, educators, and community leaders on domestic violence.

Societal-Level Strategies to Prevent Domestic Violence

At the societal level, effective responses by the police, messages in the media, and greater participation of men in activism against domestic violence can help to curb domestic violence. Media campaigns also have an important role to play in changing social norms and beliefs that perpetuate community tolerance of violence against women. A social-ecological model will focus on training media professionals on eliminating message which reinforce violence against women, and alternatively, promote messages that promote a culture of peace and tolerance.

Social influencers today must be recognized as powerful influencers of behaviours and attitudes. Therefore, networking with trusted social influencers and having them speak out against domestic violence against women can build a culture that is safe for women and girls.

A critical component of violence prevention strategies at the societal level is the need to integrate anti-violence messages within the school system. Thus, children can be exposed to age-appropriate lessons which promote respectful relationships. These lessons need to be integrated from the early childhood care centres to out-of-school programmes and tertiary level curricula.

Activism is also important to continue public sensitization and policy lobbying necessary for eliminating domestic violence against women. Training young people and women in activism to end domestic violence will ensure sustainability of the movement for a safe society for women. While many activists in Trinidad and Tobago are women, the need to involve men in activism is important. Thus, men's participation in media advocacy campaigns, protests, and policy development is important in preventing domestic violence.

The Social-Ecological Model, Domestic Violence, and Globalization

The social-ecological model, as proposed by Bronfenbrenner and modified by Heise explains that violence against women is influenced by complex factors across individual, relationship, community, and societal levels. This chapter supports the use of this model in designing approaches to addressing the issue of domestic violence against women in Trinidad and Tobago. While the model has relevance, it should be noted that globalization has had a strong influence on the behaviours and attitudes of Trinidad and Tobago citizens. Thus, globalization has the potential to also transform societies (Castles 2001), and the potential for globalization to do "contradictory work on sexed, raced, and laboring bodies: gendered family relations; and masculinized and feminized institutions, ideologies and identities" (Ferguson et al. 2008, p. 2) must be recognized. The work is of Fulu and Miedema (2015) should be considered as we apply a social-ecological model to designing approaches to domestic violence against women, as they recognize that "No longer do the drivers of violence against women stop at national borders" (Fulu and Miedema 2015, p. 1447).

Conclusion

The high number of domestic violence situations in Trinidad and Tobago begs for new approaches to be implemented. With statistics showing that one in three women in Trinidad and Tobago are victims of domestic violence, the situation calls for effective models for understanding the risk factors for both victims and perpetrators of domestic violence and challenging individual, interpersonal, cultural, and social factors which perpetuate violence against women.

While there is a need for greater understanding of risk and protective factors associated with domestic violence, there is definitely a need to go beyond the pathologizing individual characteristics of women or victim blaming, to include risk factors. The social-ecological model offers a multifaceted approach to understanding these risk factors along the individual, relational, community, and societal dimensions. In examining a case of domestic violence in this chapter, one can get a better sense of the many factors which contribute to domestic violence and the ways in which each reinforce tolerance for violence against women on the societal level.

This chapter also advances the need for multidimensional approaches to be used in intervention at the individual, interpersonal, community, and societal levels to end domestic violence. Comprehensive, multisectoral, long-term collaboration between governments and civil society at all levels of the ecological framework is necessary. The social-ecological model provides a suitable backdrop for tailoring current prevention and intervention programmes for eliminating domestic violence.

Notes

1. https://www.undp.org›unct›caribbean›docs

References

Abramsky, Tanya, Charlotte H. Watts, Claudia Garcia-Moreno, Karen Devries, Ligia Kiss, Mary Ellsberg, Henrica A.F.M. Jansen, and Lori Heise. 2011. What Factors Are Associated with Recent Intimate Partner Violence? Findings from the WHO Multi-country Study on Women's Health and Domestic Violence. *BMC Public Health* 11 (1): 1–17. http://www.biomedcentral.com/1471-2458/11/109.

Bott, Sarah, Alessandra Guedes, Mary Goodwin, and Jennifer Adams Mendoza. 2012. *Violence Against Women in Latin America and the Caribbean: A Comparative Analysis of Population—Based Data from 12 Countries*. Washington, DC: Pan American Health Organization.

Bronfenbrenner, Urie. (1994). Ecological Models of Human Development. In *International Encyclopaedia of Education*, vol. 3, 2nd ed. Oxford: Elsevier.

Castles, Stephen. 2001. Studying Social Transformation. *International Political Science Review* 22: 13–32.

Cramer, Robert J., and Nestor D. Kapusta. 2017. A Social-Ecological Framework of Theory, Assessment, and Prevention of Suicide. *Frontiers in Psychology* 8 (2017): 1756. https://doi.org/10.3389/fpsyg.2017.01756.

Ferguson, K.E., S.E. Merry, and M. Mironesco. 2008. Introduction. In *Gender and Globalization in Asia and the Pacific: Method, Practice and Theory*, ed. K.E. Ferguson and M. Mironesco, 1–12. Honolulu: University of Hawaii Press.

Fulu, Emma, and Stephanie Miedema. 2015. Violence Against Women: Globalizing the Integrated Ecological Model. *Violence Against Women* 21 (12): 1431–1455. https://doi.org/10.1177/1077801215596244.

Gibbons, A. Y. 2015. Family Violence in the Caribbean. In *Expert Group Meeting on Family Policy Development: Achievements and Challenges*. New York, NY: United Nations Headquarters. Retrieved from http://www.un.org/esa/socdev/family/docs/egm15/Gibbonspaper.pdf.

Golden, Shelley, and Joanne Earp. 2012. Social-Ecological Approaches to Individuals and Their Contexts: Twenty Years of Health Education & Behaviour Health Promotion Interventions. *Health Education & Behaviour* 39 (3): 364–372. https://doi.org/10.1177/1090198111418634.

Guedes, Alessandra, Sarah Bott, Claudia Garcia-Moreno, and Manuela Colombini. 2016. Bridging the Gaps: A Global Review of Intersections of Violence Against Women and Violence Against Children. *Global Health Action* 9 (1): 31516. https://doi.org/10.3402/gha.v9.31516.

Hadeed, Linda. 2007. Contributing Factors to Staying in Abusive Relationships: Afro-Trinidadian Women in Trinidad and Tobago. *Caribbean Journal of Social Work* 5: 106–121.

Heise, Lori. (2011). *What Works to Prevent Partner Violence: An Evidence Overview*. London, UK: STRIVE Research Consortium, London School of Hygiene and Tropical Medicine.

Hester, Marianne, Nicole Westmarland, Geetanjali Gangoli, Mike Wilkinson, Caitriona O'Kelly, Andrew Kent, and Alana Diamond. 2005. *Domestic Violence Perpetrators: Identifying Needs to Inform Early Intervention*. Newcastle: Northern Rock Foundation.

Hosein, Gabrielle, Tricia Basdeo-Gobin, Colin Robinson, Sabrina Mowlah-Baksh, Simone Leid, and Amilcar Sanatan. 2018. Gender-based Violence in Trinidad and Tobago. *UNWOMEN: Port-of-Spain*.

Johnson, Emmanuel Janagan. 2017. An Exploratory Study on the Impact of Domestic Violence on the Families in Trinidad and Tobago, the West Indies. *Journal of Evidence-Informed Social Work* 14 (1): 19–34. https://doi.org/10.1080/23761407.2016.1269709.

Johnson, Emmanuel, and Cheryl-Ann Sarita. Boodram. 2019. Exploring the Experiences of Females on Reporting Incidents of Domestic Violence in Trinidad and Tobago. *The British Journal of Social Work* 49 (8): 2226–2244. https://doi.org/10.1093/bjsw/bcy13.

Pemberton, Cecile, and Joel Joseph. 2018. *National Women's Health Survey for Trinidad and Tobago*. https://doi.org/10.18235/0001006.

Richard, Patrick, Sara Siebert, Junior Ovince, Alexandra Blackwell, Manuel Contreras-Urbina, Robert Pantzer, Eric L. Olson, and Jacquelyn Dolezal. 2018. A Community-Based Intervention to Prevent Violence against Women and Girls in Haiti. Discussion Paper No. IDB-DP-594.

Sukhu, Raquel. 2013. Masculinity and Men's Violence Against Known Women in Trinidad—Whose Responsibility? *Men and Masculinities* 16 (1): 71–92. https://doi.org/10.1177/1097184X12468102.

Sutton, Heather, and Lucciana Álvarez. 2016. How Safe Are Caribbean Homes for Women and Children? Attitudes Toward Intimate Partner Violence and Corporal Punishment. Policy Brief No. IDP-PB-258. Washington, DC: Inter-American Development Bank.

Tekkas Kerman, Kader, and Patricia Betrus. 2020. Violence Against Women in Turkey: A Social-Ecological Framework of Determinants and Prevention Strategies. *Trauma, Violence, & Abuse* 21 (3): 510–526. https://doi.org/10.1177/1524838018781104.

Wallace, Wendell C., Cherrie Gibson, N. Gordon, Rennie Lakhan, Jinnalee Mahabir, and Cassandra Seetahal. 2019. Domestic Violence: Intimate Partner Violence Victimization Non-reporting to the Police in Trinidad and Tobago *Justice Policy Journal* 16 (1): 1–30. http://www.cjcj.org/uploads/cjcj/documents/intimate_partner_domestic_violence_victimization_non_reporting_to_police_trinidad_tobago.pdf.

CHAPTER 9

Exploring Domestic Abuse in the Seventh-day Adventist Church

Edward Clarke

This chapter seeks to explore the presence of domestic abuse in the church, with special reference to the Seventh-day Adventist Church (SDAC), and failure of the local SDA church(es) and the corporate entity (conference), to provide emotional and support care services, to victims of domestic abuse. My interest in this investigation was aroused when I encountered a young married woman who experienced domestic abuse, psychological and physical, and felt unable to seek assistance from members and the church pastor. Her reluctance was based on stories she heard from other female members who sought help, but did not receive the empathy, compassion, and emotional support they needed. My interest was piqued and I wanted to verify the truthfulness of this allegation and to enquire about the occurrence of domestic abuse in the church. In addition, I assumed also, that if domestic abuse occurred, there would be support services provided by the Women's Ministries Department of the Church. Many questions engaged my mind. Was

E. Clarke (✉)
School of Social Science, University of the Southern Caribbean, Saint Joseph, Trinidad and Tobago

A. M. Bissessar and C. Huggins (eds.), *Domestic Violence in the Anglophone Caribbean*,
https://doi.org/10.1007/978-3-030-88476-5_9

the young lady I met an isolated case or a reoccurring incidence of domestic abuse in her congregation and in the wider church? Was the church uncaring and unempathetic towards members who were abused and sought emotional support? Did the church provide emotional and psychological support services to its members? If provided, were these services meeting adequately the needs of victims? There were more questions than answers. The chapter attempts to answer some of these questions by examining the lived experience of six victims of domestic abuse. It is difficult for some people to think of domestic abuse occurring in Christian families and in churches, where the sanctity of marriage is extolled and spouses are encouraged to make God the guiding force in their lives. In the absence of data on domestic abuse in a church population—specifically the Seventh-day Adventist Church—in Trinidad and Tobago and the Caribbean, and without the financial resources and time to conduct a comprehensive study of domestic abuse in Trinidad and Tobago it was decided to conduct a qualitative pilot study of domestic abuse among married women attending the SDA church in Trinidad. This initiative proved difficult because the purposive sample selected, subsequently became apprehensive and withdrew. It was later decided to use snowball sampling—a nonprobability sampling technique, in which existing subjects provide referrals to recruit samples required for the research study. This technique identified six married women in the age range 25–50, from three countries,—two women from each country respectively,—Trinidad, Barbados, and St Lucia. All the participants were "equally yoked",—married to baptised church members. Men were not selected for this explorative study because the main suffers of domestic abuse are women. Data from the Crime And Problem Analysis (CAPA) Branch of the Trinidad & Tobago Police Service (TTPS) revealed that there were approximately 11,441 reports relating to domestic violence incidents between 2010 and 2015. Approximately 75% of these reports were related to female individuals. During the same period, there were 131 domestic violence-related deaths of which 56% were female (http://www.opmgcagov.tt/gender/genderinitiatives).

Guided Questions

The following questions guided the virtual study. Based on your interaction with women in your church how widespread is domestic abuse?

Who are the main perpetrators? In your opinion what are the main causes of domestic abuse? For how long have you experienced domestic abuse? Why did you stay in an abusive relationship? Have you discussed the abuse with anyone or sought help? Did you seek help from the church? Do local churches and conferences provide the emotional support services that you need when you want to talk to someone?

Domestic Abuse

The United Nations notes that, domestic abuse, also called "domestic violence" or "intimate partner violence", can be defined as a pattern of behaviour in any relationship that is used to gain or maintain power and control over an intimate partner. Abuse is physical, sexual, emotional, economic, or psychological actions or threats of actions that influence another person. This includes any behaviours that frighten, intimidate, terrorise, manipulate, hurt, humiliate, blame, injure, or wound someone. Domestic abuse can happen to anyone of any race, age, sexual orientation, religion, or gender. It can occur within a range of relationships including couples who are married, living together, or dating "In this chapter domestic abuse refers to physical and emotional abuse/violence against an individual—mostly women. A report from the World Health Organisation, indicates that globally, 1 in 3 women will suffer abuse in their lifetime, (https://www.who.int/domestic/violence).

In a European Union survey of twenty-eight member states, 1 in 10 women experienced some form of sexual violence since the age of 15, and one in 20 (approximately 5%) has been raped. Just over one in five women has experienced physical and/or sexual violence from either a current or previous partner, and just over one in 10 women indicates that they have experienced some form of sexual violence by an adult before they were 15 years old (EU Report 2015).

In the Church

These global statistics present a chilling story about what happens to women mainly in their homes, but what about elsewhere, more specifically in church? It may be challenging for society to accept that domestic abuse can and does occur in church, the citadel of love, grace, and spiritual upliftment. Has domestic abuse has entered the church, more specifically the SDA church? In the absence of local and regional data on domestic abuse among church attendees, it was necessary to look at international data to gain an overview of the scale of the problem. A number of international studies looked at domestic abuse in the church. In 2009 the Methodist Church in the United Kingdom conducted a survey and found that, 17% of respondents had experienced domestic abuse. The main perpetrators of violence were husbands and partners (https://www.methodist.org.uk/downloads/conference).

Christianity Magazine, in conjunction with RESTORE (a non-profit organisation), conducted a survey (77% female and 23% male); 97% of whom were churchgoers. They discovered that 40% of women had suffered some form of intimidation and emotional abuse—"putdowns"—such as, being told that they "were too fat, too thin, ugly or stupid", while 16% had suffered some form of physical violence,—being pushed, slapped, or hit with an object. The majority of the respondents (87%) reported that domestic violence occurred because a partner wanted to control the relationship. "However, only 42% agreed with the statement: 'My church is a safe place for people suffering abuse,' while 40% were unsure of who to contact in their church if they, or someone they knew, were suffering domestic abuse. Rob Parsons, Chair of Care for the Family, said: 'In our experience, the second deepest hurt of those who have suffered abuse is so often having nobody who will listen to their plight".

In another study, The Evangelical Alliance UK in its "How's the Family?" report, (2012), found that of the 1219 people responding to the Survey Monkey study, 10% of women experienced physical abuse in their relationship and 7% of men admitted perpetrating physical abuse. Figures for unfaithfulness were 9%. Finally, a study done by Drumm et al. (2006) on domestic violence among Seventh-Day Adventists (SDAs) in America, sampled one thousand four hundred and thirty-one (1431) SDAs of both genders (61% female and 39% male) in 70 churches in a 5-state area in the United States and found high levels of intimate partner violence among SDAs. More specifically, the study found that, 65% reported that they had experienced controlling and demeaning behaviour at least once in their lifetime, 46% experienced common couple violence, 29% reported sexual violence, and 10% severe physical violence. These studies demonstrated that domestic abuse is present in church, irrespective of denomination.

Not in My Church Domestic abuse results from a mismanagement of the power relationship between men and women. One person believes that he or she is better or superior, and desires to control the other. This attitude often results in disagreements, conflict, exploitation, emotional, and physical abuse. To think that such thoughts and behaviours can be found in the body of Christ—the church—is an unpleasant reality for most Christians, especially Christian leaders. Consequently, a discussion about domestic abuse in the church often results in senior clergy becoming defensive, with comments and remarks such as, "Domestic violence has nothing to do with religion. 'It is about the sinful nature in people.' It is not a major problem here", I was told by a Seventh-Day Adventist administrator.

Interestingly, findings of a survey, of one thousand (1000) pastors conducted by Lifeway Research in the summer of 2018 reported that, thirty-seven (37%) of pastors said, they believe that domestic and sexual violence does NOT occur in their congregations. While being confident that their church would be a safe haven for victims of domestic violence, 47% of Baptist pastors did not know if anyone in their church had been a victim of domestic violence. Further, if pastors were aware, they often did not know how to help. Consequently, only half said they had a plan in place to help if a victim came forward (6).

The reactions of Christian leaders to domestic abuse among their congregations are not surprising. However, to assume that domestic violence is a minor issue, which does not directly affect the church, is to pursue a deceptive path that enhances the damage done by the perpetrators of domestic violence.

Lived Experiences of Female Victims of Domestic Abuse

In order to explore the dynamics of domestic abuse in the SDA, a small sample of six participants, victims of physical and emotional abuse were selected by snowball sampling. All of the female participants were married to SDAs men and were interviewed via Zoom or cell phone by the author. The names of participants, husbands, elders, and pastors mentioned in the text are aliases in order to protect the privacy and confidentiality of the respondents.

The participants in the study, were asked questions relating to: what factors caused their domestic abuse, and duration of abuse; reasons for staying in the abusive relationship; with whom did they discuss the abusive relationship; did they seek and receive emotional support from church members or clergy during the period of abuse?

Findings

In summary, responses to questions: Participants were in the age range 25–50 years, and were "equally yoked"—formerly married to baptised members of the Seventh-Day Adventist church. All of the participants were current members of the SDA church at the time of the interview. They were asked: based on your interaction with women in your church how widespread is domestic abuse? All of the respondents noted that domestic abuse was fairly widespread but was covered up. "We don't like to talk about these things, because there are not nice, we prefer to keep quiet", was one response that captured the sentiment of the respondents.

There was a unanimous agreement that men were the main perpetrators of domestic abuse. When asked what were the main causes of domestic abuse, answers included: cheating/unfaithfulness, lying, broken promises, unresolved arguments which lead to physical abuse; cell phone secrecy, intimidation, controlling behaviour, and poor communication. For howlong did you experience abuse? The period of abuse lasted between two–five years. Reasons for staying in the abuse relationship, included: "it was too early in the relationship to leave; "I hoped and prayed that he would change", "I married for the long-term", "I didn't want to bring shame on my family and the church", "I had to think about the children".

While experiencing abuse did you talk about it with anyone or sought help? There was mixed response to this question. Some respondents spoke to family members, including female siblings, mother, adopted mother, and best friend. Respondents shared their experiences with significant others they trusted, because they felt stressed, depressed, overwhelmed, confused, and unsure about what to do.

- Lack of emotional and psychological support services.
- These themes will be discussed in relationship to the lived experience of participants.

Cheating/Infidelity

Infidelity, or cheating, is the act of being unfaithful to a spouse or partner. It typically means engaging in sexual or romantic relations with a person other than one's spouse. However, it can imply inappropriate behaviour with a person of opposite gender. When Ruth discovered that her husband was having an affair she was devastated and heartbroken. "How could this happen to me," she questioned? "I am not married for one year yet!" Ruth found herself alone in her misery with destructive thoughts, struggling with her position as a role model for single girls, and newly married couples in the church.

Barbara's experience was similar. She fell in love with a Christian young man when she joined the church. It was what she had prayed for, and was full of expectation. She exclaimed, "we were so madly in love, on second thought, I think lust. I ignored all the warning signs, he was such a nice guy, everybody liked him.

One day I discovered a red bra in his car. I was nervous, dizzy and too shocked to speak about it. Two days, later I confronted him about it. He was stuck for words, and replied that he did not know how the bra was on the floor of the back seat. I knew he was lying". He offered an explanation. "It probably fell out of someone's bag, when I gave them a lift". "The main issue was his continuing lying, and cheating. I would always catch him out, then he would become angry and begin to push me around, punch me and bang my head against the wall, in an attempt to shut me up". Betty, another participant, emigrated from England to her native country because she was fed up with the British weather and lonely life. She joined the SDA church and was an active member. Two years later, she met and married the head elder of the church. He represented the spiritual uprightness that she admired and desired in a man. Reflecting on the occasion she opined, "I considered myself lucky. He was single, handsome, preached the word well, a businessman, popular among the brethren, equally yoked (she chuckled), and came from good Adventist stock, what more could I ask for".

After two years, she discovered that he was cheating and had several ladies in and out of church. This discovery was the onset of many fierce arguments, verbal, and physical assaults. She would often check his cell phone and find disturbing messages. Renell, a young aspiring lawyer and Keisha, a teacher experienced emotional and physical abuse when they confronted their spouses about These young women were disappointed, and overwhelmed by their experience and did not know what to do. Renell, who was newlywed—eighteen months—was emotionally torn between wanting to leave, and staying, with the hope that he would change. The embarrassment of leaving and the pain of staying created an unhealthy mental state which resulted in depression for Renell. All of these respondents shared a common experience, unfaithful spouses. In spite of their long-suffering attitude, they were unable to save their relationships from separation and divorce.

Suffering Silently

Suffering silently was the hallmark of these abused wives. Ruth remarked, "I was trapped in a marriage and did not knowing how to exit. The consequences were too enormous for me to consider leaving. All I wanted was to save my marriage. I liked being married. Family means a lot to me, I didn't have a family when I was growing up". "As wife of a popular pastor, how could I face the congregations? Who would believe that Pastor Matthews is a wife beater? How would I explain myself? If I talked to church members, this would cause shame and embarrassment to my family, relatives and endanger my husband's job. I also wanted to protect my children from gossip. So I continued to live a 'normal' life, pretending yet fearful, loyal yet broken".

Barbara reflecting on her experience, said, "people always ask these questions. Why did you stay? Why didn't you talk to somebody? They do not understand how difficult it is. You don't marry to get divorce. You marry for keeps. Plus you don't want people to know that your marriage is in trouble, especially in a church. The young people are looking at you as a role model and the older members are full of expectation. It is a very embarrassing situation, so you sit it out, you make a sacrifice, hope and pray for the best".

Tamara, was more forthright with her response. She noted, "I wanted to talk about it. I approached my mother's friend, but she told me not to be hasty, because it is just a phase he is going through, all men go through this phase when they just get married", she assured me. "It was difficult for me to accept that, because they was no reason for him to be cheating, and when I complain he start hitting, pushing and shoving me". Of significance is the fact that Tamara, although being assertive about her situation, endured much suffering hoping that her husband would change. Instead, the abuse worsened, and her silent acquiescence emboldened the abuser.

Betty was less fearful of the church community response, and approached senior ladies and pastor, informing them of her marital problems and need for an intervention. The leaders promised to intervene. Betty was very disappointed when nothing happened. She reminded herself that, "his brother was the senior sadministrator, and he knew what was going on, but made no attempt to assist. He never called me. They eventually removed him from his position in the church, but no one came to give me support. His family turned against me, even though they knew he was cheating". Suffering in silence should not be viewed as a badge of toughness or obedience to some scriptural principal or promise, "till death us do part", but a sign of fear which strengthens the abuser.

Support Services

None of the respondents reported being aware, that the SDA church, at local or conference (corporate) level, provided emotional and psychological support services for victims of domestic abuse. Neither were they aware of any promotional activity that informed women where to go or who to contact if they needed emotional and psychological support for domestic abuse.

However, the laity acknowledged that each church had a Women's Ministry group, but viewed this Church department as a main concern with promoting religious witnessing and programme planning.

This view was validated by a General Conference (GC) flyer which stated, "The Department of Women's Ministries exists to uphold, encourage, and challenge Adventist women in their pilgrimage as disciples of Jesus Christ and members of His world church" (https://women.adventist.org). Our findings revealed that some respondents did not know who to approach for help, others were reluctant to seek help because of distrust, while others contacted senior church members and pastor but did not receive any assistance. Personal discussion with a Woman's Ministry administrator noted that, "we have many calls for help, but without a counsellor, we refer.... we are unable to follow-up". To whom I queried? "Private practitioners", was the reply. Emotional Abuse Emotional abuse ranks as one of the most pernicious forms of domestic abuse. The scars of emotional abuse are real and long-lasting. Healing is slow and painful and often creates collateral damage to other personal relationships. While the scars of physical abuse are visible on the outside, the same cannot be said about emotional wounds. Unless a person speaks about theiremotional distress associated with being emotionally or mentally abused, there is no seeing the wounds that have scarred the victim, damaged for a lifetime.

According to David Hawkins (2018), thirty-five percent (35%) of married women experience some or all of the following aspects of emotional abuse: Constant criticism, excessive jealousy, use of power to control and overwhelm, intimidation and threats, control of finances, authority/spiritual abuse, isolation from family/friends and punishment if she doesn't comply with his wishes.

An impromptu meeting with a small group of young married women made me aware of the fact, that there are several married women in the church, experiencing emotional abuse, more than I had imagined. The women in this groupwere complaining, that their husbands were disrespectful, controlling, verbally abusive at times, and engaged in threateningbehaviour. One of the participants Gloria, experienced emotional abuse from her husband. Gloria is a forty-year-old entrepreneur, managing her own cosmetic business with fifteen (15) employees, for the past six (6) years. Always well-dressed, educated, articulate, and self-confident, a role model to many young women in the church and her community. Gloria lived two very different lives. In the office, she was an assertive, self-assured entrepreneur, at home a cowed nervous wreck, who subsequently became very ill. Although she was the main income earner for the family she lacked respect and validation from her husband. He displayed an aggressive attitude and would verbally abuse and be little her in front of their children complaining about her poor parenting skills, style of dressing, and hair extensions which he disliked. "I think he is cheating on me" she muses, "but I am afraid to confront him because he might get aggressive and create a lot of confusion, it is best to let sleeping dogs lie, I'll just keep praying". She had spoken to her mother and sister about her domestic problems but did not get the emotional support from family members that she needed. When asked if she had contacted anyone in church she replied, "I am not sure how they can help. I don't know who to talk to". Not knowing who to contact when help is needed is a critical factor in help-seeking behaviour of many victims. Who can victims trust to self-disclose? In most churches the pastors are males and older women occupy senior positions. Do these conditions enable confidence in victims? Gloria's inability to identify someone with whom she could self-disclose about her domestic problems raised a number questions. From whom should Gloria seek assistance and advice? Gloria admits that she is not ready to separate or divorce her spouse, but would like them to have counselling sessions, to address their problems before it gets worse. During my conversation with Tamara, she recounted many unpleasant instances and told me of other young women in church who were experiencing similar emotionally abusive marital relationships. What should Tamara do? From whom should she seek assistance and advice in the church? Is there a dedicated, experienced, trustworthy person to whom she could speak about her or deal? Should she continue to pray for her abusive husband and trust God to deliver her? What is the role of the church in such situations? Personal investigation revealed that in SDA churches, there is no formal support services for abused women. The informal service is not promoted or staffed by qualified professionals.

The Role of the Church in Domestic Abuse

The Church should provide an intervention role in treating the issue of domestic abuse. In keeping with its ethos of nurturing and unifying families, the church has a critical role in ensuring that the family is supported spiritually, emotionally, and psychosocially. The church needs to provide at a basic level, emotional support to members who are hurting, more specifically, victims of domestic abuse.

Laura Hughes (2017) defines emotional support, as listening and offering, "empathy and compassion to someone when they are communicating how they are feeling to us; it is about being non-judgemental and allowing someone to express themselves in a safe and supported relationship or interaction. It is about not imposing our views or opinions on someone, but letting them feel accepted for expressing the way they feel—warts and all". Unfortunately, as witnessed in reports from participants, the church seems detached and inactive, oftentimes unaware that families are hurting and children are being impacted by family violence, either because the church community is fractured, pastoral counselling services are unavailable, or privacy and confidentiality is suspect. Additionally, if the church does become aware, there is usually hesitancy or refusal to get involved when victims cry for help. The Bible, on which church practices are founded, promotes what a loving relationship between a married couple should be. It is, the essential requirement, for

> "Husbands, to love your wives, and do not be harsh with them". Colossians 3:19.

> "live with your wives in an understanding way; showing honour to the woman as the weaker vessel, since they are heirs with you of the grace of life, so that your prayers may not be hindered". 1 Peter 3:7

Not withstanding this, the disclosure of infidelity and abuse by a victim is seldom taken to clergy. The Church must be proactive. While some may excuse the church's reluctance to get involved with family matters, others hold the view that it is necessary to provide appropriate pastoral care and support for victims and abusers, and not subject them to further victimisation, blame, and shame. What can the local church do to assist victims of domestic abuse? End it now, a global initiative by SDAs posits, that the church can be a refuge for women fleeing domestic abuse. But sometimes they can help perpetuate abuse by failing to offer support when needed. Sometimes it's because church leaders simplydon't understand—or are not willing to accept—that domestic abuse occurs within their congregations (8).

The respondents in this study did not perceive the church as a safe place to go for support. When there is abuse in the family, the victims usually donot know who to contact, there are no designated support services for victims and survivors of abuse. Additionally, there are issuesaround privacy and confidentiality, basic components of counselling service.

The Seventh-Day Adventist church, regards thefamily as an essential building block of church and society, the church has a responsibility to care for, protect the most vulnerable members, women and children, and deal with domestic abuse as it should with other wrong doings. "Call sin by its right name. Declare what God has said in regard to lying, Sabbath breaking, stealing, idolatry, and every other evil", (including adultery, my emphasis).... "the church must show that she does not sanction their deeds, or she herself dishonours her Lord"—Ellen White, Desire of Ages.

Is the Church Responsive?

The question that remains unanswered, is church administrators aware of the prevalence or incidence of domestic abuse in the church? If they are, what is being done about it? Is the church responsive to the needs of domestic abused members? Has the church provided the services abused victims require? Natalie Hoffman posits that, for the church: "the first priority, marriage, is held in revered esteem regardless of whether it is toxic or healthy; the investment is in being the Saviour of the marriage, the focus is to change the abuser in order to achieve, save, the number one priority, the marriage; the marriage itself is worshiped while the human lives and souls within the family are treated with less importance; women of faith, in toxic marriages are afraid to tell people at church. They don't want to embarrass their husbands or be seen as a bad wife who is "tearing down her husband", and bringing shame to the family, therefore the church is uninformed and doesn't respond; often emotional abuse lies under the radar, few persons know about it, victims are reluctant to talk about it, "everyone knows, but no one knows", others may be oblivious to what is happening, because domestic/emotional abuse is not easy to spot, and it is usually viewed as the normal 'ups and downs' of married life; they are worried that nobody will understand what they are going through, and that complaining would worsen their situation". The testimonies of participants in the study, inferred that they were either not aware of emotional support services, or that these services were not available in the local SDA churches they attended. It is important to note that in some churches their members who are professional counsellors and social workers, who can assist if asked.

Outcomes

If domestic abuse is left unresolved, the marital relationship deteriorates, threatening the survival of the marriage, often resulting in one of the spouses not attending church. This was the reality for Patricia, one of my respondents—who was not included in the study, for whom emotional abuse was ignored and developed into severe physical abuse resulting in her ending the abuser's life in self-defence.

The SDA Corporate Response to Domestic Abuse

The SDA church is not ignorant of the severity and magnitude of treating the issue of domestic abuse. At the highest administrative structures—General Conference (GC), Division, Union and Conference levels, workshops are held,—presentations made, marches and annual campaigns are conducted, by "End It Now",—which had a struggle inception,—are initiatives utilised to treat with the issue of domestic abuse at a global level. However, these activities are not translated into visible services at the local church level.

The Seventh-Day Adventist corporate position on domestic abuse, states emphatically that there is "no room among Christ's followers for tyrannical control and the abuse of power or authority. The church, 'household of faith,' functions as an extended family, offering acceptance, understanding, and comfort to all, especially to those who are hurting or disadvantaged".

While acknowledging that family violence occurs in many Christian homes, "it can never be condoned, by the church", because, "it severely affects the lives of all involved and often results in long term distorted perceptions of God, self, and others. It is our belief that the Church has a responsibility". Therefore it is critical for the church: "To care for those involved in family violence and to respond to their needs by: (a) Listening to and accepting those suffering from abuse, loving and affirming them as persons of value and worth. (b) Highlighting the injustices of abuse and speaking out in defence of victims both within the community of faith and in society. (c) Providing a caring, supportive ministry to families affected by violence and abuse, seeking to enable both victims and perpetrators to access counseling with Seventh-day Adventist professionals where available or other professional resources in the community. (d) Encouraging the training and placement of licensed Seventh-day Adventist professional services for both church members and the surrounding communities. (e) Offering a ministry of reconciliation when the perpetrator's repentance makes possible the contemplation of forgiveness and restoration in relationships" (11).

In addition, the SDA church declared that such abusive behaviour is a violation of Seventh-Day Adventist Christian standards. Any indications or reports of abuse must not be minimised but seriously considered. "For church members to remain indifferent and unresponsive, is to condone, perpetuate, and possibly extend family violence" (12).

Given these committed statements and clear objectives, why is there limited, and in most cases no, visible or tangible evidence available to validate, and demonstrate the implementation of programmes, structures, and systems to treat with victims of domestic abuse in a holistic manner?

The Way Forward

The findings from our survey have demonstrated that domestic abuse is occurring in the church, more specifically the SDA church. In addition, the corporate policies, admonitions, and pronouncements on domestic abuse have not been translated into tangible action in the churches, and remain more idealistic than realistic. Consequently, there are no established support services for victims of domestic abuse in any of the local churches within the countries from which the participants live. It is therefore incumbent on church leaders at regional and local levels to recognise the need for emotional support services and to establish these services in each church within the Caribbean Union of Seventh-Day Adventists. We have had enough meetings and workshops, action is required.

What can local churches do, in the absence of guidelines from conferences? End it now, a global initiative of the Seventh-Day Adventists to raise awareness and advocate for the end of violence around the world, recommends that: "local churches can ask the pastor or some other qualified person to preach asermon on violence prevention. Ask those who have the main prayer during the worship service to pray for those in thecongregation who are abused. Apply the principle of confidentiality when dealing with victims, Compile complete, up-to-date information about all resources in your community available to victims of any type of gender-based violence. Make sure the information is easily available to members and others. Collect funds and provide your church leaders with educational materials on gender violence. Organise a group to assess the needs in the local community. Present sermons and workshops to the congregation and the community on issues of gender-based violence, relevant to your community. Offer to present age-appropriate information in local schools. Care for hurting people in our church. Be non-judgemental. Develop support groups. Help raise awareness. Share materials about gender-based violence with your community".

RESTORE, a programme of Planned Parenthood, working to transform relationships and end violence against women, identified three activities that the church can implement—*Be Aware, Be Engage and Support* (14). These activities would be beneficial to the establishing of services in churches.

Awareness

Creating awareness, at the church level is critical in laying the foundation for all the services that will be offered. The church must be aware that violence and abusive behaviour are no strangers to families attending our local church. Kudakwashe Nyakudya, a domestic-abuse survivor, notes that "many Christians will not accept the problem, that there is domestic abuse in the church. Where you have domestic abuse, you have deception by the perpetrator, and people need to see the truth. I've seen churches that are trying their best, it's because the pastor has some kind of knowledge". This knowledge must be shared with the laity/congregation, everyone needs it to be aware. Therefore, "the church must take an intentional stand on the issue of abuse and, regularly, provide messages in sermons, workshops, seminars and classes that domestic abuse is inappropriate, un-Christlike and wrong" (15).

"It is important to commit to pray for those affected (victims & perpetrators). The local church can provide a variety of promotional resources-posters, cards, leaflets and the church's website to publicly indicate that domestic abuse is unacceptable and against God's plan for Christian families". Finally, "the church must acknowledge the real pain and victimization caused by physical and emotional abuse and provide opportunities for healing and reconciliation for those who have been injured" (16).

Be Engage

Being engaged, involves the church becoming a safe place, with more considered actions taken by the congregation and leadership.RESTORE asserts that, "Church leaders, (especially directors of Women and Men Ministry my italics) should improve theirunderstanding of domestic abuse by consulting the various online resources, e.g. Thirty-one: eight, (formerly Churches ChildProtection Advisory Service (CCPAS), RESTORE and read books on the subject to be better informed. In addition, "engage and Educate the church by inviting local and international domestic abuse specialist, to do presentations and/or training. Reserve a dayon the church calendar, (Nov. 25 is the international day of action to end violence against women), when your church will focus on increasing awareness of issues linked to domestic abuse issues".

It is commended that "Women Ministry should workcollaboratively with Men's Ministry to plan special workshops and training for boys and men on "what it means to be a man, that is,walking in the footsteps of Jesus". RESTORE (2016) Finding a safe place is the desire of most victims of domestic abuse, a place of reflection, a refuge from the frequent abuse and emotional turmoil. A place where empathy, spiritual comfort, and reassurance can be found. The church needs to be that place, where victims find support.

Support RESTORE recommends that, the church should, "work together with local service providers to establish systems, procedures and clear pathways for referral of survivors and perpetrators". Support for these initiates should be a budgeted item on the annual financial Plan. There is a need to provide trained staff and first responders in church, who can facilitate and provide comfort, guidance, and reassurance to victims. These non-professionals should be supported with good clinical supervision. In-church support services should ensure safety and confidentiality, for women and their children. The lack of confidentiality was identified as a significant deterrent for abused persons not seeking assistance from church services and leaders.

In addition **RESTORE** (2016) has identified the "4Rs" that the Church can implement in responding to domestic abuse: Recognise, Respond, Refer, and Record "RECOGNISE, implies being socially aware, acknowledging that domestic abuse occurs in church families and it is a sign of power and control in a relationship".

RECOGNISE, implies being socially aware, acknowledging that domestic abuse occurs in church families and it is a sign of power and control in a relationship.

RESPOND, "accept the victims statements and respond empathetically, 'I believe you' is a helpful first response. Do not ask for proof of violence, assure the victim of your interest and concern, let her know that it is not her fault. It is critical that privacy and confidentiality is maintained, but do not forget to explain the boundaries of confidentiality".

REFER, "if the church lacks the support services or the professional expertise to manage abuse situation(s) victims should be referred to qualified local professionals".

RECORD, "keep a record (dates, times, quotes, actions, and process notes of important information shared by the victim".

In most abusive situations, men play a central role, therefore it is essential that the church provides support services for abusers. It is important to get men to understand their role in the family and the need for mutual respect and dignity between partners/spouses.

Conclusion

Finally, the study revealed that there is domestic abuse in the SDA church, the extent of which remains concealed and unexplored. The local church(es) are not equipped to provide emotional and psychological support services to victims of domestic abuse, consequently victims suffer silently.

International studies have established that domestic abuse is present in "the body of Christ"—the church. Findings from studies done in the UK among Methodist and Evangelicals found that 17% and 10%, respectively, of the samples, experienced domestic abuse. A pioneering study done by Drumm et al. (2006) among Seven-Day Adventists in 70 churches in 5 States, reported that 65% of the sample (1431), experienced controlling and demeaning behaviour at least once in their lifetime, 46% experienced common couple violence, 29% reported sexual violence and 10% severe physical violence. Findings, from the lived experience of respondents in the pilot survey, revealed that church attendees in the SDA church experience domestic abuse. This study is small and a general conclusion cannot be drawn about domestic abuse in the SDA church.

Abuse victims in the study, were hesitant to seek support from the church because of: a perceived distrust of church members and clergy, personal feelings of shame, stigma and guilt, "what would they think about me", Ruth reminds me: protection of husbands' reputation and a socioreligious conviction, that marriage is a life commitment.
An important factor limiting help-seeking behaviour of victims of domestic abuse, is the absence of emotional and psychological support services at local churches and conferences, in the three countries in which respondents live. Personal communication from a senior administrator at one of the conferences, revealed that there are no professional services available at the churches because of financial resources, so referral becomes the main option. The corporate policy of the SDA church states emphatically that there is "no room among Christ's followers for tyrannical control and the abuse of power or authority. It can never be condoned, by the church because, it severely affects the lives of all involved and often results in long term distorted perceptions of God, self, and others". The SDA church through its agency Enditnow, is a global advocate to stop domestic violence. However, this initiative is not implemented at local churches in Trinidad and Tobago, Barbados, and St Lucia.

This study highlights the need for a comprehensive study of domestic abuse in the church, across denominations, in Trinidad and Tobago and the Caribbean. The church has a socioreligious and societal responsibility to provide a place of emotional comfort, healing, and safety for the—hurting, broken, lonely—victims of domestic abuse.

References

Adventist Women's Ministries. https://women.adventist.org.

Ashley Madison. Affairs and Discreet Marriage Dating. htpps://www.ashleymadison.com.

Brenda Branson and Paula Silva, *Pastor's Guide-Dealing with Domestic Violence.*

Church Times, 2021, June 17, Thursday. Clifford Steve.

David Hawkins, Marriage 911 (2018).

David Williams, Effectively Confronting the Challenge of Domestic Violence.

Drumm, R.D., M. Popescu, D. McBride, G. Hopkins, J. Thayer, and J. Wrenn. 2006. Intimate Partner Violence in a Conservative Christian Denomination. *Social Work & Christianity* 33: 233–252.

Ellen White, Education, p. 57. https://ellenwhite.info.

Ellen White, Desire of Ages, p. 805. https://ellenwhite.info.

European Union Report (2015). *Violence Against Women: A European Wide Survey.*

Global Status Report on Violence Prevention (2014). https://www.who.int/domestic/violence.

Hoffman, N. 2018. *Is it Me Making Sense of Your confusing Marriage?: A Christian Woman's Guide to Hidden Emotional and Spiritual Abuse.* Rosemount, MN: Flying Free Media.

How's the Family?' Evangelical Alliance Report 2011.

How's the Family?' Evangelical Alliance Report 2012. https://www.eauk.org/church/resources/snapshot/hows-the-family.cfm.

Laura Hughes, Amber Counselling (updated 2017). *The difference between Counselling and Emotional Support.*

Lifeway Research. Baptist Press, Bob Smietana, Church Response to Domestic Violence focus of study, 2017. https://lifewayresearch.com

Lucinda van der Hart (2013). Domestic violence and the UK Church, Premier Christianity.

Martin, Grant L., Counselling for family Violence and Abuse.

National Coalition Against Domestic Violence's website at www.ncadv.org.

Nyakudya, Kudakwashe. Founder of Kahrmel Wellness, Cited in Church Times, Churches urged to tackle Domestic Violence by Gavin Drake, 2014.

Office of National Statistics. 2014. *Crime Survey England and Wales 2013–2014.* London: Office for National Statistics.

Restored, Ending Domestic Abuse, 2016.

Seventh-Day Adventist-Position on Domestic Violence. *General Conference of Seventh-Day Adventists Administrative Committee (ADCOM) on August 27, 1996.*

CHAPTER 10

Escape to Safety: Seeking Shelter from Domestic Violence—The Case of *Madinah House* (1999–2019)

Amina Ibrahim-Ali and Nura Amina Ali

Introduction

Madinah House, a temporary shelter, was founded in 1999 in Trinidad to respond to the needs of battered women and their children who, having escaped their abuse, were forced to deal with practical issues such as housing and safety. In 2019, after having housed more than 1200 clients and their children, the shelter was closed due to insufficient funding to manage its daily expenses and to complete outstanding repair work on its building. This chapter provides information on the day-to-day operations of *Madinah House*, and, in so doing, contributes to an under-researched area related to gender-based violence in the Caribbean, i.e. safe houses. The two authors, former board members, follow a narrative approach

A. Ibrahim-Ali (✉) · N. A. Ali
University of the West Indies, St. Augustine, Trinidad and Tobago
e-mail: amina.ibrahim-ali@sta.uwi.edu

A. M. Bissessar and C. Huggins (eds.), *Domestic Violence in the Anglophone Caribbean*,
https://doi.org/10.1007/978-3-030-88476-5_10

in examining individual client files, journals, and letters, and conducting interviews with former shelter managers. Findings document the 20-year contribution of *Madinah House* and deepen the understanding of the circumstances of battered women, and the key interventions which afford them support.

In 2001, a review was conducted of the ten Caribbean OAS member states, including Trinidad and Tobago, who had, in June 1994, adopted the Inter-American Convention on the Prevention, Punishment, and Eradication of Violence Against Women[1] (Chin and Dandurand 2001). The scarcity of women's shelters was noted and, so too, that those and other crisis services which existed, were under-resourced and did not sufficiently meet the needs of victims. The physical location of shelters was found to be unable to guarantee the safety of women and their children who felt threatened and frightened by acts of retaliation by their abusers. While the police had begun to ensure the safety of shelter occupants from further acts of violence, the review noted that physical safety, in conjunction with emotional support and skills training, was necessary for battered women to be financially independent of their abusive spouses/partners. The review also remarked on the dearth of reliable data on the nature of violence against women, the relationships between battered women and their abusers, and the consequences of their victimization.

More recent information on Trinidad and Tobago's status with respect to the 1994 Convention showed compliance in some key areas. The *Trinidad and Tobago Country Report* (2017) remarked on the existing number of civil society organizations which were managing domestic violence issues, the introduction of a national domestic violence hotline, 800-SAVE, which had been established through the Office of the Prime Minister (Gender and Child Affairs), and the availability of shelters run by non-governmental bodies.

The question of reliable data on gender-based violence was, however, still of concern in 2018. A green paper issued by the Government of Trinidad and Tobago in that year, attributed the lack of knowledge about gender-based violence to insufficient data, as had the aforementioned 2001 review, although the poor coordination and evaluation of programmes on gender-based violence were also considered to be causal factors. The causes, consequences, and response mechanisms to reduce the incidence of gender-based violence were therefore not fully understood, and those mechanisms led by non-governmental organizations remained under-resourced and under-supported. Among the policy measures to be instituted, mentioned in the government publication, were the amendment of legislation and response mechanisms to counteract gender-based violence. These included the Domestic Violence Act 1999, the Sexual Offences Act 2000 and the Children's Authority Act, and protection orders, counselling services, and shelters which supported the legislation (*National Policy on Gender and Development* 2018).

Shelters were, not solely dependent on government subventions, but also sourced funds from the corporate and private sectors and held fundraising events throughout the year. Chairman of *The Shelter for Battered Women and Children*, Scott Hamilton, said, that maintaining women and children on a daily basis required significant funding. This was in spite of increased outreach and fundraising activities. Hamilton spoke of the provision of nutritious meals, clothing, transportation, healthcare, equipping children for school, and assisting women in sourcing suitable housing and employment.

In 2020, the running of shelters for battered women in Trinidad and Tobago was notably affected by issues of funding. Of the 14 shelters in operation, four were forced to close. President of the Coalition Against Domestic Violence, Roberta Clarke, announced the closure of *Madinah House*, and the founder of *Conflict Women*, Asiya Mohammed, declared that, although the 2019/2020 national budget had made provision for the building of more shelters for women, additional state support was essential for those shelters that were currently in operation[2] (Kong-Soo 2020).

Background

Madinah House, a non-profit company incorporated under the Companies (1995) Act, was a shelter located on leased premises in Trinidad which serviced battered women and their children from February 1999 to October 2019.[3] *Madinah House* was established by a group of Muslims called "MusServ" (Muslims in Service) under Guidance Officer in the Ministry of Education of Trinidad and Tobago, Gayaz Rajab. Rajab's postgraduate education in Counselling, Human Services, and Social Work afforded him the opportunity to work with schools in the Central Education Division and to recognize the pressing need for safe spaces for battered women and their children. In 2005 and 2007, respectively, *Madinah House* was registered as a non-governmental and non-profit organization.

Over the twenty years of its existence and in the interest of safeguarding the protection of its clients, *Madinah House* kept its location hidden from the general public. The shelter was permitted the use of St. Kevin's College in San Fernando as its mailing address. Referrals were initially made by other non-governmental bodies and government offices. Thereafter, in the interest of accountability, all cases were directed to the police station and a receipt was obtained before the police contacted 800-SAVE to find suitable shelter accommodation.

The shelter was managed by a board of Muslim women under the patronage of former First Lady, Zalayhar Hassanali, with its day-to-day operations dependent on a manager and two matrons who served as in-house counsellors. By December 2018, *Madinah House* had sheltered 1208 people; 480 women and 728 children, including victims of human trafficking. In October 2019, the shelter was forced to close owing to inadequate funding. State subventions had been granted between 2009 and 2014, after which time, state grants became inconsistent. Incoming donations from the corporate and private sectors and monies generated from fund-raising activities were insufficient to cover recurring expenses and to maintain the premises which were in need of repair.

Research Questions

The research questions for this chapter were as follows:

1. What were the physical and operational structures of *Madinah House*?
2. What services did *Madinah House* offer over its twenty-year period of existence?
3. Who stood to benefit from these services, and what were their circumstances?
4. What were the challenges encountered in keeping women safe and providing assistance to them?

Literature Review

Other chapters in this volume focus on domestic violence in its various forms as authors bring to light some of the distinctive outcomes of primarily gender-based violence. As Modeste-James and Huggins

(Chapter 1) and Clarke (Chapter 9) discuss the impact of domestic violence on children, and the contradiction between religion and the abuse of girls and women respectively, they bring the question of violence against women and children into focus. This chapter will also elucidate some of the key elements involved in violence against women and children, given that during the twenty-year period of its operation *Madinah House* provided shelter for both women and their children. In accordance with the findings in the present study, the bulk of this review will: (1) examine the phenomenon of child abuse and demonstrate its association with domestic violence; (2) elucidate the concept of family in the Caribbean in conjunction with family violence, and (3) elaborate on the relationship between both real, or suspected infidelity or romantic jealousy (RJ) and intimate partner violence (IPV).

Any form of actual or potential neglect or maltreatment which causes harm to the development, dignity, health, or survival of an individual under the age of 18, is construed to be child abuse. This includes all forms of emotional, physical and sexual abuse, neglect, and negligence, as well as commercial, or other, exploitation. The propensity of parents and caregivers to maltreat children may increase if they suffered maltreatment as children, have a mental or neurological disorder, are unknowledgeable about child development, and have unrealistic expectations of children. Adults who illtreat children tend to have easy access to, and misuse, drugs and alcohol, are involved in criminal activity, are unemployed, and exist in poor living conditions (*Child Maltreatment* 2020).[4]

Even in those cases where they are not the intended targets, children are affected by violence in the home. In fact, those children who witness domestic violence may be affected in the same way as those who suffer physical and sexual abuse. Children are often threatened or victimized in situations where they are used as a means by an abuser of exerting control over a partner, and they may be unintentionally injured when acts of violence are carried out on the intended victim in their presence. Some shelters have reported that the primary reason that battered women flee their homes is that their abusers were also attacking their children (The relationship between Domestic Violence and Child Abuse).

Child marriage, which was outlawed in Trinidad and Tobago in 2017, also falls within the ambit of child abuse. Child marriage is reported to primarily affect girls, who, as a result of discontinued education and early childbearing, suffer far worse economic and health outcomes than their unmarried peers (UNICEF for Every Child). The Central Statistical

Office of Trinidad and Tobago reported that 8400 girls and 1300 boys under the age of 19 were married between 1997 and 2007 (Mendes-Franco 2017). Between 1996 and 2016, 3478 child marriages were reported in Trinidad and Tobago, with evidence from marriage certificates showing that girls aged 11 and 12 were married to men in their thirties, forties, and fifties. Babies born to children in Trinidad and Tobago between 1999 and 2015, were 15,231 in number (Baboolal 2017). While child marriage is often associated with religious beliefs, the phenomenon of child marriage refers to both formal and informal unions between a child under the age of 18 and an adult, or another child (UNICEF for Every Child).

Informal or "non-marital unions" are noted to be accepted norms in the Caribbean where general statistics reveal that some 80% of children are born to unmarried couples and where the prevalence of "multiple mating patterns" is remarked (Gibbons 2015). The term "family" in the Caribbean can refer to people belonging to different races, religions, and cultures and may include both formal and informal unions across various households. Family violence is a broader understanding of violence which is related to a wide spectrum of formal and informal "family" relationships. These include, but are not limited to, dating and married couples, sibling and sibling, child and parent, parent and (foster, adopted) children, aunts or uncles and their nieces or nephews, and younger family members and their elders.

The issue of "multiple mating patterns" in the Caribbean (Gibbons 2015) is a useful consideration in the discussion of how real or suspected infidelity, or romantic jealousy (RJ) relates to intimate partner violence (IPV). Having interrogated 51 peer-reviewed and published papers from 28 countries between 2009 and 2019, Pichon et al. (2020) made a sturdy contribution to this dimension of domestic violence. The authors explained that infidelity or RJ serves to threaten traditional gender norms. Such norms are associated with male dominance, control, possessiveness, social acceptance of their own infidelity and violent behaviour; and the corresponding subservience of women whose opportunities outside of the home are controlled and limited. The "established" gender norms are therefore upturned when women: (1) question male infidelity; (2) are themselves unfaithful, and, (3) gain employment. In such cases, traditional gender norms which are underpinned by male dominance, sexual conquest, and family provider, are threatened.

From a biological perspective in the context of RJ and IPV, while men are driven to have as many sexual partners as possible, they protect their partners from other males whom they view as their competitors. Suspected infidelity by their female partner often results in their becoming sexually coercive to increase the likelihood of reproduction, or using IPV to end a pregnancy when paternity is doubtful.

Naturally, diminished dominance and control will drive abusive men to seek out their partners who have escaped to safety. A woman's escape from a violent relationship is mainly the reason why she is killed (Häggblom and Möller 2007), and according to Baddam (2018), a woman who flees an abusive partner is more likely to be murdered by him in the first few weeks of her escape than at any other time. It has, however, become increasingly difficult to keep shelter locations confidential, particularly in light of technological advances such as Google Maps which have been noted to reveal their locations (Zara 2015). The same is true of tracking devices on smartphones (Baddam 2018).

The issue of whether shelter locations should be kept confidential has, in the past few years, become controversial. In spite of the risk factors involved, where perpetrators may return to inflict further harm on their victims, there are some shelters which have deliberately begun to reveal their locations. Their rationale is that keeping abused women hidden stigmatizes them (Belluck 1997). Other arguments in favour of making shelter locations public are that the facilities available to victims of abuse and their children become identifiable, and accessible, particularly through public transportation in poor weather conditions; and that, once the presence of a shelter is recognized, the likelihood of neighbourhood watch groups to assist in securing the safety of its occupants would increase. Public shelters were also believed to be more inclined to draw more monetary donations and volunteers than those that remained private. Aside from search engines, shelter locations can be revealed by former occupants, by taxi drivers, and other transport services, as well as by neighbours and observers (Thurott 2020).

In Trinidad and Tobago, persons who are eligible to apply for a protection order include women, children, and parents who share a household with the respondent, as well as anyone who is currently or was formally in a visiting relationship with any member of that household.[5] A protection order[6] is issued by a court magistrate and is valid for three years. It prohibits the respondent from: (1) being on any premises frequented by the victim, (2) threatening to inflict, or inflicting violence on the victim;

and, (3) engaging with the victim through direct or indirect communication. A protection order can prohibit the respondent from his/her own home, and demand that s/he relinquish any firearm or weapon in his/her possession or under his/her control. In cases of monetary damage, s/he can be ordered to pay compensation, to pay child support, and to receive professional counselling (Clarke 2019).

Methodology

This chapter aims to provide information on the day-to-day operations of *Madinah House* (1999–2019) and, in so doing, contributes to under-researched support facilities established in response to gender-based violence in the Caribbean, i.e. safe houses. The methodology section will begin by defining and justifying the use of narrative inquiry in the qualitative research design, and will then describe the research tools used in the data-gathering process viz: (1) individual client files; (2) interviews with former managers, and, (3) a published autobiography of a former client and manager. The methodology will then delineate the data reduction process to explain how findings were achieved, and conclude with ethical considerations, and matters of credibility and dependability.

A Narrative Approach

Both author-researchers had rendered voluntary service to *Madinah House* before serving on the Executive Board of Management for a two-year period. As such, they were familiar with the issues related to the administration and upkeep of the shelter. The investigation therefore centred upon a specific community in their own society, and not a distant and unfamiliar culture where "gaining entry" to the information site posed difficulty. The use of participant observation in an ethnographic approach was, however, not an option afforded to them, given that the shelter was closed at the time of writing. There was no opportunity for the authors to function as primary research tools (Evans 2012, 98) by becoming involved in the social world and its participants being investigated, in order to describe "how its culture [ticked]" (Goldbert and Hustler 2005, 16).

A narrative approach which rests on the qualitative system of inquiry was considered to be the best alternative to address the research questions about former shelter occupants, their circumstances, and the services afforded to them. Such narratives or stories arising out of the shelter were anticipated to reflect the reality which members of the institutional environment, the shared community, or culture, experienced. Further, these accounts would capture intergroup relations and represent other such social settings to some extent (De Fina 2016).

Research Tools

Access to client files was granted in December 2019 to the author-researchers, shortly after the shelter had been closed. Individual client files in hard-copy format were 465 in number and represented the non-elicited, written narratives (De Fina 2016) used in data gathering. Client files had been grouped according to year. There were seven files for 1999, 18 for 2000, 29 for 2001, and 22 for 2002. For 2003, 2004, and 2005 there were 30, 26, and 17 files, respectively. There were 25, 24, and 24 client files representing the years 2006, 2007, and 2008, respectively, and 12 representing 2009. Files labelled 2010, 2011, and 2012/2013 were 15, 26, and 28 in number. For 2013, 2014, and 2015 there were 25, 15, and 35 files, respectively. For 2016, 2017, 2018 and 2019, there were 31, 23, 21, and 12 files.

Each file contained signed consent for the shelter to disclose information, a waiver form, and a client intake form. The intake form comprised referral information, personal and offspring data, a personal history of the abuse suffered, and signs of physical abuse. The client's financial information, her medical history, and discharge data were included here. The file was also used to record pertinent information during her stay such as safety and familial concerns, counselling sessions and medical care, court appointments, and visits to social welfare offices. Odd journal entries written onsite by the clients, and letters received from them after their discharge from the shelter were also stored in these files. Client files, in essence, provided life-story and biographical information and served to reveal the topics and perspectives that were unique to the community under study (De Fina 2016) therefore representing, to a large extent, the day-to-day history of *Madinah House*. These files were examined over a three-month period for content in the first instance, and over a ten-day period for demographic information in the second.

Interviews, classified as elicited, oral narratives (De Fina 2016), were conducted with three of the five former shelter managers who had supervised the home for a combined period of 18 years. The managers who lived in the community in Trinidad where *Madinah House* was located, had also served as board members. The pseudonyms assigned to them and the periods of time they served as managers are as follows: (1) Raeesa 1999; (2) Faryal 2000–2011; and (3) Dalia 2011–2017. Although Raeesa formally managed *Madinah House* for one year only, she was involved in a practical capacity until the closure of the shelter in 2019.

The following questions were used to guide the interviews with the managers:

i. How would you describe the physical layout of Madinah House?
ii. Who was eligible for the services of Madinah House?
iii. What was the admission procedure?
iv. What were the clients' rights and responsibilities?
v. What was the discharge policy and procedure?
vi. What services were available at the home to support clients and their children?
vii. How would you describe a typical day at Madinah House?
viii. What were the challenges in keeping women and their children safe?
ix. How did MH assist their clients in managing their legal matters, accessing social services and accessing medical attention?

Interviews were arranged via telephone. The questions which guided the interview process were sent beforehand to Raeesa and Dalia via WhatsApp Messenger. Both agreed to be interviewed through Zoom. Faryal, on the contrary, who did not have access to social media, was interviewed by telephone. The interviewer read the questions to her during the initial telephone conversation and used them to guide the interview process itself. Without the opening and closing comments and casual conversation, each of the three interviews lasted approximately one hour. With the permission of the interviewees, the zoom interviews were recorded and uploaded to OneDrive for safekeeping. All interviews were audio-recorded and uploaded to Google Drive.

Sarah, who managed the shelter for a brief period in 2011, and was a shelter occupant in 2004, directed the author-researchers to her published autobiography (Winters 2020), which contained two chapters narrating her experience both as a client and manager of *Madinah House*.

Data Reduction

The most common of the approaches in the narrative method, i.e. a narrative thematic analysis (Butina 2015), was used in data reduction and analysis. Site documents in the form of 465 client files for the 20-year period were critically examined. Journal records and incoming letters were scanned and stored. During the first examination round, copious notes were made with respect to content. The notes made from candidate files, including journal records and letters, were read over a period of one and a half weeks as the researchers explored the literature on domestic violence and, using a memo format, began to group the information into broad themes.

The second examination round of site documents took place to capture demographic information which had not been included in the original notes made, but which was considered to be necessary in relaying a full picture of the shelter's operations.

The recordings from the manager interviews were organized and prepared for analysis (Butina 2015) through the transcription of the data. The two chapters in the written, autobiographical account of Winters (2020) during the time that she was a client and subsequently a manager of the shelter, were studied in the context of the whole publication, and notes were made. The information from the interviews and two book chapters were then grouped into themes in conjunction with what the research questions were asking, and in light of what the client files, journals, and letters had revealed.

Ethical Considerations, Credibility, and Dependability

The client files which were examined for the purposes of this study were entrusted to this chapter's authors, former members of the Board of *Madinah House* who understood and maintained a high regard for client privacy and confidentiality. Although clients had consented in writing for the shelter to disclose their information, the files were carefully stored in such a way as to limit their access to the researchers only, so as to guard former clients against any unwanted exposure, harm, or embarrassment. The researchers also refrained from contacting the clients whose current circumstances were unknown and could not be compromised.

The anonymity of former managers of *Madinah House* was also maintained. Raeesa, Dalia, and Faryal were assured that only the researchers themselves would access the recordings of their interviews. The recordings were destroyed once the interviews were transcribed and both researchers were satisfied that the transcriptions fully captured the accounts therein.

The chapter's credibility hinges on its methodological triangulation where the day-to-day running of *Madinah House* was investigated through different measures, and using three research tools. Its dependability is evident in the careful steps followed and outlined by the researchers with respect to data gathering, and the rigour which was applied to data reduction and analysis.

Findings

Research Question One: What Was the Physical and Operational Structure of **Madinah House?**

The only physical shelter provided by *Madinah House* comprised a two-storey concrete structure with a basement, at an unlisted location. While this building could house a maximum of seventeen (17) clients at once, upon the request of police, temporary accommodation could be arranged for up to twenty (20) clients. Each storey of this building was fully utilized in Madinah House's efforts to make a client's stay at the shelter a comfortable one.

The First Storey

The main entrance of the shelter was accessible at street level. This was situated on the first storey of the building and welcomed clients who were usually escorted in for registration by a female police officer. This level of the shelter comprised a sitting area, living and/or dining room, kitchen, office, matron's room, and washroom. Clients were welcomed into the shelter by the matron on duty and their names and those of any accompanying children were registered by the accompanying police officer. A quick background was elicited and any health-related concerns would be addressed before deciding on the length of stay; the relevant long- and short-term forms would be filled out once the clients had had sufficient time to adjust to their new surroundings. Clients were allowed to stay at the shelter beyond six months. Upon registration, they would be offered light refreshments as well as over-the-counter pain medication and, at this point, matrons would supervise any children while clients would go upstairs to the second floor to shower and put away their belongings.

The Second Storey
Three bedrooms were situated on the second storey of the shelter. Clients were given a grace period of three days to rest before they were asked by matrons to do some light chores. These would of course include caring for their children as well as cleaning their rooms, doing their laundry, and contributing to the cooking of meals. There was also, on this floor, a sitting area, a bathroom, and a closet, as well as a small hallway that could be converted into a room for additional clients when needed.

The Basement
The basement provided recreational activities for clients and their children. It comprised an open space divided into two rooms; one room was used as a play area with a library that would also allow for in-house schooling of clients' children. The second room was divided into two smaller rooms; one was reserved for counselling sessions and the other was a stock room for supplies donated to the shelter.

At the back of the building was a laundry area which clients could make use of at their convenience. There was a play area with a swing and slide for children, a garden used for entertainment and parking, with a capacity for six (6) cars at the back of the building and three (3) cars at the front of the building.

Research Question Two: What Services Did Madinah House *Offer Over Its Twenty-Year Period of Existence?*

Board members and shelter managers of *Madinah House* participated regularly in training offered by the Network of NGOs of Trinidad and Tobago for the Advancement of Women. This equipped them with the practical knowledge and ability to manage the shelter and to disseminate information to educate the general public about domestic violence.

The subsidiary objects of the shelter are set out in Section 3 of the Constitution of *Madinah House* where the following services offered to clients are listed.

Counselling for Victims of Domestic Violence

An external family counsellor was commissioned for individual counselling sessions with clients and their children. While she provided training for Board members who maintained a system of telephone counselling, the family counsellor developed a case management plan suited to each client's history and individual circumstances. Clients reported that these sessions were productive, but only the few who stayed at the shelter for the entirety of the duration of the case management plan, fully benefitted from the system. One such client pursued Early Childhood Education and became a preschool teacher. Those clients wishing to continue counselling after they had left the shelter, were referred to the Rape Crisis Society of Trinidad and Tobago.

Skills Enhancement Programmes Aimed at Empowering Women and Support Groups

Matrons on duty capitalized on their own hobbies and interests to host group sessions with clients which involved art, craft, exercise, make-up application, meal preparation, sewing, and spa treatments. These sessions were popular with clients who would sit together in a circle and look forward to sharing and participating in various conversations relating to women's wellness, health, and development. The sessions served as a much-needed form of diversion. A skilled instructor was hired to provide computer literacy training.

Children Services

In a few cases, girls seeking shelter at *Madinah House* from abusive relationships were transferred to the Islamic Home for Children in Gasparillo. However, in cases where they appeared too mature to be transferred and would soon become adults, managers made efforts to facilitate their stay at the shelter.

For those children accompanying their mothers at the shelter, efforts were made to ensure their continued education. Matrons would seek to acquire the relevant documents, including birth certificates, where children needed to be transferred to a school closer to the shelter. School uniforms and transport were arranged for children. In one documented case, a teacher assisted in picking up and dropping a child back to the shelter to ensure that her Secondary Entrance Assessment preparations were not disrupted.

For those children not enroled in school, or who were at the shelter temporarily, a tutor would visit the shelter to volunteer lessons in mathematics and reading. Clients who had attained the requisite secondary level mathematics and English qualifications would also volunteer their time to tutor other clients and their children.

Relocation of Clients and Job Placement

Start-up rent of two months, grocery items, and medical fees where necessary, were usually given to discharged clients to help them relocate. A transition home, outfitted with furnishings and appliances, was also constructed next to the shelter to assist clients in restarting their lives. However, one client's decision to disclose the location of the transition home to her partner and former abuser, led to him breaking into the home to retrieve her. It was later discovered that furnishings which had been placed in the transitional space had been stolen.

Matrons and managers were instrumental in securing passports for clients who were able to reside temporarily with friends and relatives living abroad. This gave these women the opportunity to devise long-term arrangements for their lives without their partners. A few housekeeping jobs were also secured for clients seeking financial independence from their partners upon their departure from the shelter.

Legal Services

An attorney-at-law provided pro bono legal advice to clients. Where issues were more complex, clients would be referred to the Legal Aid and Advisory Authority. Common-law relationships were prevalent among clients at the shelter but, in cases where married clients were desirous of a divorce, matrons would assist with making the relevant court arrangements, phone calls, and escorting clients to and from court appointments with police. Matrons would also facilitate access of children to their fathers by taking them to and from designated locations.

Medical Services

Clients in need of medical attention were transported by matrons to a nearby medical clinic. Matrons tried to ensure the safety of clients and stayed with sick clients throughout their period of attendance at the clinic. Administrative arrangements were made by matrons for clients attending medical clinics for specific conditions to be transferred to the one nearest to the shelter.

Research Question Three: Who Stood to Benefit from the Services of Madinah House *and What Were Their Circumstances?*

Demographics

Age was listed in 422 of the total number of client files. There were 18 girls between the ages of 13 and 17 who were relocated to a children's home. There were 15 who were 18 years of age; 9 who were 19 years of age; and 15 who were 20 years of age. Client numbers were 159 in the 21–30 age group, and decreased in each successive age range. There were 154 clients in the 31–40 age group, 48 in the 41–50 age bracket, and 4 clients in the 51–60 age range.

Race was listed in 371 files according to six given categories, viz. "African", "East Indian", "Mixed", "White", "Chinese", and "Other". The "East Indian" category was predominant, and represented 210 clients, followed by "Mixed" with 85 clients, "African" with 73, and "Other" with three 3. Nationality was noted in the case of non-residents and non-nationals, and applied in particular to victims of human trafficking. The nationalities recorded were Cuban, Guyanese, Indian, and Venezuelan.

Although the given categories for religion were "Roman Catholic", "Anglican", "Hindu", "Islam", and "Other", clients were more specific about their religious affiliations in 346 of the client files. Christians accounted for 116 clients (6 Anglican, 10 Baptist, 1 Gospel, 1 Jehovah Witness, 1 Methodist, 13 Pentecostal, 5 Presbyterian, 76 Roman Catholic, and 3 Seventh-Day Adventist). The pre-existing "Other" and "Hindu" categories were listed in 94 and 81 files respectively. "Muslim" was recorded 54 times, and "Atheist", once.

Education level was included in a revised version of intake forms, which may have explained why it was listed in only 18 client files, as follows: 1 primary, 15 secondary, 1 tertiary, and 1 diploma. Employment status was recorded for 189 clients (143 unemployed, 7 on public assistance, 3 disability pension, 3 self-employed, and 32 employed). A client with secondary-level education had worked as a customer service representative, marketing promoter, and library assistant. Other clients worked in fast-food outlets, in bakeries, as grocery packers, and as babysitters and maids. Some worked as city, customs, and library clerks, and others were security guards and soldiers (in training). Two were hairdressers, one was a "chadon beni"[7] vendor, and others sold car parts, confectionary and dairy products.

Family Violence

Clients who sought shelter at Madinah House had suffered and witnessed acts of violence in their family settings and extended households where drug and alcohol abuse were rampant. Girls and young women were victims of incest and/or rape by fathers, step-fathers, uncles, brothers, cousins, and friends of their parents; and, in a fair number of cases, they bore children from these "relationships". One client who was impregnated by her father fled her home after she gave birth because her mother wanted her and the baby to drink Gramoxone.[8] Maltreatment at the hands of their mothers caused clients as young as 16 years old and up to more than 30 years of age to access the services of the shelter but, overall, violence was inflicted predominantly by male relatives. One client witnessed her father beat her mother to death, and another reported that her common-law husband had killed her sister. One client revealed that her mentally challenged mother had been raped by her brother-in-law, while another said that her mentally challenged brother had sexually molested her preschool child. A client who sought refuge from the abuse inflicted by her husband and father-in-law, was hit and cursed, prohibited from speaking to anyone, and forced to sign her child over to her in-laws. A 60-year-old client who accessed the services of *Madinah House* had applied for a protection order from her in-laws, her children, and grandchildren who physically and verbally abused her and took her money, food, and belongings.

A pressing concern for some clients, and a reason for their decisions to seek shelter, was that they were in unions with men who threatened, beat, and, "interfered with"[9] their children. Clients fled from domestic circumstances in which they suspected sexual "interference" with their children, were afraid to leave their young children under their husband's care, and were forced to interrogate their children. While a few abusers intimidated their family members with guns, there were several cases of men who physically abused and terrorized their wife and children with cutlasses and knives, while threatening to kill them. In one case, a man threatened to kill and bury the members of his family and drew pictures of them dead in boxes. It was not uncommon for a client to report that her pregnancy was terminated as a consequence of physical abuse, or that her baby was admitted to hospital after receiving an "accidental blow", or for burns to be visible on an infant at the time of registration. One client described her domestic circumstances in which she was forced to have sexual intercourse for hours while her children were left unattended; and another spoke of engaging in sexual activity while watching pornography in a room shared with the children.

Romantic Jealousy (RJ) and Intimate Partner Violence (IPV)
Clients who provided registration information recounted the controlling and possessive tendencies of their partners which led to violent behaviour and physical injury. This kind of behaviour was triggered when the client worked late, or responded to a social invitation from a friend, or registered for a course, or chose not to answer her cellphone during an after-work "lime".[10] Abusers, who were in multiple relationships, accused their wives and girlfriends of having sexual relations with, and being impregnated by, other men, including their own sons, their brothers-in-law, fathers-in-law, or stepsons. Clients spoke of the open infidelity of their partners who brought other women home. Some clients who were sexually involved with a married man were expected to live in the same house as him and his family.

Client Medical History and Physical Condition
The medical history of clients and their physical conditions at the time of registration served to further elucidate their circumstances. Notes on medical history revealed that two women had been formerly hospitalized; one for a psychiatric condition and another for having attempted suicide by ingesting a weedicide (Gramoxone). One woman who was due for an STD test reported brain dysfunction with "shaking head and hands" and two children at the shelter who accompanied their mothers were brain damaged and had hydrocephalus (a buildup of fluid in the brain), respectively. A client and her spouse, as well as a ten-year-old child were recorded to be HIV positive. Some of the visible signs of abuse noted upon entry into the shelter, were bruises on the buttocks, face and body, cigarette burns on the face, red and swollen eyes, cuts on the head, missing teeth, oozing scars, and "a shifted neck and the displacement of the top right incisor". Other medical conditions recounted by registering clients were asthma attacks, chest pain, depression insomnia, "nerves", and thyroid issues.

Research Question Four: What Were the Challenges Encountered in Keeping Women Safe and Providing Assistance to Them?

Lack of Cooperation from the Police Service

Madinah House relied heavily on police assistance for the transportation and escorting of clients to the shelter and to court hearings. Police officers were often tardy in carrying out these duties. This resulted in long wait times at police stations for clients as well as missed court hearings. Further, due to inadequate preparation from police on the operations of a shelter, women would often opt not to register upon arriving at *Madinah House*.

Police officers were also liable for breaching their duty of trust and confidentiality to clients at *Madinah House* by revealing their exact location to partners enquiring about clients' whereabouts. This would lead to husbands as well as common law husbands visiting the shelter in order to make attempts to take clients back home. Matrons would deny that the client was at the home and efforts would then be made for clients to be relocated privately.

For those fortunate enough to make it to court in time for their scheduled hearings, police officers would have to make attempts to get clients safely out of courtrooms before they could be followed by their partners. In one case, at the conclusion of a matter, a police officer privately requested that a magistrate delay the respondent so that there would be sufficient time for the client to leave the court without being followed.

Unsuitable Location and Building Issues

The shelter's close proximity to a street and its construction below street level was, according to one manager, not conducive to clients' safety and security. As a result, nearby residents were very much aware of the shelter and its operations. Although the building was fenced, passers-by would be able to look into the shelter, especially with the building lit at night, to confirm clients' identities.

Client files cited the presence of bats and centipedes as a major hindrance to the shelter's activities. Matrons also complained of the shortage of refrigerator space to cater to each client's needs.

Lack of Funding

Madinah House was responsible for footing the cost of manager and matron salaries monthly, counselling fees, utilities, groceries, toiletries, medication, and repairs to the premises. Transportation of clients to and from court hearings, to hospitals, to school, and to social services agencies to access various grants proved a significant cost and one that could not be sustained by *Madinah House*.

Disconnect Between Board of Madinah House *and Staff*
According to one manager, issues at the home level were difficult for the Board to understand and address due to their lack of first-hand experience with the daily activities of *Madinah House*. For instance, recommendations were made by managers to the Board of Madinah House to install galvanized sheets around the shelter to prevent people in the area from looking in. However, when presented to the Board it was felt that this would not be aesthetically pleasing.

Client/Matron/Manager Conflict
Many clients were not prepared for the rules that *Madinah House* implemented to ensure their safety. These included a no smoking, no alcohol, and no cellphone policy. Matrons tried to facilitate clients by allowing a few cigarettes per day. Yet, these rules resulted in strained relationships between clients and matrons, especially in one case where a client was found in possession of marijuana. One manager felt that there was a need for hiring younger staff at Madinah House to reduce the age gap between matrons and clients. However, there were many challenges encountered in hiring personnel for the shelter.

Additionally, managers struggled with matrons who were verbally abusive and they tried to deal with matrons who had developed relationships with men residing close to the shelter. This was considered to be a safety risk for clients at *Madinah House*.

Conclusion

In 2001, physical safety, emotional support, and skills training were acknowledged as necessary for battered women in Trinidad and Tobago to be independent of their abusive partners. But insufficient data was noted with respect to the nature of violence against women, the relationship between them and their abusers, and the consequences of their victimization (Chin and Dandurand 2001). Some seventeen years later, in 2018, the causes, consequences, and response mechanisms to reduce the incidence of gender-based violence in Trinidad and Tobago were still not fully understood and it was remarked that those support systems such as shelters, which were being operated by non-governmental organizations were under-resourced and under-supported (*National Policy on Gender and Development* 2018).

Madinah House was nonetheless recognized both by the Network of NGOs of Trinidad and Tobago for the Advancement of Women and by the State for community service. In 2011, former Vice President, Rasheeda Ibrahim, received the Faith Wiltshire Award from the Network of NGOs for excellence in delivery of care to victims of domestic violence. In 2013, Ibrahim was awarded the Chaconia Gold for Community Service. In 2016, former Executive Member, Neeza Hallim received the Hummingbird Silver also for Community Service; and in 2017 the Public Service Medal of Merit Silver for Education and Community Service was awarded to President, Lydia Rosalie Choate.

This chapter elaborated on the twenty-year operations of *Madinah House,* a women's shelter in Trinidad which functioned from 1999 to 2019, limited resources and limited support notwithstanding. Life-story and biographical information gleaned from client files and interviews with former managers of *Madinah House* served to generate data on the women who stood to benefit from the services of the shelter and their peculiar circumstances. Evidence is presented on the relationship between family structure in the Caribbean and the concept of family violence which is also meted out in its various forms against children. Issues of romantic jealousy in intimate partner violence (Pichon et al. 2020) are linked to the phenomenon of child marriage, and the multiple mating patterns said to be characteristic of Caribbean society (Gibbons 2015).

These narratives, situated against the day-to-day operations of *Madinah House* served to substantiate the purpose of "safe houses", an under-researched support system in addressing gender-based violence in the Caribbean. This chapter described the physical and operational structure of Madinah House. It outlined the services rendered by the shelter during its 20-year existence and recounted the challenges encountered in keeping women safe, and in providing assistance to them.

Notes

1. This was called the Convention of Belém do Pará. On 8 May 1996 Trinidad and Tobago ratified the Convention https://www.oas.org/juridico/english/treaties/a-61.html.

2. In 2000 the United National Inter-Agency Campaign on Gender Violence Against Women and Girls National Report—Trinidad and Tobago, recognized the lack of monetary support from the State and the public with respect to the sustainability and quality programmes being offered by Mizpah House, a Christian oriented institution for battered women. The tendency for religious bodies to establish and manage battered women's shelters including Madinah House was also noted (Reddock and Barclay 2000).
3. According to the Madinah House Constitution, incorporation occurred on 21 June 1999.
4. See Section 22 (1A) of the Children's Authority Act Chap. 46:10.
5. This is cited in section 4 of the Domestic Violence Act Chap. 45:56. https://rgd.legalaffairs.gov.tt/laws2/alphabetical_list/lawspdfs/45.56.pdf.
6. This is cited in section 6 (1) of the Domestic Violence Act Chap. 45:56. https://rgd.legalaffairs.gov.tt/laws2/alphabetical_list/lawspdfs/45.56.pdf.
7. A herb similar to cilantro used in cooking.
8. Gramoxone is a unique, fast acting, non-selective, contact herbicide whose active ingredient is paraquat. It is often ingested in Trinidad and Tobago by individuals attempting to commit suicide. https://pubmed.ncbi.nlm.nih.gov/10407970/.
9. 'Interfere' is a term used in Trinidad English Creole, which equates to the Standard English, "to sexually molest".
10. 'Lime' in Trinidad English Creole (TEC) refers to a get together of friends.

References

Baboolal, Yvonne. 2017. AG: 3,748 Child Marriages in 20 Years. *Trinidad and Tobago Guardian*, January 11. https://www.guardian.co.tt/article-6.2.348481.fa7accd1c5.

Baddam, Brenda. 2018. Technology and Its Danger to Domestic Violence Victims: How Did He Find Me? *Albany Law Journal of Science and Technology* 28 (1): 73–93.

Belluck, Pam. 1997. Shelters for Women Disclosing Their Locations, in Spite of Risk. *The New York Times*, sec. 1, p. 1. August

10. https://www.nytimes.com/1997/08/10/us/shelters-for-women-disclosing-their-locations-in-spite-of-risk.html.

Butina, Michelle. 2015. A Narrative Approach to Qualitative Inquiry. *Clinical Laboratory Science* 28 (3): 190–196. https://doi.org/10.29074/ascls.28.3.190.

"Child Maltreatment." 2020. *World Health Organization*, 8 June. https://www.who.int/news-room/fact-sheets/detail/child-maltreatment.

"Child Marriage." *UNICEF for Every Child*. Updated 8 March 2021. https://www.unicef.org/protection/child-marriage.

Chin, Vivienne, and Yvon Dandurand. 2001. *National Programs to Prevent, Punish, and Eradicate Violence Against Women in Ten Caribbean Countries*. Violence in the Americas: A Regional Analysis. Sub-Regional Analyses CIM. https://www.oas.org/es/mesecvi/docs/Violence_in_the_Americas-EN-Caribbean.pdf.

Clarke, Roberta. 2019. Protection Orders and Legislation: Madinah House, 'More Than Just a Shelter' 1999–2019.

De Fina, Anna. 2016. Narrative Analysis. In *Research Methods in Intercultural Communication: A Practical Guide*, ed. Zhu Hua, 327–342. Chichester: Wiley

Evans, Gillian Margaret. 2012. Practising Participant Observation: An Anthropologist's Account. *Journal of Organizational Ethnography* 1 (1): 96–106. https://doi.org/10.1108/20466741211220697.

Follow-Up Mechanism Convention of Belém do Para/(MESECVI). Fourteenth Meeting of the Committee of Experts (CEVI). 2017. *Trinidad and Tobago Country Report. Third Round*. https://www.oas.org/en/mesecvi/docs/FinalReport2017-TrinidadTobago.pdf.

Gibbons, Allison. 2015. Family Violence in the Caribbean. Presented to *Expert Group Meeting on Family Policy Development: Achievements and Challenges, United Nations Headquarters*, New York, 14–15 May 2015. New York, NY: United Nations. https://www.un.org/esa/socdev/family/docs/egm15/Gibbonspaper.pdf.

Goldbert, Juliet, and David Hustler. 2005. Ethnography. In *Research Methods in the Social Sciences*, ed. Bridget Somekh and Cathy Lewin, 16–23. London: Sage.

Häggblom, Anette M. E., and Anders R. Möller. 2007. Fighting for Survival and Escape from Violence: Interviews with Battered Women. *International Journal of Qualitative Studies on Health and Well-Being* 2 (3): 169–178. https://doi.org/10.1080/17482620701296259.

Kong Soo, Charles. 2020. Shelters Need $$ to Save Women's Lives. *Trinidad and Tobago Guardian*, February 8. https://www.guardian.co.tt/article/shelters-need--to-save-womens-lives-6.2.1049895.202903fe9e.

Mendes-Franco, Janine. 2017. Child Marriage Is No More in Trinidad and Tobago. *Global Voices* [Blog], June 12. https://globalvoices.org/2017/06/12/child-marriage-is-no-more-in-trinidad-tobago/.

Pichon, Marjorie, Sarah Treves-Kagan, Erin Stern, Nambusi Kyegombe, Heidi Stöckl, and Ana Maria Buller. 2020. A Mixed-Methods Systematic Review: Infidelity, Romantic Jealousy and Intimate Partner Violence Against Women. *International Journal of Environmental Research and Public Health* 17 (16): 5862. https://doi.org/10.3390/ijerph17165682.

Reddock, Rhoda, and Rosalie Barclay. 2000. *Inter-Agency Campaign on Violence Against Women and Girls. UNIFEM-UNDP-UNICEF-UNFPA-ECLAC-UNHCR-UNAIDS-UNHCHR. National Report: Trinidad and Tobago [Preliminary]*. National Reports on the Situation of Gender Violence Against Women, RLA/97/014UNDP.

Thurott, Stephanie. 2020. Should Shelter Locations Be Made Public? *Domestic Shelters*, September 14. https://www.domesticshelters.org/articles/housing/should-shelter-locations-be-made-public.

Trinidad and Tobago. Office of the Prime Minister. 2018. *National Policy on Gender and Development. A Green Paper*. Trinidad and Tobago. Office of the Prime Minister. http://www.opm-gca.gov.tt/portals/0/Documents/National%20Gender%20Policy/NATIONAL%20POLICY%20ON%20GENDER%20AND%20DEVELOPMENT.pdf?ver=2018-03-08-134857-323.

Winters, Sarah. 2020. *Why I stayed in an Abusive Marriage: Live, Love, Learn, and Leave*. Bloomington, IN: Balboa Press.

Zara, Christopher. 2015. Google Maps Accused of Revealing Secret Locations of Domestic Violence Shelters. *International Business Times*, June 1. https://www.ibtimes.com/google-maps-accused-revealing-secret-locations-domestic-violence-shelters-1946808.

CHAPTER 11

Shifting from Domestic Violence to Transformative Gender Justice: A Template for Public Accountability and Inclusion

Jewel Amoah

Introduction

If a new course of action is to emerge from the centuries of gender violence that impacts Trinidad and Tobago and the Commonwealth Caribbean as a whole, what is required is a new engagement with the language and constructed frameworks of gender. Unless there is true accountability for the consequences of domestic violence, there will be no individual or societal impetus to address it. This accountability has

J. Amoah (✉)
University of the West Indies, St. Augustine, Trinidad and Tobago
e-mail: jewelamoah@me.comf

A. M. Bissessar and C. Huggins (eds.), *Domestic Violence in the Anglophone Caribbean*,
https://doi.org/10.1007/978-3-030-88476-5_11

been lacking at the domestic level and so it is argued that the international arena may be the forum in which true accountability can be upheld and gender justice meted out.

The COVID-19 pandemic context has been a common pervasive global experience from March 2020 throughout most of 2021. The pandemic has exposed and made connections to long-standing challenges such as gender violence and discrepancies in access to healthcare, education and a myriad of social services. Regardless of how long it lasts, the COVID-19 pandemic will have a permanent impact on the trajectory of social interactions in the private sphere, citizen–state interactions in the public sphere and state-to-state interactions in the international arena. The pandemic has paved the way for sustainable change. The opportunities of this moment should not be lost.

Throughout this chapter, reference made to "gender violence" is intended to encapsulate gender-based violence, domestic violence or violence against women. The rationale is two-fold: undeniably the conversation is about violence. But it is not only about those who are directly victimized or impacted by the violence. Violence in the way that it is implied in this chapter engages a whole host of actors in both the public and private spheres and across the gender spectrum. Any attempt to address gender violence, must focus on remedies and supports for those who survive the violence, as well as ways to remediate the behaviour of those who perpetuate the violence, and those who support either directly or indirectly, the continuation of the violence. Secondly, gender is the portal through which the violence is either witnessed, experienced, perpetuated or denied. Gender, its manifestations and interpretations have been at the core of the problem; similarly, reconstructions and transformative approaches to gender must be at the core of the solutions.

Insofar as this chapter takes a transformative approach to gender violence, it further proposes a template for accountability. This template contemplates that a broadening in the understanding of who is identified as aggressor and survivor in the gender violence dynamic also leverages the public sphere and existing public mechanism to hold aggressors accountable and to provide substantive protection for survivors. The point here is that "the state, even if it does not directly commit the harm, often acquiesces to and ratifies such acts when its agents—police, persecutors and judges fail to adequately respond. Such inaction means that the state is an accomplice in the causing of harm and is therefore implicated in its commission".[1]

Part I—History of Domestic Violence in Trinidad and Tobago

The scourge of gender-based violence has been a challenge throughout the Caribbean since the colonial era of late-nineteenth century and has continued unabated in the post-colonial independence era of the mid-twentieth century and beyond into the current twenty-first century.[2] Gender-based violence is itself derived from the general culture of violence that embodied Trinidad from the end of the slave trade in the nineteenth century to the middle of the twentieth century. In building on the work of Trotman, Brereton explains that,

> [t]he legacy of history and the nature of the colony's society bred — a pattern of violence which was both impulsive and implosive: that is, it manifested itself as the violent actions of irrational men [and women] wreaking havoc on themselves rather than on the source of their frustrations and oppression. ... Colonialism and racism made possible atrocious living conditions and a low quality of life, which in turn promoted a milieu in which violence and aggression were salient. [footnotes omitted][3]

Gender violence seems to have evolved from general societal violence, which was itself derived from the racist and colonial frameworks that both defined and restricted the evolution of Trinidad and Tobago. Further,

> [b]y the middle of the twentieth century, a culture of violence was clearly entrenched in the colony, even if it had not yet taken on all the characteristics of the contemporary (early 21st century) period. While the culture of violence in many respects transcended both ethnicity and gender, there is no doubt that a gender dimension was salient. Violence against women, especially murderous attacks and marital abuse ("wife-beating") by men, was a pervasive feature of the society, and the latter at least was widely accepted, by women as well as by men.[4]

Given this history, confrontation with gender-based violence within the homes and private spheres of Trinidad and Tobago is not new. In the effort to alleviate and hold accountability for gender violence within the intimate private sphere, there must first be a reckoning of broader societal violence.[5] This reckoning can begin with a deconstruction of the basis for the violence. The mere distinction of gender can be seen as the trigger, so the project of addressing gender violence is indistinguishable from the project of gender equality. In this contemporary moment, it is argued that what is required is a broadening of the understanding of who is identified as a perpetrator and the broad spectrum of gender identity of those who are victimized by violence in the private sphere.[6] The urgency of this inquiry is highlighted by Michelle Thomas's reflection that,

> African slavery and East Indian indentureship instilled a culture of violence on the island. To date, the legacy of domestic violence remains part of Trinidadian society and yearly emerging statistics attest to its prevalence in the intimate relationship. It has therefore become important and necessary to explore why Trinidadian men perpetrate domestic violence against women. Failure to examine this is to suggest that men, the primary perpetrators of domestic violence in Trinidad, do not play a role in the perpetuation of this social ill. Not only that, but by turning a blind eye to this gender group is to suggest a subtle participation in the furtherance of labelling this social issue as belonging only to women. Finally, by ignoring the reality that it is perpetrators who give victims their victim title keeps in motion the cycle of domestic violence.[7]

The objective of this chapter then is to not only reflect and reconsider the roles in the victim-aggressor dynamic and how these are expressed in gendered dimensions, but to examine these gendered dimensions, both in the intimate private sphere and the broader public sphere and theorize a framework for justice, accountability and ideally, the elimination of gender violence.

a) *Gender Violence in the COVID-19 Contemporary Context*

The COVID-19 global pandemic has laid bare all instances of social vulnerability that were previously masked in denial and lack of priority. The pandemic made it difficult to continue to ignore the stark inequities that are tied to social identity. Not least among these inequities is violence against women. But also noticeable is violence directed towards sexual and gender identity minorities.[8] The instinctive global coping mechanism for the coronavirus pandemic was to limit forms of public social and physical interaction—schools, workplaces, shopping centres, parks, playgrounds, sporting and concert venues, etc., and require people to contain themselves to their homes for as long as possible.[9] This global containment or shutdown, meant that people were isolated in their homes for months. For some who were able, this meant working from home, facilitated through online communication technology. For those who were able to work from home, not much changed, particularly not economic class status or social positional power. For those who work in the direct service provision industry, such as retail or restaurants, or market vendors, or street hawkers, or taxi drivers—this meant no or drastically reduced work and income and a corresponding increase in anxiety and frustration that is associated with these losses. The dominos continued to fall, and the stress and the anxiety of the uncertainties of the trajectory and length of the pandemic coupled with severe national and household economic challenges meant that the level of violence in the private domestic sphere escalated and intensified—quickly and ferociously.

It is not new that data reveals that the incidence of domestic violence and violence against women generally takes on a particular character in the Caribbean and this trend certainly continued throughout the pandemic.[10] Without running the risk of over-generalizing, it can be said that Caribbean societies, national economies and individual households exist on the cusp of economic peril.[11] This economic peril extends to a personal safety and security peril for women who are victimized not through any fault of their own, but because society has relegated them to the position of repository of frustrations. Crudely put, one's gender is a general indicator of the extent to which one will be the victim or bearer of social frustration.

The gendered impact of the COVID-19 pandemic, it is recognized that this is more aptly described as a pandemic within a pandemic: a pandemic of gender (and racial) inequity with a health pandemic (all set against a backdrop of a climate change pandemic). Socially constructed gender inequities replicate and exacerbate disparities. These replications and exacerbations create wider gaps of disparity that become increasingly difficult to bridge. Hence, transformative gender justice must be focused on bridge-building and gap filling. In this way, there is both a responsive and a proactive nature to gender justice.

To be a woman in the Caribbean is to live in a constant state of pandemonium. This refers to a series of ongoing and intersecting pandemics that problematize the lack of access to gender justice. This lack of access is also characterized by a lack of acknowledgement of the conditions of inequality under which Caribbean women live; and notwithstanding these challenges, through which they thrive. For example, women the world over are challenged by the persistent pandemic of patriarchy—and the Caribbean generally is no exception. For example, "men in the Caribbean have always been more privileged than women. The literature shows that Caribbean men were born into a system of patriarchy and masculine privilege; naturally they were vested with having more privileges over women."[12] Historically, patriarchy in the Caribbean has been such that "masculine privilege allowed men, whether deserving or undeserving, to hold higher positions of standing, power and access to resources. Trinidad's culture of gender socialization is responsible for perpetuating a system reflective of a male–female dichotomy".[13] The COVID-19 pandemic has laid bare globally the structures of oppression and inequality that disproportionately impact women. This negative disproportionate impact is exacerbated by intersections of race, education, family status and socio-economic status.

b) *Identifying the "Many Faces of Domestic Violence"*

Traditionally, reference to domestic violence has implied spousal or intimate partner abuse and more specifically, violence committed by male partners towards female partners.[14] Violence in the household or intimate sphere is a product of broader gender inequality and male dominance in society at large—the household is merely a microcosm, or an intensified arena of attitudes and relationships in society. But this traditional conception itself belies structural inequities and exclusions. The traditional domestic violence framework presumes a heteronormative framework between parties in the household. And further, there is a presumption, not only of heteronormativity, but also of marital status.[15] If there is to be a substantive transformation of the remedies to address gender justice, there must first be a transformative understanding of the relational construct between parties in the domestic violence sphere. Transformative gender justice must consider that violence within the household or the private sphere can contemporaneously be classified as intimate partner violence. Within the context of intimate partners, the nature of the relationship is not limited to heterosexual partners but can include partners who individually or jointly identify as gay, lesbian, transgender or bisexual. The aggressors and the victims within the intimate partnership context can be male or female or transgender. A contemporary justice construct of gender justice must be reflective of contemporary constructs of gender and gender relationships.

c) *Defining the Domestic Sphere*

The language of domestic violence in the Caribbean is not new and has been a phenomenon for as long as the Caribbean region has been studied.[16] According to Thomas, "as a product of stereotypical gender socialization in Trinidad and other parts of the Caribbean, the bread-winner role was strictly assigned to men while women were nurtured into assuming caregiver and domestic roles".[17] But despite the historical grounding of violence against women throughout the Caribbean and in fact, the world, the focus in this chapter in identifying transformative human rights-based approaches to address this long-standing concern, is first to consider a shift in language. Domestic violence or violence against women both suggest a polarization between public and private spheres and between men as aggressors and women as survivors.[18] These polarities further complicate identifying and addressing the issue because there is an increasingly blurred distinction between the domestic/private and public spheres in this contemporary age. Similarly, there is an evolving blur in the nexus between men as perpetrators and women as victims. Moreover, there is also a lack of clarity around the historical polarities of male and female. Contemporary gender identities recognize both the social construction (and hence, deconstruction and reconstruction) of gender and the way in which gender, its expressions and interpretations are increasingly fluid.[19] In advocating for "transformative gender justice", this chapter emphasizes not only the need for transformative language of gender that is untethered from the traditional polarities of victimhood as being distinctly female and aggressor as being male, but emphasizes that it is not so much biological sex that gives way these roles in the dynamic (although it does feature prominently), but also the social construction of biology into gendered roles.

Transformative gender justice,[20] other than recognizing the blurred gender roles, also recognizes blurred constructions of gender. For example, the gender violence framework must also consider the engagement of transgender individuals, and their susceptibility to violence—in both public and private spheres—as well as the evolving nature of the relationships in which gender-based violence occurs. For example, this can include same-sex relationships, including those where, regardless of biology, parties in the relationship take clearly identifiable masculine and feminine gendered roles, and these clear roles may or may not align with traditional gender-based constructions of perpetrator and victim. In a transformative gender violence framework, all traditional stereotypes and identity-based roles are upended in favour of a broader contextual case by case analysis that focuses primarily on the attainment of justice (within Caribbean parameters).

Part II—Overview of Contemporary Legislative Framework

With the 1991 passage of the *Domestic Violence Act*,[21] Trinidad became the first Caribbean island to have legislation on domestic violence.[22] Before the introduction of specific legislation to address domestic violence, issues were "infrequently legally filed as criminal matters of assault and battery".[23] In this historical iteration, there was arguably a heightened degree of state accountability for processing these matters, and they were not confined to the purview of the private realm. This specific legislative change in 1991 was attributed to "women's coming to consciousness and their struggle for equality that was responsible for igniting and setting in motion the process of crafting specified legislation for domestic violence in Trinidad. The Trinidadian leaders' response to the plight of women's activist groups came as a result of their feeling pressured and forced to do something, and not of a genuine concern for women and human rights".[24]

In July 2020, the government of Trinidad and Tobago enacted the Domestic Violence Amendment Act,[25] which aimed primarily to:

- amend several key definitions
- expand the category of persons who can apply for protection orders[26]
- make provision for Emergency Protection Orders
- establish the National Domestic Violence Register for Domestic Violence Complaints.

This discussion will not offer protracted commentary on these amendments, but will simply note the recency of the changes—particularly definitions and the continuing gap in recognizing the full spectrum of gender identities that are involved in relationships contemplated in the letter and spirit of the act, but are not specifically listed in the expanded definitions. This was a lost opportunity to validate and same-sex relationships and support the dignity of those involved. Although both a literal and broad interpretation of the language in the amendment undoubtedly provides protection to those in same-sex relationships,[27] the lack of explicit mention is still arguably a nod to the status quo.

This is not to say that the amended definitions do not reflect some progress. It is simply argued that more could have been done. For example, the amended definition of "domestic relationship" includes a person who is the spouse of former spouse of the respondent (the person who is the recipient of the protection order), or a person who is a cohabitant or former cohabitant or a person who has agreed to marry the respondent (regardless of whether that agreement has been terminated).[28] These definitions do avoid strict gender (binary) references and to that effect, they can be broadly interpreted as applying to a range of gender identities, so that is good. But the broad interpretive range is not intentionally listed—there is an option to read-in the broad scope, it is not explicitly laid out. In many ways, this openness is inclusive, whereas detailed lists are often boundaries of exclusion.

When we speak of contemporary legislative and policy responses, it is best to narrow down the field to those that have been proven to be positively impactful. It is noted that not all legislation functions as an effective sword against injustice. In fact, particularly, in the Commonwealth Caribbean, where so much deference is given to colonial laws and ideologies, it is often the case that laws and policies continue to exist as shields of an era that was undoubtedly unjust.

An area of historical controversy in Trinidad and Tobago's *Domestic Violence Act* is the way in which protection orders are granted by courts and enforced by police.[29] Both aspects speak to who is entitled to protection from whom and without which contexts. These determinations, although in theory, applied against objective parameters to guide determinations of enforcement, are largely driven by subjective assessments of gendered power relations. The core of the controversy is the way in which the subjective determinations of victimization provide protections for non-traditional "victims" such as those in same-sex relationships which belie traditional assignments of gendered and gender performance roles, or in those situations where men are victims.

Entrenchment of gender roles, and the policing of these roles by different components of the state is itself a form of violence.[30] Thus the vulnerable are victimized by violence within the domestic sphere and further victimized by the state and the way in which it interprets or polices victim status. These challenges are attributed to difficulties in being able to consider gender identities outside of the traditional paradigms and require a broader and more open reflection—not only of gender identity itself but the way in which the law functions to protect and serve gender. This function is rooted in what was discussed in Part I as the value that is ascribed to masculine and feminine gendered constructions within the parameters of patriarchy. For example, "the greater valuing of those qualities associated with dominant masculinities in both public and private spheres has differential and unequal impacts on women while also negatively affecting men. It creates power hierarchies between women and men as well as amongst groups of women and groups of men".[31] These power hierarchies then become determinative in the way in which the gender-based violence is constructed. The proposal then is to untether gender justice from these traditional and binary gender constructions and be open and responsive to a broader spectrum of gender identities, behaviours and power relationships. Such openness will lead to a more expansive analysis that is grounded in human rights and not traditional narrow frameworks of hierarchy. The language of human rights speaks to honouring the realities of the individual and not conflating these into the familiar and comfortable understanding of the group. Further, a substantive human rights analysis also recognizes the agency of individuals to name what they need and seek in the form of protection, and requires those responsible for managing this protection to pay heed. Joseph et al. argue that the effectiveness of domestic violence legislation can be significantly improved if the following six conditions are met and sustained:

1. Enact and implement comprehensive legislation recognizing domestic violence as a criminal offence. They should recognize it separately from assault and battery and treat it as a distinctive crime.
2. Expand the categories of relationships under legislation. The type of relationships covered under domestic violence legislation varies from country to country.
3. Expand the categories of acts of domestic violence and that constitute domestic violence.

4. Provide easy access to long-term enforceable protection orders.
5. Make clear the penalties for breach of protection, such as fines, imprisonment or both.
6. Outline court procedures and encourage the use of victim-sensitive judges and other personnel.[32]

This chapter endorses these six conditions and proposes further that an international human rights framework and analysis will be vital in not only transforming the approach to gender violence, but will also function to minimize the occurrences of gender violence and mitigate its long-term impacts. It should be noted that the above six conditions were proposed in 1998—and many of them remain points of controversy today, preventing robust revision of domestic violence legislation or frameworks of approach.

Historically, the inability of legislation to be the magical panacea to address the issue of gender violence has been rooted in "the intimacy of the relationship between the aggressor and the abused. However, an additional explanation for this schism is that the law cannot address something that has been inaccurately conceptualized".[33] Meyersfeld emphasizes here that if the very framework through which gender violence is conceived, is flawed, then it cannot be properly addressed. And so if the legal framework does not provide scope for variations in terms of how the roles of aggressor and abused are conceptualized in a relational gender paradigm, then most likely anything that does not fit squarely within the parameters of the acceptable or common paradigm will be incorrectly and unfairly interpreted. An example of this is the incorrect legal characterization of all forms of intimate violence under the rubric of "domestic violence"—essentially because this domestic realm has been considered to be shielded by the bounds of privacy and outside the range of public accountability. All of that changes with the leveraging of an international framework that holds states accountable for the way in which they are able to serve the needs of citizens within their public borders. When states are held accountable as states for the well-being of their citizens, the "domestic realm" is catapulted into the broader public realm where state accountability is associated with legislative processes, law enforcement and the judiciary. This public catapult counteracts the traditional frame in which family violence usually takes place in secret and the suffering of its victims takes place in silence.[34] Specifically, Myeresfled notes that

> Increasingly, states are being held responsible for certain harmful conduct of their citizens. In this sense, the requirement of official involvement for international human rights violations has been broadened to include state compliance, complicity, or acquiescence. Such state liability for failure "to take reasonable steps to prevent or respond to an abuse" has been framed as a "failure to exercise due diligence and to provide equal protection in preventing and punishing such abuses by private individuals."[35]

The "abuse" referenced here also gets constructed in such a way that it is perceived as "torture" and attracts the international response framework that attaches to torture.

Part III—Transformative Gender Justice to Demand Public Accountability

The ongoing challenges related to mistrust of the police and police inaction regarding domestic violence complaints broadly, and particularly, those which may reflect an element of gender variance or gender diversity in terms of the complainant/victim, suggest that much of the challenge around accountability is the police as an obstacle to justice. If the police are not held accountable, justice cannot be achieved.[36]

Given the realities of the COVID-19 global pandemic and the context of social inequity and gender-based vulnerability that it has exposed, the proposed framework of analysis of gender justice to address gender violence must be focused on the contemporary challenge of navigating through the pandemic and at the same time laying the groundwork for a transformational and empowering post-pandemic future that demands accountability for gender violence. It is clear that such accountability must be constructed as transformative gender justice. Anything less than transformation will lead to a repetition of the same patterns of violence and inequity. And anything less than justice will be devoid of what is required for substantive accountability.

a) *Shifting from the Private to the Public Sphere*

Not only has the incidence of violence in the private sphere increased during COVID-19 shutdowns,[37] but the shut down itself has migrated much of living and working and interacting onto online platforms. Similarly, the online environment—which is very much a public environment, has become a platform for both generalized and targeted gender-based violence.[38] The initial conception of this paper sought to consider how to elevate public accountability for domestic violence in the private sphere—and that is certainly a key objective. But the COVID-19 shut down has also inspired a need to secure public accountability for actions and harm in the public sphere. And certainly, we have seen this since the end of May 2020 and the energy that has galvanized the #BlackLivesMatter movement and protests for broader social equality and specific accountability for the systemic racism that is disproportionately experienced by Black and Indigenous peoples. The global reckoning of systemic racism can stimulate a parallel and interesting platform for addressing gender justice.[39]

In considering the link between gender justice and public accountability, a key consideration is who constitutes the public. In addition to outdated conceptions of gender norms, roles and responsibilities, a large part of the reason why gender justice has largely been so elusive—not just in the Caribbean, but the world over—is because those making the decisions about accountability are not the ones who are victimized by gender violence and inequality. Violence perpetuated by men or masculine personalities against women or feminine personalities is largely fueled by a lack of accountability for this harm.

b) *Template for Accountability*

The notion of accountability is not new and is broadly constructed of justice and equality.[40] What is evolving, however, is the specificity of this accountability and how it factors into monitoring, enforcement and revised impactful action. The notion of accountability is broadly the purview or responsibility of the state—both in terms of state/government responsibility to its citizens in the domestic realm—and states' accountability to one another in the international realm. In the domestic realm, state accountability is through the ballot box—at least in those states that reflect democracy and citizen engagement. But rarely is there an immediate or contemporaneous process that directly connects citizen dissatisfaction with government on a particular issue to an immediate vote. In some instances, political opposition parties exercise the role of citizen accountability, but this is only effective where minority governments are obliged to satisfy the critiques of political opposition. In instances where state or local governments have outright majorities, immediate accountability in the political process is difficult to affect. In the international context, states may hold one another accountable through political persuasion or economic sanctions. The efficacy of these tools is fluid and shifting and depends on the political and economic landscapes and where best interests lie in exercising this form of accountability. In short, whether it be domestic or international, existing frameworks of accountability are milquetoast, ineffective and inconsistent. This is not to suggest that aspirations of substantive accountability ought to be abandoned, but that they should be constructed in an innovative and novel way.

c) *Transformative Language for Gender Justice, Understandings and Accountability for Gender Violence*

An initial step in establishing a transformative framework and analysis to secure gender justice is to modify language. Gender-based violence and domestic violence are reflected in the common parlance on violence in the domestic or private sphere. But specifically, what we mean in the realm of privacy or domesticity is intimate partner violence. There is violence that occurs in private that may not be contextualized by a domestic partnership or spousal arrangement, so we are not intentionally broadening our scope of study, but rather, narrowing it to violence that occurs on the basis of gendered identities within the context of an intimate partner relationship.

A key component in shifting from the current conception of gender-based violence or intimate partner violence as a series of individual (private) acts, for which it is difficult to institute systemic state action and accountability, to a framework that sees gender-based violence as an issue that threatens and diminishes human dignity on the basis of gender, is a transformative understanding that a series of seemingly isolated events in the private sphere are easily woven together to reveal a public pattern of complicity warranting state action. The effort to catapult gender violence from the private intimate sphere into the public sphere is leveraged by an understanding that differential treatment on the basis of gender is a human rights matter. Essentially, this transformation in understanding (resulting in transformed accountability and ultimately gender justice) hinges on education. Broad awareness, sustained discussion and debate are key. All of these can be stimulated and supported by the state.

Although international conventions such as CEDAW and the Rome Statute[41] acknowledge violence against women as a form of torture constituting human rights violations, the limited construction of violence against women should be expanded to gender-based violence in order to provide fulsome protection and accountability. This shift in understanding from violence against women to gender violence supports the pursuit of gender justice and honours a human rights framework that speaks to the spectrum of gender identity, rather than the polarizing binary construction of men and women within the narrative of domestic violence. Such a shift acknowledges the reality that violence in the private sphere relates to a host of identities and relationship dynamics within the private sphere and does not restrict accountability because of stereotypical assumptions of who is being harmed by whom. This transformative approach not only assures justice for a broader scope of private relationships, but also dispels the myth that there are sectors that are immune from state action to protect human rights. Such a transformation, however, does not diminish the sanctity of the private sphere, nor collapse it into the public sphere. But rather this transformation also clarifies that the borders of public and private spheres are fluid and transposable where human rights are found to require a very public commitment to response and redress.

At the forefront is CEDAW: Convention on the Elimination of Discrimination Against Women.[42] This international convention is based on the spirit of collective aspirational morality. A universalist conception that it is wrong to disadvantage women simply because they are women. Embedded in this universalist ideal is also the recognition that local histories and cultures and often laws may pose the largest obstacles to this commitment to equality.[43] It is all well and good to pronounce that where domestic legislation and enforcement mechanism fall short, the international framework provides more traction, but it might be helpful here to provide a brief overview of the scope of this international protection framework.[44]

At the core of a transformative understanding of accountability for gender violence is a willingness to shift the definitional framework outside of the traditional nuclear family binary of male–female roles and power relationships within the private sphere. This shift creates space for same-sex relationships that can be viewed as entities unto themselves and not as queer recreations of the familiar binary. For example, "the difficulty that the culture and the courts have in imagining 'woman-as- abuser' impairs the perceived credibility of the lesbian victim of intimate violence. Insufficient credibility may have severe material consequences. The claims made by one woman to fear the violence of another woman may go unheeded, and she may be denied the help she needs to escape or survive her traumatic circumstances."[45] Transformative gender justice is dependent upon transformative imaginings that are a precursor to broader constructions of womanhood. Similarly, "a battered gay man may be even more disadvantaged. While the law has typically portrayed self-defense as arising between two men, these paradigmatic individuals have not been gay men involved in an intimate relationship. The dynamics of the traditional self-defense confrontation are not the prolonged cyclical dynamics of relationships marred by repeated violence. Even more problematically, both the domestic violence movement and the law envision the abused partner to be female".[46] So a transformative framework is not only beneficial to a broader population of women, but to men as well. And in this way, this transformed framework offers remedial accountability for men who were not only physical (and perhaps emotionally and psychologically) harmed in the private sphere by their male partners with no processes for redress, but they were also harmed and undignified by a legal system that could not accept them as being in a position of victimization.

Goldfarb makes the point that "the failure of both the legal system and the dominant domestic violence literature to consider the problem of intimate violence in gay and lesbian relationships illustrates the power of what Leigh Leonard calls 'the heterosexual presumption'". Implicit in this presumption is the notion that everyone affected by an issue is heterosexual, or if lesbians or gay men are affected, it is "in situations essentially similar to those of heterosexual women so that no specific consideration is warranted".[47] [footnotes omitted]. The transformative solution is part language, part ideology, but is wholly grounded in human rights. "Domestic violence violates the principles that lie at the heart of this moral vision: the inherent dignity and worth of all members of the human family, the inalienable right to freedom from fear and want, and the equal rights of men and women".[48]

Part IV—International Solution to Counteract Traditional Gendered Frameworks

The international law solution to counteract traditional gendered frameworks, must oddly enough, itself be tempered by an intentional and layered gender analysis. As Wilets explains, "although international law is gender neutral in theory, in practice it interacts with gender-biased domestic laws and social structures that relegate women and men to separate spheres of existence: private and public".[49] In order to address the change of rigid constructions of gender, there must be an intentional framework that incorporates the broadest possible scope of gender recognition and identity and order to honour individual dignity—a key foundation of human rights—and to fashion an appropriate remedy. The reliance on an international law framework is done in recognition that international human rights law is the law of the "lowest common denominator".[50] The Universal Declaration proclaims in its Preamble that the international community's "recognition of the inherent dignity and of the equal and inalienable rights of all members of the human family is the foundation of freedom, justice and peace in the world".[51] It follows then that the focus on the individual's identity—including gender identity—is about honouring the individual that is at the centre of the international human rights analysis. This emphasis on the individual and their unique identity intersections is a means of shifting away from the conflated interpretation of identity to a manner that is more responsive to individuality and in this way, more supportive of inherent dignity.

Even though international law is assistive in terms of reframing gender definitions and constructs, the reality is that domestic violence—the particular characterization of gender-based violence that is the focus of this discussion—is focused primarily in the private sphere and international law as a tool of redress and enforcement is the domain of the public realm. And so our basis of transformative justice continues to situate gender-based violence in the public sphere, and not exclusively within the private realm. This is not a difficult stretch. For example, in its traditional or current construction, accountability or redress for gender-based violence is managed by various state/public entities. To begin with, the legislative framework that details the scope of redress or illegality of action is within the public sphere. Legislative processes, interpretation and application are primarily public acts—police, or other law enforcement officials as well as judges, all perform public functions. So, the nuance is that even if the act of domestic violence itself takes place within the private realm, accountability and sanction are without doubt the very public role of the state. With this public characterization of gender violence, it is less of a challenge (if even one at all) to rely on an international human rights framework for a transformative solution. It should also be noted just as states are accountable for their own actions, as well as for failing to secure accountability for individuals who are engaged in the gender violence dynamic, state accountability also arises for the acts or omissions of non-government actors.[52] Hence there is an expectation that states will really exercise all that is within their ability to prevent violence—or risk accountability by the international community. As Arnott explains, "when viewed through an international human rights lens, domestic violence is not an individual problem for which our country has no responsibility, but rather, as some state laws explicitly recognize, it is a societal problem that the government has a vital interest in and a responsibility to address".[53]

Simply put, "domestic violence is in fact a violation of a woman's human rights".[54] If domestic processes are insufficient to protect women's human rights, then international systems can be engaged—and this would apply not only to the "grass roots" violence that is being exhibited, but also to the state-level violence in not addressing this violence at its source. In this case, then the state is accountable in the international arena on two counts: its initial failure domestically and breach of its international commitments.

a) *The Gender Binary Problematic*

If the solution to enhanced accountability for and protection from gender violence is rooted in a reframing of langue and analytical context, then it is helpful to begin with outlining what is problematic in the original framework of gender analysis. It was noted earlier that the challenges with binary gender constructs are not new, nor are they unique to the Caribbean. It is in fact that global pervasiveness of the gender binary problematic that gave rise to the suggestion in this chapter that an international human rights framework might provide some traction for transformation. In considering the pervasiveness of this global problematic, Nurse suggests that

> Gender is considered to be one of the main conflict formations in the modern world-system. The masculine/feminine schism is one of the fault

> lines in the modern human condition that facilitates epistemic violence and compromises social justice and harmonious global relations. Masculinism is the dominant philosophical value system in the gender framework. It is a totalizing philosophy in that it operates with a high level of consensus, as a well-constructed myth and as an instrument of disciplinary power. In the nature of myths, it goes largely uncriticized and unquestioned. The pervasiveness and seeming permanence of masculinism is explained by the fact that gender, like other arenas of oppression, "is not only 'out there' structuring activities and institutions, and 'in our heads' structuring discourse and ideologies; it is also 'in here' – in our hearts and bodies – structuring our intimate desires, our sexuality, our self-esteem and our dreams."[55] [footnotes omitted]

Although Nurse provides this foundation to focus specifically on the problems that masculinity poses in the context of other system frameworks such as capitalism, sexism and imperialism, his premise here is relied on to demonstrate the power of the perpetuated myths—not specifically of masculinity but of the notion of the purity of gender binaries.

b) *Gender Violence as Torture*

The rationale for proposing an international human rights framework to provide for stronger recognition and remedies for gender violence is not only to benefit from the broader definition of gender that prevails in the international arena, but also to benefit from a broader understanding of the nature of the violence itself. In advocating for stronger state accountability to assist those who are impacted by gender violence, Meyersfeld explains that gender violence can be interpreted as meeting the definition of torture.[56] Of course, the initial consideration is that even if the extent or magnitude of gender violence constitutes torture, this is arguably torture in the domestic realm and there are huge variations in how states deal with this level of violence in the public sphere. Nevertheless, "private torture like official torture, is an international human rights violation and its remedy should be addressed by international committees, tribunals, and potentially, by international courts".[57] Given that generally, the international community does hold states accountable for the mistreatment of their citizens. Within this context, the argument can be made that the absence of a robust and functioning system of reporting, investigation, punishment for perpetrators and supports for survivors—the absence of this system of accountability for justice for gender violence is itself an act of torture perpetuated by the state.

The argument to view gender justice within an international human rights law framework (of which torture is a part) does not seek to alter the relationship between state and citizen, but rather to leverage a system of accountability whereby states must honour their commitments to citizens.[58] Gender violence is seen firstly as a cycle of abuse between abuser and survivor, but the circle does not close there; it extends to include a cycle of inadequate or non-existent processes and resources managed by the state. In many ways, the prevalence of domestic violence is a public health challenge.

The argument that a solution to the gender violence issue in Trinidad can be addressed through an international framework that deconstructs gender stereotypes is applicable not only to Trinidad and Tobago, or the broader Caribbean region, but in fact, this global challenge can be addressed through a solution with global reach and application. A key tool aimed at addressing gender stereotypes is the Convention on the Elimination of All Forms of Discrimination Against Women (CEDAW). The Introductory comments to CEDAW note that "cultural patterns which define the public realm as a man's world and the domestic sphere as women's domain are strongly targeted in all the Convention's provisions that affirm the equal responsibilities of both sexes in family life and their equal rights .... The Convention provides a comprehensive framework for challenging the various forces that have created and sustained discrimination based upon sex".[59] Gender violence is but one manifestation of discrimination on the basis of sex. Promotion of equality of all gender identities and the elimination of cultural stereotypes that support rigid gender roles is imperative in the effort to eliminate gender violence.

Conclusion

The opposite of gender violence is gender justice. Just as gender is at the core of what renders people vulnerable to violence, similarly, gender must be at the forefront of what liberates them to a fully just and equitable experience of equality. Gender violence is not unique to the Caribbean or even post-colonial societies. This is clearly a problem that has plagued cultures and societies the world over for centuries.

There is a need for a new approach to what has been a deep-rooted regional and cultural challenge to address gender violence. There is a particular manifestation of gender-based violence in the post-colonial Caribbean context that necessitates a unique approach that highlights the need for accountability.[60] The private realm is a protected realm, and this chapter has not sought to challenge that. But it has sought to challenge the construction of the private realm that is beyond the scope of accountability by those in the public arena.

Just as the COVID-19 pandemic has revealed that sustainable solutions and health require a coordinated international approach that recognizes the interconnected and interlocking impact of all citizens of all nations, similarly, a substantive and transformative approach to gender justice must recognize that the solution is a global commitment to recognize and address gender-based violence not as a private domestic matter, but a public health issue that requires strategic and coordinated public health interventions. The lessons from COVID-19 extend to the domestic violence framework in the sense of identifying the need to focus on identity categories of vulnerability and implement a system of state response and accountability that is grounded in a human rights framework supporting the individual.

The proposed template for accountability that will guide the aspirational objective of transformative gender justice involves the following:

1. Broad definitions of gender identity that are not limited to biological sex and traditional gender roles and stereotypes;
2. A broad understanding of what constitutes violence and the range of actors involved in the violence dynamic;
3. Reference to international conventions, adjudicative committees/treaty bodies and their inherent reporting functions that create reporting and accountability avenues for states as well as non-governmental bodies;
4. Recognition that there is public/state accountability for violence that occurs in the domestic/private sphere and that these artificial distinctions of jurisdiction do not alleviate the obligation of states to be accountable for the wellbeing of all citizens;
5. Despite the reference to international frameworks to leverage state accountability, recognize that there may be a face of gender violence in the Caribbean that is distinct in manifestation to other parts of

> the world. Which also means there will be distinct representations of gender across the Caribbean and these should be acknowledged.

The lesson of the COVID-19 health pandemic is not only that we all share common vulnerabilities, but that this collective global period of pause and reflection creates opportunities to truly leverage transformative gender justice in a way that not only provides redress, but that creates spaces for revisioning empowerment and agency. In the words of Arundhati Roy, the pandemic is a portal, "a gateway between one world and the next. We can choose to walk through it, dragging the carcasses of our prejudice and hatred, our avarice, our data banks and dead ideas, our dead rivers and smoky skies behind us. Or we can walk through lightly, with little luggage, ready to imagine another world. And ready to fight for it".[61]

Notes

1. Margaret Maisel, "Have Truth and Reconciliation Commissions Helped Remediate Human Rights Violations against Women—A Feminist Analysis of the Past and Formula for the Future" (2011) 20(1) Cardozo Journal of International and Comparative Law 143 at 181.
2. See generally Valerie Yousef, "The Culture of Violence in Trinidad and Tobago: A Case Study" (2010) 4 Caribbean Review of Gender Studies (available at: https://sta.uwi.edu/crgs/february2010/abs tracts/editorial.pdf); M. Jacqui Alexander, "Not Just (Any) Body Can Be a Citizen: The Politics of Law, Sexuality and Postcoloniality in Trinidad and Tobago and the Bahamas" (1994) 48 Feminist Review, The New Politics of Sex and the State, pp. 5–23; Eudine Barriteau, *Confronting Power Theorizing Gender in the Caribbean*, UWI Press, 2003 at pp. 3–24; Stacy-Ann Elvy, "A Postcolonial Theory of Spousal Rape: The Caribbean and Beyond" (2015) 22 Michigan Journal of Gender and the Law 89.
3. Bridget Brereton, "The Historical Background to the Culture of Violence in Trinidad and Tobago" (2010) 4 Caribbean Review of Gender Studies 1 at 8 quoting D.V. Trotman, *Crime in Trinidad* Knoxville: University of Tennessee Press, 1986 at pp. 134–139.
4. Bridget Brereton, "The Historical Background to the Culture of Violence in Trinidad and Tobago" (2010) 4 Caribbean Review of Gender Studies 1 at 14.

5. For contemporary media discussion of gender violence in Trinidad and Tobago see: https://globalvoices.org/2021/02/23/trinidad-tobagos-problem-with-gender-based-violence/.
6. See Ella Kuskoff and Cameron Parsell, "Striving for Gender Equality: Representations of Gender in "Progressive" Domestic Violence Policy" (2020) 27 Violence Against Women pp. 470–488; See also Sophie King and Eleni Sifaki, "Ending Domestic Violence: The politics of Global Norm Diffusion" in Sohela Nazneed, Sam Hickey and Eleni Sifaki, eds., *Negotiating Gender Equity in the Global South: The Politics of Domestic Violence Policy*, (Routledge: London, 2019) at pp. 44–66.
7. Michelle A. Thomas. 2018. Balancing the domestic violence equation: Exploring Trinidadian men's perspectives on male marginalization and why men perpetrate domestic violence. Doctoral dissertation. Nova Southeastern University. Retrieved from NSUWorks, College of Arts, Humanities and Social Sciences—Department of Conflict Resolution Studies. (97) at p 12. Available at: https://nsuworks.nova.edu/shss_dcar_etd/97.
8. See UN Women Campaign, The Shadow Pandemic: Violence Against Women During COVID-19, available at: https://www.unwomen.org/en/news/in-focus/in-focus-gender-equality-in-covid-19-response/violence-against-women-during-covid-19; See also Shivam Gulati, Simrat Kaur Sarai and Steven Lippmann, "COVID-19 and Domestic Violence" Internet and Psychiatry, October 8, 2020 available at: https://www.internetandpsychiatry.com/wp/editorials/covid-19-and-domestic-violence/.
9. Varying degrees of ongoing or successive lockdowns and service restrictions were in place from March 2020 until the second quarter of 2021. For those nations that were able to fully vaccinate populations quicker, these lockdown restrictions have been eased or removed entirely. But for the vast majority that have not had access to vaccines, restrictions and the frustrations that they produce continue. See Harman S, Erfani P, Goronga T., et al., "Global Vaccine Equity Demands Reparative Justice—Not Charity" *BMJ Global Health* 2021; 6:e006504 (available at: https://gh.bmj.com/content/6/6/e006504).
10. See: https://www.globalcitizen.org/en/content/domestic-violence-covid-19-latin-america-carribean/ and

https://trinidadexpress.com/opinion/editorials/violence-behind-locked-doors/article_8760fad4-8815-11ea-beed-77a3c2767b9b.html which detail trends of increases in domestic violence in the early months of the first year of the pandemic. The trend continued and intensified well into the second year: https://trinidadexpress.com/domestic-violence-the-pandemic-within-the-pandemic/article_5f2c8418-c796-11eb-a226-1382a60af25e.html; https://globalvoices.org/2020/04/10/stay-at-home-orders-accompanied-by-rise-in-domestic-violence-in-trinidad-tobago/.

11. In considering the importance of restructuring post-pandemic economies, Kevin Durant, Ian Durant, Director of Economics at the Caribbean Development Bank has stated that:

> …the Region's economies were small with no reserve currencies and were heavily reliant on imports to maintain standards of living. "This means that increasing gross domestic product, increasing incomes and improving standards of living in a sustainable way requires export growth. But this export growth must be diverse to ensure that there are not major setbacks when one export industry is affected by a shock. In turn, diversification requires enhanced competitiveness."

See "CBD Calls for Improving Competitiveness for Strong, Inclusive Growth after COVID-19" (available at: https://www.caribank.org/newsroom/news-and-events/cdb-calls-improving-competitiveness-strong-inclusive-growth-after-covid-19, accessed June 22, 2021).

In this way, Durant comments on the pre-pandemic struggles that were inherent in small island developing states and connects this to a need to stablish and sustain a post-pandemic economy. It is important to note that the characteristics of the economy that Durant challenges will not necessarily impact the ordinary person on the street or in the marketplace, and so the small scale challenges of the informal economy that place pressure on domestic households of these small scale actors may not be radically transformed in any post-pandemic theorizing or economic structures.

12. Michelle A. Thomas. 2018. Balancing the domestic violence equation: Exploring Trinidadian men's perspectives on male marginalization and why men perpetrate domestic violence. Doctoral dissertation. Nova Southeastern University. Retrieved from NSUWorks, College of Arts, Humanities and Social Sciences—Department of Conflict Resolution Studies. (97) at p 12. Available at: https://nsuworks.nova.edu/shss_dcar_etd/97. See also Keith Nurse, generally in speaking on the construction of masculinities, expresses that, "[w]e start from the premise that masculinism is a gendered ideology that is socially constructed and therefore not static or immutable but shaped by the historical and cultural context." It can be inferred then that the femininity expressed by women reflects the opposite of the power endowed to masculinities. See Keith Nurse, "Masculinities in Transition: Gender and the Global Problematique" in Rhoda E. Reddock, ed., *Interrogating Caribbean Masculinities: Theoretical and Empirical Analyses* (Trinidad & Tobago: UWI Press, 2004) 3 at p. 5.
13. Michelle A. Thomas. 2018. Balancing the domestic violence equation: Exploring Trinidadian men's perspectives on male marginalization and why men perpetrate domestic violence. Doctoral dissertation. Nova Southeastern University. Retrieved from NSUWorks, College of Arts, Humanities and Social Sciences—Department of Conflict Resolution Studies. (97) at p. 12. See also Richard B. Felson, *Violence and Gender Reexamined*, American Psychological Association: Washington, DC, 2002, pp. 31–49 where he explains that violence in domestic relationships is rooted in existing tensions. Felson's discussion also comments on the extent of violence in heterosexual relationships as compared to same sex relationships. Available at: https://nsuworks.nova.edu/shss_dcar_etd/97.
14. See Michelle A. Thomas. 2018. Balancing the domestic violence equation: Exploring Trinidadian men's perspectives on male marginalization and why men perpetrate domestic violence. Doctoral dissertation. Nova Southeastern University at p. 11, available at: https://nsuworks.nova.edu/shss_dcar_etd/97
15. See generally Michelle A. Thomas. 2018. Balancing the domestic violence equation: Exploring Trinidadian men's perspectives on male marginalization and why men perpetrate domestic violence. Doctoral dissertation. Nova Southeastern University at p. 13,

available at: https://nsuworks.nova.edu/shss_dcar_etd/97; See also Nancy Knauer, "Same-Sex Domestic Violence: Claiming a Domestic Sphere While Risking Negative Stereotypes" (1999) 8 Temple Political & Civil Rights Law Review 325–350.

16. See Allison Y. Gibbons, "Family Violence in the Caribbean", presentation to Expert Group Meeting on Family Policy Development: Achievements and Challenges, UN Headquarters, New York, May 14–15, 2015; Roanna Gopaul, Payla Morgan, Rhoda Reddock and Roberta Clarke, "Origins and Structure of the Caribbean Family 1838–1950 in *Women, Family and Family Violence in the Caribbean: The Historical and Contemporary Experience with Special Reference to Trinidad and Tobago* (UWI: Centre for Gender and Development Studies, 1994), pp. 3–7; Case Study Family Violence in Trinidad and Tobago in the 1990s, 51–61.
17. Michelle A. Thomas. 2018. Balancing the domestic violence equation: Exploring Trinidadian men's perspectives on male marginalization and why men perpetrate domestic violence. Doctoral dissertation. Nova Southeastern University. Retrieved from NSUWorks, College of Arts, Humanities and Social Sciences—Department of Conflict Resolution Studies. (97) at p 13. Available at: https://nsuworks.nova.edu/shss_dcar_etd/97.
18. For a discussion of the shifting language from victim to survivor, see Jennifer Andrus, "Storying the Victim/Survivor: Identity, Domestic Violence, and Discourses of Agency" in *Narratives of Domestic Violence: Policing, Identity, and Indexicality*, (Cambridge: Cambridge University Press, 2020), pp. 119–156; See also Kristen Lee Discola, "Constructing Victim, Survivor, and Transgender Identities", in *Redefining Murder, Transforming Emotion: An Exploration of Forgiveness and Loss Due to Homicide* (London: Routledge, 2020), pp. 110–140.
19. See generally, James D. Wilets, 'Conceptualizing Private Violence against Sexual Minorities as Gendered Violence: An International and Comparative Law Perspective' (1997) 60(3) Albany Law Review 989–1050; Rhoda E. Reddock, ed., *Interrogating Caribbean Masculinities: Theoretical and Empirical Analyses* (Trinidad & Tobago: UWI Press, 2004), pp. 3–104.
20. In the current context, transformative justice is defined as a means to "provide people who experience violence with immediate safety and long-term healing and reparations while holding

people who commit violence accountable within and by their communities". See Sara Kershnar, Staci Haines, Gillian Harkins, Alan Greig, Cindy Wiesner, Mich Levy, Palak Shah, Mimi Kim and Jesse Carr, *Toward Transformative Justice: A Liberatory Approach to Child Sexual Abuse and other forms of Intimate and Community Violence* (Generation Five, June 2007) at p. 5. Available at: https://www.transformativejustice.eu/wp-content/uploads/2010/11/G5_Toward_Transformative_Justice.pdf.

21. Domestic Violence Act 27 of 1999 (as amended to 2016).
22. Michelle A. Thomas. 2018. Balancing the domestic violence equation: Exploring Trinidadian men's perspectives on male marginalization and why men perpetrate domestic violence. Doctoral dissertation. Nova Southeastern University. Retrieved from NSUWorks, College of Arts, Humanities and Social Sciences—Department of Conflict Resolution Studies. (97) at p 16. Available at: https://nsuworks.nova.edu/shss_dcar_etd/97.
23. Michelle A. Thomas. 2018. Balancing the domestic violence equation: Exploring Trinidadian men's perspectives on male marginalization and why men perpetrate domestic violence. Doctoral dissertation. Nova Southeastern University. Retrieved from NSUWorks, College of Arts, Humanities and Social Sciences—Department of Conflict Resolution Studies. (97) at p 16. Available at: https://nsuworks.nova.edu/shss_dcar_etd/97.
24. Michelle A. Thomas. 2018. Balancing the domestic violence equation: Exploring Trinidadian men's perspectives on male marginalization and why men perpetrate domestic violence. Doctoral dissertation. Nova Southeastern University. Retrieved from NSUWorks, College of Arts, Humanities and Social Sciences—Department of Conflict Resolution Studies. (97) at p 18. Available at: https://nsuworks.nova.edu/shss_dcar_etd/97.
25. *Act to amend the Domestic Violence Act, Chap. 45:56 to provide for emergency protection orders and for related matters*, Act 18 of 2020.
26. Expanding the category of persons is one thing; providing adequate training and raising awareness of judges and magistrates who would be assessing the situations in which protection orders are to be issued is another thing entirely.
27. See Colin Robinson, "Answers on the Domestic Violence Bill)" July 5, 2020, https://newsday.co.tt/2020/07/05/answers-on-the-domestic-violence-bill/

28. *Domestic Violence Amendment Act* 18 of 2020, s. 3 definition of "domestic violence" (a)(i), (ii) and (vi).
29. See Janice Joseph, Zelma Weston Henriques and, Kaylene Richards Ekeh "The Legal Response to Domestic Violence in the English Speaking Caribbean Countries" (1998) 3 Caribbean Journal of Criminology and Social Psychology 174–175; 179.
30. Gabrielle Jamela Hosein, "'Ketch Dis'—Envisioning Alternatives to Gender Based Violence in the Caribbean" (2010) 4 Caribbean Review of Gender Studies 1.
31. Gabrielle Jamela Hosein, "'Ketch Dis'—Envisioning Alternatives to Gender Based Violence in the Caribbean" (2010) 4 Caribbean Review of Gender Studies 1 at 2.
32. See Janice Joseph, Zelma Weston Henriques and, Kaylene Richards Ekeh "The Legal Response to Domestic Violence in the English Speaking Caribbean Countries" (1998) 3 Caribbean Journal of Criminology and Social Psychology 174 at p. 184.
33. Bonita C. Meyersfeld, 'Reconceptualizing Domestic Violence in International Law' (2003) 67(2) Albany Law Review 371 at pp. 373–374.
34. Bonita C. Meyersfeld, 'Reconceptualizing Domestic Violence in International Law' (2003) 67(2) Albany Law Review 371 at p. 384.
35. Bonita C. Meyersfeld, 'Reconceptualizing Domestic Violence in International Law' (2003) 67(2) Albany Law Review 371 at pp. 409–410.
36. However, it is noted that the issue of accountability is not limited to the police, but extends to the courts, social service agencies and anything that can broadly be seen as falling within the purview of the public arm of the state. The accountability argument is not to hold these individual actors accountable, but to hold the state accountable (at the international level) so that it can coordinate, dictate and monitor/provide oversight over its various components that engage with gender-based violence.
37. Find global data/statistics to show the increase in incidents of domestic violence since March 2020. It will also be interesting to comment on whether those increase is disproportionally high in the Caribbean.
38. Although myriad sources generally indicate that there has been a rise in gender-based violence during the COVID-19 pandemic,

sources also suggest that there has been a rise in online violence in particular. See Ingrid Brudvig, Chenai Chair and Adriane van der Wilk, World Wide Web Foundation,"Covid-19 and increasing domestic violence against women: The pandemic of online gender-based violence", which was submitted to the UN Special Rapporteur on Violence Against Women, available at: http://webfoundation.org/docs/2020/07/WWWF-Submission-COVID-19-and-the-increase-of-domestic-violence-against-women-1.pdf; See also, UN Women, "Online and ICT-facilitated Violence Against Women and Girls During COVID-19" (available at: https://www.unwomen.org/-/media/headquarters/attachments/sections/library/publications/2020/brief-online-and-ict-facilitated-violence-against-women-and-girls-during-covid-19-en.pdf?la=en&vs=2519).

39. Since its founding in 2013, the founders of Black Lives Matter have always put LGBTQ voices at the centre of the conversation. The movement was founded by three Black women, Alicia Garza, Patrisse Cullors and Opal Tometi, two of whom identify as queer. Although in recent years, particularly after May 2020 with the police killing of George Floyd, the Black Lives Matter movement has been the voice of criticism of police killing of Black men and boys, the origins of the movement lay in the gender violence experienced by Black members of the lesbian, gay, trans and queer communities.
40. See Ved Nanda, Meera Nayak, and Jeremy Goldstein, "Global Efforts to Realize the Essential but Elusive Goal of Gender Equality and Women's Empowerment (SDG 5)" (2020) 48(1) Denver Journal of International Law and Policy 1 at pp. 17, 33.
41. The Rome Statue is an international treaty that was adopted in 1998 to establish the International Criminal Court (ICC). The Rome Statute established four core international crimes that could be referred to the ICC for adjudication: genocide, crimes against humanity, war crimes and the crime of aggression. The full text of the Rome Statute is available here: https://www.icc-cpi.int/nr/rdonlyres/ea9aeff7-5752-4f84-be94-0a655eb30e16/0/rome_statute_english.pdf. For the present purposes, the issue would be whether state non-compliance of international human rights treaty obligations which provide for the human rights and gender equality of citizens, and particularly

the right to be free from violence would fall within the purview of one of these four areas. The space and focus limitations of the present chapter do not permit an elaborate discussion of this issue.

42. Convention on the Elimination of All Forms of Discrimination against Women (CEDAW). Adopted and open for signature on signature, ratification and accession by General Assembly resolution 34/180 of 18 December 1979, entry into force 3 September 1981, in accordance with article 27(1) (available at: https://www.ohchr.org/Documents/ProfessionalInterest/cedaw.pdf).
43. See Elene G. Mountis, "Cultural Relativity and Universalism: Reevaluating Gender Rights in a Multicultural Context" (1996) 15(1) Dickinson Journal of International Law 113–150; See also, Sally Engle Merry, "Gender Violence and the CEDAW Process" in Sally Engle Merry, *Human Rights and Gender Violence: Translating International Law into Local Justice* (Chicago: University of Chicago Press, 2006) at pp. 72–102; See also Barbara Stark, "Inequality, COVID-19, and Human Rights: Whose Lives Matter?" ILSA Journal of International and Comparative Law 27 (2021), pp. 251–274.
44. See generally, Stacy-Ann Elvy, "A Postcolonial Theory of Spousal Rape: The Caribbean and beyond", (2015) 22 Michigan Journal of Gender and the Law 89 at 144–166. Also for a discussion of the legal standard of state responsibility for gender violence, see: https://caribbean.unwomen.org/en/caribbean-gender-portal/caribbean-gbv-law-portal/gbv-country-resources/trinidad-and-tobago; See also Gabrielle Hosein, et al., *Gender-Based Violence in Trinidad and Tobago: A Qualitative Study* (UN Women, Government of Trinidad and Tobago, 2018), available at: https://www.undp.org/content/dam/unct/caribbean/docs/20181011%20AF%20Trinidad%20and%20Tobago%20Health%20for%20digital.pdf.
45. Phyllis Goldfarb, "Describing without Circumscribing: Questioning the Construction of Gender in the Discourse of Intimate Violence" (1996) 64 George Washington Law Review 582, at p. 607.
46. Phyllis Goldfarb, "Describing without Circumscribing: Questioning the Construction of Gender in the Discourse of Intimate Violence" (1996) 64 George Washington Law Review 582, at p. 611.

47. Phyllis Goldfarb, "Describing without Circumscribing: Questioning the Construction of Gender in the Discourse of Intimate Violence" (1996) 64 Geo Wash L Rev 582, at pp. 612–613.
48. Dorothy Q. Thomas and Michele E Beasley, "Domestic Violence as a Human Rights Issue" (1995) 58(4) Albany Law Review 1119 at p. 1120.
49. James D. Wilets, "Conceptualizing Private Violence against Sexual Minorities as Gendered Violence: An International and Comparative Law Perspective" (1997) 60(3) Albany Law Review 989 at p. 991.
50. James D. Wilets, "Conceptualizing Private Violence against Sexual Minorities as Gendered Violence: An International and Comparative Law Perspective" (1997) 60(3) Albany Law Review 989 at p. 1017.
51. James D. Wilets, "Conceptualizing Private Violence against Sexual Minorities as Gendered Violence: An International and Comparative Law Perspective" (1997) 60(3) Albany Law Review 989 at 1017.
52. Stephen R. Arnott and Margaret C Hobday, "It's a Human Right: Using International Human Rights Principle to Assist Employees Experiencing Domestic Violence" (2014) 18(1) Employee Rights and Employment Journal 1 at p. 20).
53. Stephen R. Arnott and Margaret C Hobday, "It's a Human Right: Using International Human Rights Principle to Assist Employees Experiencing Domestic Violence" (2014) 18(1) Employee Rights and Employment Journal 1 at p. 33.
54. Margaret Maisel, "Have Truth and Reconciliation Commissions Helped Remediate Human Rights Violations against Women—A Feminist Analysis of the Past and Formula for the Future" (2011) 20(1) Cardozo Journal of International and Comparative Law 143 at pp. 180–181.
55. Keith Nurse, "Masculinities in Transition: Gender and the Global Problematique" in Rhoda E. Reddock, ed., *Interrogating Caribbean Masculinities: Theoretical and Empirical Analyses* (Trinidad & Tobago: UWI Press, 2004) at pp. 3–4.
56. "A foundational principle of human rights law is that violent and extreme harm should never be justified. If the harm caused by private torture is such that it constitutes an invasion into

the humanness inherent in the definition of torture in international law, it may be possible to argue that dire instances of 'domestic violence' meet the requirements of the revered status of international human rights violations". See: Bonita C Meyersfeld, "Reconceptualizing Domestic Violence in International Law" (2003) 67(2) Albany Law Review 371 at pp. 424–425.

57. Bonita C. Meyersfeld, "Reconceptualizing Domestic Violence in International Law" (2003) 67(2) Albany Law Review 371 at p. 425.
58. Bonita C. Meyersfeld, "Reconceptualizing Domestic Violence in International Law" (2003) 67(2) Albany Law Review 371 at 422.
59. Introduction to CEDAW, available at: https://www.un.org/womenwatch/daw/cedaw/text/econvention.htm.
60. See Gabrielle Jamela Hosein, "'Ketch Dis'—Envisioning Alternatives to Gender Based Violence in the Caribbean" (2010) 4 Caribbean Review of Gender Studies 1; See also Mindi Lazarus-Black, "The (Heterosexual) Regendering of a Modern State: Criminalizing and Implementing Domestic Violence Law in Trinidad" (2003) Law and Social Inquiry 979–1003.
61. Arundhati Roy, Azadi: Freedom, Fascism, Fiction (Toronto: Hamish Hamilton, 2020), p. 214.

References

Alexander, M. Jacqui. 1994. Not Just (Any) Body Can Be a Citizen: The Politics of Law, Sexuality and Postcoloniality in Trinidad and Tobago and the Bahamas. *Feminist Review, the New Politics of Sex and the State* 48: 5.

Andrus, Jennifer. 2020. *Narratives of Domestic Violence: Policing, Identity, and Indexicality*. Cambridge: Cambridge University Press.

Arnott, Stephen R., and Margaret C. Hobday. 2014. It's a Human Right: Using International Human Rights Principle to Assist Employees Experiencing Domestic Violence. *Employee Rights and Employment Journal* 18 (1): 1.

Barriteau, Eudine. 2003. *Confronting Power Theorizing Gender in the Caribbean*. Trinidad: UWI Press, UWI Press.

Brereton, Bridget. 2010. The Historical Background to the Culture of Violence in Trinidad and Tobago. *Caribbean Review of Gender Studies* 4: 1.

Discola, Kristen Lee. 2020. *Redefining Murder, Transforming Emotion: An Exploration of Forgiveness and Loss Due to Homicide*. London: Routledge.

Elvy, Stacy-Ann. 2015. A Postcolonial Theory of Spousal Rape: The Caribbean and beyond. *Michigan Journal of Gender and the Law* 22: 89.

Gibbons, Allison Y. 2015. Family Violence in the Caribbean. Presentation to Expert Group Meeting on Family Policy Development: Achievements and Challenges, UN Headquarters, New York, May 14–15.

Goldfarb, Phyllis. 1996. Describing without Circumscribing: Questioning the Construction of Gender in the Discourse of Intimate Violence. *George Washington Law Review* 64: 582.

Gopaul, Roanna, Payla Morgan, Rhoda Reddock, and Roberta Clarke. 1994. *Women, Family and Family Violence in the Caribbean: The Historical and Contemporary Experience with Special Reference to Trinidad and Tobago*. UWI: Centre for Gender and Development Studies.

Hosein, Gabrielle et al. 2018. *Gender-Based Violence in Trinidad and Tobago: A Qualitative Study*. Port of Spain: UN Women, Government of Trinidad and Tobago.

Hosein, Jabrielle J. 2010. 'Ketch Dis'—Envisioning Alternatives to Gender Based Violence in the Caribbean. *Caribbean Review of Gender Studies* 4: 1.

Joseph, Janice, Zelma Weston Henriques, and Kaylene Richards Ekeh. 1998. The Legal Response to Domestic Violence in the English Speaking Caribbean Countries. *Caribbean Journal of Criminology and Social Psychology* 3: 174.

King, Sophie, and Eleni Sifaki. 2019. Ending Domestic Violence: The politics of Global Norm Diffusion. In *Negotiating Gender Equity in the Global South: The Politics of Domestic Violence Policy*, ed. Sohela Nazneed, Sam Hickey, and Eleni Sifaki. London: Routledge.

Kuskoff, Ella, and Cameron Parsell. 2020. Striving for Gender Equality: Representations of Gender in "Progressive" Domestic Violence Policy. *Violence against Women* 27: 470.

Lazarus-Black, Mindie. 2003. The (Heterosexual) Regendering of a Modern State: Criminalizing and Implementing Domestic Violence Law in Trinidad. *Law & Social Inquiry* 28 (4): 979.

Maisel, Margaret. 2011. Have Truth and Reconciliation Commissions Helped Remediate Human Rights Violations against Women—A Feminist Analysis of the Past and Formula for the Future. *Cardozo Journal of International and Comparative Law* 20 (1): 143.

Merry, Sally Engle. 2006. *Human Rights and Gender Violence: Translating International Law into Local Justice*. Chicago: University of Chicago Press.

Mountis, Elene G. 1996. Cultural Relativity and Universalism: Reevaluating Gender Rights in a Multicultural Context. *Dickinson Journal of International Law* 15 (1): 113.

Myersfeld, Bonita C. 2003. Reconceptualizing Domestic Violence in International Law. *Albany Law Review* 67 (2): 371.

Nanda, Ved, Meera Nayak, and Jeremy Goldstein. 2020. Global Efforts to Realize the Essential but Elusive Goal of Gender Equality and Women's Empowerment (SDG 5) (2020). *Denver Journal of International Law and Policy* 48 (1): 1.

Nurse, Keith. 2004. Masculinities in Transition: Gender and the Global Problematique. In *Interrogating Caribbean Masculinities: Theoretical and Empirical Analyses*, ed. Rhoda E. Reddock. Trinidad & Tobago: UWI Press.

Paust, Jordan J. 1999. Human Rights Purposes of the Violence against Women Act and International Law's Enhancement of Congressional Power. *Houston Journal of International Law* 22 (2): 209.

Reddock, Rhoda. 2004. *Interrogating Caribbean Masculinities: Theoretical and Empirical Analyses* Trinidad & Tobago: UWI Press.

Roy, Arundhati. 2020. *Azadi: Freedom, Fascism, Fiction*. Toronto: Hamish Hamilton.

Stark, Barbara. 2021. Inequality, COVID-19, and Human Rights: Whose Lives Matter? *ILSA Journal of International and Comparative Law* 27: 251.

Thomas, Dorothy Q., and Michele R. Beasley. 1995. Domestic Violence as a Human Rights Issue. *Albany Law Review* 58 (4): 1119.

Thomas, Michelle A. 2018. Balancing the Domestic Violence Equation: Exploring Trinidadian Men's Perspectives on Male Marginalization and Why Men Perpetrate Domestic Violence. Doctoral dissertation, Nova Southeastern University: Department of Conflict Resolution Studies.

Trotman, D.V. 1986. *Crime in Trinidad*. Knoxville: University of Tennessee Press.

Weissman, Deborah M. 2015. *University of Miami Race and Social Justice Law Review* 5 (2): 635.

Wilets, James D. 1997. Conceptualizing Private Violence against Sexual Minorities as Gendered Violence: An International and Comparative Law Perspective. *Albany Law Review* 60 (3): 989.

Yousef, Valerie. 2010. The Culture of Violence in Trinidad and Tobago: A Case Study. *Caribbean Review of Gender Studies* 4: 1.

Websites

https://www.un.org/womenwatch/daw/cedaw/text/econvention.htm.

https://www.ohchr.org/Documents/ProfessionalInterest/cedaw.pdf.

https://www.undp.org/content/dam/unct/caribbean/docs/20181011%20AF%20Trinidad%20and%20Tobago%20Health%20for%20digital.pdf.

https://www.icc-cpi.int/nr/rdonlyres/ea9aeff7-5752-4f84-be94-0a655eb30e16/0/rome_statute_english.pdf.

https://globalvoices.org/2021/02/23/trinidad-tobagos-problem-with-gender-based-violence/.

https://gh.bmj.com/content/6/6/e006504.

https://www.globalcitizen.org/en/content/domestic-violence-covid-19-latin-america-carribean/.

https://trinidadexpress.com/opinion/editorials/violence-behind-locked-doors/article_8760fad4-8815-11ea-beed-77a3c2767b9b.html.

https://trinidadexpress.com/domestic-violence-the-pandemic-within-the-pandemic/article_5f2c8418-c796-11eb-a226-1382a60af25e.html.

https://globalvoices.org/2020/04/10/stay-at-home-orders-accompanied-by-rise-in-domestic-violence-in-trinidad-tobago/.

https://nsuworks.nova.edu/shss_dcar_etd/97.

https://www.unwomen.org/en/news/in-focus/in-focus-gender-equality-in-covid-19-response/violence-against-women-during-covid-19.

https://www.internetandpsychiatry.com/wp/editorials/covid-19-and-domestic-violence/.

https://www.transformativejustice.eu/wp-content/uploads/2010/11/G5_Toward_Transformative_Justice.pdf.

http://webfoundation.org/docs/2020/07/WWWF-Submission-COVID-19-and-the-increase-of-domestic-violence-against-women-1.pdf.

https://www.unwomen.org/-/media/headquarters/attachments/sections/library/publications/2020/brief-online-and-ict-facilitated-violence-against-women-and-girls-during-covid-19-en.pdf?la=en&vs=2519.

https://newsday.co.tt/2020/07/05/answers-on-the-domestic-violence-bill/.

Index

A. M. Bissessar and C. Huggins (eds.), *Domestic Violence in the Anglophone Caribbean*,
https://doi.org/10.1007/978-3-030-88476-5

Printed in the USA
CPSIA information can be obtained
at www.ICGtesting.com
LVHW051511110923
757848LV00005B/101